Finding Sparkle in the Sh*t Show

All attempts have been made to preserve the stories of the events, locales, and conversations contained in this collection as the author remembers them. The author reserves the right to have changed the names of individuals and places if necessary and may have changed some identifying characteristics and details, such as physical properties, occupations, and places of residence, in order to maintain their anonymity.

Published by St. Petersburg Press
St. Petersburg, FL
www.stpetersburgpress.com

Design and composition by St. Petersburg Press and Isa Crosta
Cover design by Amanda Dugger and Isa Crosta
Cover photo by Jon Knobelock
As told to, story architect Emily Claire Schmitt

Print ISBN: 978-1-964239-39-2
eBook ISBN: 978-1-964239-40-8

First Edition

Finding Sparkle
in the
Sh*t Show

AMANDA DUGGER

PROLOGUE:
GENUINELY PISSED
I HAVE CANCER AGAIN

"I have a lump in my breast and a five-month-old baby at home."

I was leaning over the reception desk at the mammogram clinic, having been turned away from the last one, outwardly calm and inwardly panicking. The day before, my doctor had discovered a lump in my breast about the size of a raspberry. The kind that makes them go all serious before forcing a smile and saying, "Let's not jump to conclusions," followed immediately by words like "emergent imaging" and "breast mass 12 o'clock position." Then they scribble some serious-looking notes on a clipboard, press the automatic door-opening button (seriously, is it *that* hard to just use a door handle?), briskly walk out of the room, and leave you sitting alone half naked in your paper gown to ponder your own mortality. Modern medicine – it's all so warm, fuzzy, and reassuring.

"I already have a mammogram scheduled for tomorrow," I told my doctor, feeling fortunate. I'd been the recipient of an annual squeeze, as well as breast MRIs, since surviving a blood cancer, Hodgkin Lymphoma, at nineteen (the chemotherapy and radiation from that treatment drastically increased my odds of developing subsequent cancers, most notably breast cancer), and I'd had a few scares over the years. I was actually overdue for this one, thanks to nine months of pregnancy followed by the failure to successfully breastfeed our baby girl after six long weeks.

"Good," the doc said. "I'll change the order from a routine mammogram to a diagnostic one." However, when I arrived at my usual mammography clinic, I learned that they didn't do diagnostics. Shit. When I asked the nurse what to do next, she "helpfully" told me to go away. "You need to call the registration hotline for a new appointment with one of our clinics that offer diagnostic mammograms," she advised, sounding bored. "I might have cancer," I explained. Surely, if she understood how urgent the situation was, she'd be more helpful. "That's what the hotline is for," she replied. Fair enough. And perhaps medicine is not that woman's calling.

When I called the hotline, I learned there wasn't an opening for another two days. Shit again. I went ahead and made the appointment, but I didn't have a babysitter for two days from now. I had a babysitter today. Plus, I knew something was wrong. I could feel it intrinsically. You get a sense of these things when you've had cancer before. You also learn pretty quickly that you have to advocate for yourself. Every second that cancer is not being treated, it has the potential to spread. I hopped into the car and drove across town, determined to advocate for myself, determined to get a diag-damn-nostic mammogram today. Little did I know, this would not be the last time I would take on such a mission.

Nearly in tears upon arrival at the next clinic, I explained all of this to a rather startled secretary who saw the desperation in my eyes and took pity on me. Thank God for people who care. She looked in her computer for cancellations, explained my situation to her supervisor, and she made sure I got my test that day, scheduling be damned. Sweet relief! Within thirty minutes of that mammogram, during which the radiologist himself came in to speak with me, an immediate ultrasound was ordered. Shit. Shit. Shit. All that sweet relief turned instantly back to panic and dread. It was time to prepare for battle. Again. And that made me genuinely pissed.

People often ask me how I manage to stay positive in the face of so much bullshit. My knee-jerk response: Sometimes I don't.

Having cancer for the second time is like a slap to the face. After everything I've been through – losing my parents, infertility, That Other Thing – I felt like I'd finally gotten my life on track. "The year of the Dugg" we would say! I was just named CEO, for crying out loud! I'm supposed to be the face of the company we founded over 12 years ago alongside my husband, Jason, but instead I'm laid up in bed draining nasty liquid from tubes where my nipples used to be. It's not exactly my idea of a good time. Plus, I lost my boobs. They're definitely not the most precious things cancer has stolen from me, but I did pay good money for them. So, yeah, I'm pissed.

Then there's Ellington. She's five months old, with spikey brown hair and cheeks so big there's no room for her lips. Jason and I went through a lot to bring her into the world. She's the living embodiment of a dream, a physical and spiritual connection to my parents, who I miss fiercely. She's the brand-new center of my life, and now I can't even lift her out of her crib for six weeks. Being a parent changes every calculation. Ellie needs me more than any human being has ever needed me, which says a lot considering I was once the sole manager of my dad's exhaustive list of chronic medical conditions, including all twenty-one medications he choked down on a daily basis. Ellie also has no idea that I'm sick, which is a real blessing. I don't have the option of wallowing, and I really don't have the option of dying.

So, revisiting the question of how I stay positive, a better answer might be "because I have to." Is there really another choice? The alternative is giving up, and there's no way in hell that's going to happen. I still have a lot of shit to accomplish. I saw a meme recently that said, "Just because I carry it well, doesn't mean it isn't heavy," and that really spoke to me.

Fortunately, everything I've been through so far has prepared me well, both for the whole cancer thing and the whole life-throws-a-curveball thing. When it comes to project-managing a crisis, I'm a bona fide expert. So, I dive head-first into what I do best: Getting Shit Done.

Right after my diagnosis, I began researching my type of breast cancer (Invasive Ductal Carcinoma: Hormone Receptor Negative, HER2 Positive), interviewing cancer treatment centers, and figuring out my COBRA insurance situation. I examined every possible angle. Would getting divorced help my insurance benefits? (Fortunately, no.) Have I reached my lifetime limit for radiation? (Unfortunately, yes.) Should I have surgery or chemo first? (It's a toss-up that even my doctors couldn't initially agree on.)

The last time I went through this, Dad was by my side. God, how I miss him. My dad, Ed Carter, always knew exactly how to cheer me up. He always had a good joke (or digital cake) up his sleeve and ham in the fridge. (My husband Jason and I had a running bet on how long after stepping into his home he would offer us a slice of ham. I always took the under, and I always won.)

Dad had a tendency to overshare. He'd tell you all about his colonoscopy, for example, or describe – in painstaking detail – the process of getting his car washed. So, if you had told me growing up that Dad had secrets, I probably wouldn't have believed you. He was too honest and genuine for that. He was what I call a *Genuine Human*. Of course, what I know now doesn't change any of that. It just leaves me with so many questions I wish I could have asked him...

"*Focus.*" I told myself, pushing away the memories. "*It's time to Get Shit Done.*" I had to figure out how to be a CEO, a mom, a wife, start a non-profit, and go through cancer treatment all at the same time (during a global pandemic).

But first, I'm going to take a step back. Let me tell you about the time my friend and I stole our neighbor's car...

A Slice of Ham: *You're going to be learning a lot about Ed Carter in the following pages. For now, all you need to know is that Ed Carter was my dad, and he loved me to pieces.*

CHAPTER 1

THANK YOU FOR BUYING
AN AMERICAN CAR

My family is as quintessentially American as a Norman Rockwell painting. I mean that literally - Norman Rockwell painted my great-grandmother.

She's featured front-and-center with her hands clasped in prayer and her silver hair piled in a bun on the crown of her head. According to my grandpa, she always wore it that way. The words "SAVE FREEDOM OF WORSHIP! BUY WAR BONDS!" are emblazoned in black-on-white block letters around the frame. You can't get more American than that.

I grew up in Glasgow Village, an unincorporated, suburban carve-out just north of St. Louis. The houses there were small, but the lawns were pristine. My friends and I roamed in bicycle gangs down streets lined with neat squares of bright green grass separated by concrete driveways. A couple times a week, I would walk to the neighborhood candy store with my best friend and next-door neighbor, Adam. We always paid my Grandma Carter a visit on the way. She'd be so delighted to see us that she'd give us each a dollar. Considering tootsie rolls were a penny each, this was more than enough to secure the sugar high we were searching for. These visits were both premeditated and symbiotic.

As a kid, summers consisted of swimming in the pool, jumping on the trampoline in the backyard, and watching Days of Our Lives with Adam. Occasionally, we'd organize spelling bees with the neighborhood kids, fierce competitions that I, a chronically abysmal speller, inevitably lost to my bookworm older sister, Heather. While most kids might give up, I remained convinced that someday, somehow, I might win. I was hooked on competition, clearly not on phonics, cementing our sibling rivalry early on. Heather and I were polar opposites: she a quiet redhead and me a dark-haired troublemaker. If you didn't know better, you'd never guess we were related. Ever the goody two-shoes, she'd turn away in disgust when Adam and I stole half-smoked cigarette butts from our parents' ashtrays and proceeded to smoke them. While twirling our cigarettes, we'd do exaggerated impressions of our parents, our teachers, and our favorite soap stars and laugh until our sides hurt.

The worst part of growing up in Glasgow Village, from my perspective at least, was how hard it was to get into trouble. Even before cell phones, my parents usually knew where I was. If our neighbors weren't friends, they were relatives, so there were spies everywhere. But one evening, the summer after eighth grade, we got lucky. Adam's parents were out of the house, and his older brother had been picked up by a friend. That meant his Oldsmobile was left behind, unattended.

"You know," Adam confided, "I've been teaching myself to drive." Sweeter words were never spoken.

We swiped the keys from the kitchen drawer and were off like bandits.

I sat in the passenger seat, white-knuckling the ceiling "oh-shit" handle, while Adam slowly backed out of the driveway inch by inch. Turning onto the street was the most exhilarating feeling. We started out slowly. I held my breath as we made a right onto Shepley Drive and then another onto Lilac Drive, gradually picking up speed and confidence along the way. (When Dad told me the best way to learn was on the job, he probably didn't mean this.) Eventually, we got up enough courage to leave our neighborhood and merge onto the "outer road," a service road that ran alongside the highway. Now we were really cruising. We breezed past the vet's office and the Schnuck's grocery store, where my mom worked as a cashier. We made a pit stop at one of Adam's classmates' houses, giving ourselves the opportunity to show off just how cool we'd become.

Everything was going great until we came upon an intersection with a grassy median cutting down the center of the street. Not being exactly up to date on the intricacies of traffic laws, we did what felt natural - making a wide right-hand turn around the far side of the median – and found ourselves staring into a pair of oncoming headlights. I screamed, horns blared, and Adam thought fast. He made a sudden U-turn across the median, sending the Oldsmobile bouncing over curbs, flowerbeds, and bushes, and we somehow landed unharmed on the other side. Miraculously, the car survived without a scratch. We cut our losses, went directly home and were never caught.

I come from a proud line of troublemakers. My mother's father, Louis Giraud (aka Grandpa Louie), was born in The Bronx. His mom, Mable, was a single mother of five. During the Depression, the Federal Government decided it would be useful to move some of the starving masses from overcrowded New York out west to Arkansas. They gave Mable the deed to a random plot of land and sent them on their way. The family survived the journey via a Model T Ford by stealing apples and the occasional loaf of bread from farms and food stands along the mostly dirt roads, a skill that would come in handy for Louie later. When they finally arrived in Thida, Arkansas, however, they couldn't find the land they had been promised. Either it never existed, or the description of its location was incorrect. Fortunately, there were several abandoned homes in the area. Most likely, the previous occupants had chosen to move on to more fertile soil. So, Mable selected a house that didn't appear occupied and started squatting. This is where my grandfather and his siblings grew up.

Eventually, Grandpa Louie would go off to WWII, where he'd meet his wife and my grandmother, a German war bride named Irmgard Opitz. After briefly going AWOL to stay with her family, he negotiated with his commanding officer that he would return to his post if he was allowed to marry her. It was a very German wedding, and her parents did not look happy in the 2x3-inch photo we have commemorating the event. When the newlyweds returned to the US, Grandpa had many odd jobs before eventually finding work on the Union Pacific railroad in St. Louis and settling down. Little by little, he saved and eventually bought a home in Glasgow Village, where my mom grew up.

Grandpa was frequently in trouble at the railroad for drinking on the job or stealing materials. He heisted large beams of wood or iron that he used to construct, piece by piece, a new house for his mother. With his bare hands, he'd build an entire wall in his front yard, drive it down to Arkansas, and then return home to construct the next piece with more stolen goods. Eventually, he was forced into early retirement – the union kept him from being fired outright – but not until he met and befriended Elmer Carter, another resident of Glasgow Village who also worked on the railroad.

Elmer and Ida Carter lived only a few blocks away from the Girauds, and the couples soon became close friends. They boated together in the summers and attended the same neighborhood BBQs. When Irmgard's parents were killed suddenly in an automobile accident, the Girauds left their daughter, Sonja, to stay with the Carters while they attended the funeral in Germany. I can't be certain, but I believe this was the beginning of the flirtation between my parents. Unsurprisingly, considering her father's antics, Sonja was the neighborhood wild child. By the time she was thirteen, she was already smoking, sneaking out, and breaking boys' hearts. In contrast, Ed Carter was a quiet, shy boy. Despite being a few years older, he was completely intimidated by Sonja. It's possible he never would have asked her out at all if their parents hadn't conspired to make it happen. Somehow, Louie was baffled by his daughter's behavior and begged his friend to have his steady, upstanding son ask her out. Elmer may have thought Ed would be good for Sonja... Perhaps Elmer hoped that Sonja would bring Ed out of his shell.

Through a family friend, Ed got a job directly out of high school on the assembly line at General Motors. Landing a union job was a big deal, and he was grateful and excited for the opportunity. Plus, now he had some extra money to spend impressing his new girlfriend, who liked his fancy GTO sports car and his motorcycle. But all this was short-lived. After working only six months at General Motors, Ed was drafted for Vietnam and went straight to basic training. I think both sets of parents expected the fairly new romance to end there, but Ed and Sonja stayed in touch. Then, Ed had a stroke of luck. Out of the 200 recruits who trained together on the Pershing Missile at Ft. Sill, Oklahoma, he was one of only two selected to stay behind to be an instructor. He remained there as cohort after cohort was sent on to Vietnam, and many never returned. He always believed that this stroke of good fortune saved his life.

After two years of service, Ed returned home, and his relationship with Sonja picked up in earnest. At this point, Louie started to wonder if perhaps setting the kids up had been a mistake. Everyone in the neighborhood thought Ed should wind up with someone quiet and responsible, like him. The last thing my grandfather wanted to do was saddle Ed with a relationship he couldn't get out of. Eventually, Louie decided to take matters into his own hands.

"I wouldn't blame you if you didn't want to marry Sonja," he advised my shocked father. "She's a lot to handle, even for me." But Dad was already head-over-heels in love.

My parents finally married in 1970 and moved into the house across the street from my grandma and Grandpa Giraud. Eventually, that 927 square-foot box would become home to four humans, four show dogs, two cats, and three enormous birds. (We'll get to dissecting some of this zoo later.) The Girauds would later move to a farm in Bowling Green, Missouri, and the couple that took their place would become best friends with my parents. Typical Glasgow Village stuff.

Grandpa built his new house on the farm the same way he built his mother's house: by hand with stolen railroad materials. My earliest memories, which exist largely because they're recorded on VHS, are of that Bowling Green farm. Heather and I were riding Wendy, a pony – an actual pony – around Grandpa's front yard with my light brown wavy hair so long it lay on Wendy's back. Those same VHS videos also comprise the only memories I have of my grandmother Irmgard. She's lying in bed, rendered nearly comatose by a rare cancerous brain tumor. Grandpa spent the last year of her life brushing her teeth, bathing her, and feeding her from a tube. He may have been more renegade than saint, but he was a very loving husband.

My earliest memories of my dad, not caught on VHS, are of waiting by the front window every day at 4 p.m. for him to get home from his job on "the line" at General Motors. Often, I was in trouble with Mom and praying "the paddle" wouldn't come out before Dad arrived. Mom used the tools she had to keep me in check, the same tools her German mother used on her. Sometimes, her tough love leaned a little hard on the tough side of things. Dad, however, was a big softie.

"Daddy's home!" I'd shout, as soon as I caught a glimpse of his black Ford pickup and the billowing smoke pumping out of the exhaust. Then,

I'd run to the kitchen door to greet him, the ultimate Daddy's Girl. As a kid, I had no concept of a blue-collar vs. white-collar job. To hear Dad tell it, what he did was extremely important. He built cars, after all. Any time he saw a shiny new Pontiac cruising down the street, he'd remark proudly that he may have helped assemble it. Once he had a family, the only new car he ever bought himself was a Pontiac Grand AM manufactured in his own plant. Long after he retired, he was a proud ambassador for the "Buy American" cause.

Dad would frequently walk up to strangers at the gas station or grocery store and say, "Thank you for buying an American car!" I'd hide my face in embarrassment as he'd launch into a passionate speech about the importance of American manufacturing and the unique qualities of the car in question. Before long, he and this stranger would be chatting like old friends. His sincerity always won them over.

Despite how much he loved it, General Motors was not the most stable job. The threat of layoffs loomed ominously over every day. When the downtown plant closed, Dad was transferred to the new plant in Wentzville, which meant long commutes and even longer days. Moreover, union strikes were frequent. Strikes meant extended periods surviving on heavily truncated paychecks. Dad would always take another job to make up for these gaps. He'd go to work at his uncle's carpet store, deliver drugs for the local pharmacy, or do home repairs. We were also taught at a young age to never cross a picket line. He wanted to demonstrate that there was dignity in hard work, and he did. From early on, no matter what other trouble I might get into, I was determined to imitate my dad's work ethic. But even with all his efforts, money could sometimes be a struggle. On at least one occasion, my parents were forced to borrow from money saved in Heather's starter bank account to make ends meet. She was too young to even notice, and they made sure to pay her back with interest.

Eventually, Dad would take an early retirement package from GM. At first, he went to work with Mom at Schnuck's. Then, it was a series of odd jobs until, finally, in his mid-50s, he landed his dream job: Classic Auto Trim. Think Pimp My Ride but for retired union dudes in suburban Missouri. They'd soup up cars with leather interiors, sunroofs, remote start, and other aftermarket features. Each time they went to retrieve a car at a dealership, they'd drive up in a beat-up old chase car they dubbed the Hooptie. A few times, they even got to fly to their destination. On top of all this glory, Dad got work alongside his best friends from "the line" (GM assembly line that is). After generations of hard work and grit, we were living the American Dream. Mom and Dad had a motorcycle, and we had an above-ground pool and a trampoline in our backyard.

If all of this sounds a little too Norman Rockwell, I get it. The truth is, it wouldn't be classic Americana if there wasn't something darker under the surface. In this case, the darker element of serene Glasgow Village was quite literally under the surface – that is, in the groundwater. It turns out that all these memorable moments – the neighborhood romance, the bicycle rides, waiting by the window for Dad – took place on soil that was making us sick.

Starting in 1942, Mallinckrodt Chemical Works processed roughly one ton of pure uranium per day in downtown St. Louis. It was then shipped to labs across the country for the top-secret Manhattan Project that created the first nuclear bomb. Radioactive process byproducts were stored at a 21.7-acre area adjacent to Lambert-St. Louis Airport, which is now referred to as the St. Louis Airport Site (SLAPS). In 1966, certain SLAPS wastes were purchased, moved, and stored on Latty Avenue in Hazelwood, Missouri. Part of this property later became known as the Hazelwood Interim Storage Site (HISS). During this move, improper handling and transportation of the contamination caused the spread of materials along haul routes and to adjacent vicinity properties.

Rather than storing this waste securely, it was kept in containers above ground, unprotected and often in uncovered barrels. Worse, this dump site sat right beside Coldwater Creek, which runs through North St. Louis County and eventually feeds into the Mississippi River. When the creek inevitably flooded, groundwater became contaminated with nuclear waste. I think you know what happened next. The rapid development of residential subdivisions in the North St. Louis County area during the 1960s and 1970s completely changed the creek's downstream landscape from sparsely populated farmland to thriving suburban communities. The construction booms in the 1950s and 1960s led to soil re-grading and the process redistributed the contaminant materials (that had been sent downstream by runoff), possibly creating potential modes of human exposure through inhalation and ingestion.

It's extremely difficult to hold a company like Mallinckrodt Chemical Works responsible because it's nearly impossible to pinpoint the cause of a specific case of cancer. There are a million factors that come into play, including genetics, lifestyle, and just plain bad luck. What I can say for certain is that out of about twenty houses within a four-block radius, there were more than twelve cases of cancer, all of them different and many of them rare. This includes the brain tumor that killed my grandmother and, eventually, my own cancer at a young age. In 2019, after years of pressure from activists and researchers, North St. Louis County finally released a Health Assessment confirming what we already knew: areas near Coldwater Creek were the site of a major cancer cluster. However, the confines of that assessment didn't include my neighborhood, and many individuals never reported their cancer cases to public officials. Most likely, they've barely scratched the surface of the harm done to our community.

As of July 2025, legislation was signed into law expanding the Radiation Exposure Compensation Act (RECA) to include 21 zip codes in St. Louis, Missouri. To be eligible for compensation, individuals must have developed specific illnesses related to radiation exposure, such as certain cancers. Unfortunately, as of current, our zip code didn't make the list.

It's strange to think that so many events in my life may be the result of a careless decision made decades before I was born. Life can be that way, sometimes. The decisions we make can have ripple effects far beyond what we ever imagined. Taking the easy way out can have serious consequences, and covering up mistakes tends to make them worse. Secrets, both large and small, have a way of wearing people down. This includes big secrets, like what happened at Coldwater Creek, and smaller, more personal ones.

Which brings me to my Aunt Ingrid. She was the younger daughter of Louie and Irmgard Giraud and, unlike my mom, responded to the mischievous chaos of her family by embracing a strict code of personal discipline and profound honesty. You'll never meet a straighter shooter than Ingrid, and I mean that literally as well as figuratively. She spent twenty years in the military, a fact that comes as absolutely no surprise to anyone who meets her. She has a solid voice, deep yet feminine, and ends all her sentences with a slight upward lilt, like she's holding back a joke. You can easily imagine her yucking it up with the guys at the bar, keeping up with every dirty joke without missing a beat. She is the most direct person I've ever known, so lying is excruciating for her. But she's also a fiercely loyal person who always keeps her promises. So, when our family asked her to keep a secret, she did.

My childhood, sweet and idyllic as a Norman Rockwell painting, was built on a foundation of secrecy and stood on contaminated ground.

NEW UD
GREATER ST. LOUIS
TRAINING CLUB
MAY 7, 1994
ALLEN BIERMAN PHOTO

A Slice of Ham: *Dad's contribution to our family's dog-show competitions was, not surprisingly, a car. Specifically, an enormous blue GMC van called the Dog-Mobile. The Dog-Mobile had only two front seats and a cavernous rear end, which we'd pack full of humans, canines in dog crates, and show equipment – jumps, grooming tables, a "tack box" of grooming supplies, lawn chairs, you name it. Dad would haul us around from show to show, blasting Mom's favorite Manilow music and laying on the horn. By the time it was sold, the Dog-Mobile had over 200,000 miles on it and was being used as a third shed on my parents' property. It was towed away by a sketchy guy from Craigslist who paid us $500 and probably converted it into a meth lab.*

CHAPTER 2

THIS DOG
HAS BEEN PAINTED

Mom dedicated many years of her life to the quest for the perfect hobby. One year, it was macramé and boy did we have macramé. She made plant hangers. She made house décor. Lawn chairs. Keychains. Oven mitts. Our home was a wonderland of macramé. Another year, it was garden gnomes. Suddenly, we had dozens of hand-painted garden gnomes in every corner of the yard. At one point, we had a hundred cactuses in the house. If Mom was into something, she was all in, and we were all along for the ride. Dad did his best to support her, safe in knowing that every phase was temporary. That is, until she discovered her one true passion: dog shows.

Having pets was nothing new for my family. My parents' first dog was a Lab-mix named Major. There are pictures of me as an infant lying on Major's back and as a toddler crawling over him. When I was in first grade, Major passed away, and my mom got another Lab mix, Dudley. Labs are notoriously rambunctious animals, so despite being an experienced pet owner, she decided to take him to obedience classes. On her very first day, she met Marilyn. Marilyn was younger with a short, spiky haircut and a spunky attitude to match. She also had an absolute hellion of a Dalmatian named Checkers. Checkers had failed the beginner's obedience class twice before, so this was her third try at training that stubborn dog.

The two women hit it off right away and agreed to continue taking classes together. Intermediate courses led to advanced courses, which led, inevitably, to dog shows. They were hooked. In those days, you could only show pure-bred dogs, so naturally, Mom solved that by getting a second dog, a Golden Retriever named Brandon. Despite her past manias for collecting things, she assured Dad that the number of canines in our home would not exceed two. Famous last words.

At first, Mom took Heather and me along to competitions because she didn't want to leave us home alone. The first time Marilyn saw me, I was curled up fast asleep inside a dog crate. I loved sleeping in the crate. It was cozy in there, and dog shows started really damn early. My first memory of Marilyn is watching her and her majestic Greyhound earn a ribbon in an Obedience competition. When I watched that judge call out her armband number to a wildly applauding crowd, I thought she was the coolest person I'd ever met. Surely, there could be no higher calling. I caught the dog show bug, and I caught it bad.

I looked up to Marilyn because she was an ace at dog shows, but Mom looked up to her because she embodied all Mom's dreams for her girls. It's not that Mom wasn't happy with her life, but there were things she never had the chance to do, namely, go to college and move out of North St. Louis County. Marilyn had done both and more. She lived in a big house in a nice neighborhood. She had a "professional job," having already worked decades at Edward Jones. She wore high heels and suit jackets to work.

Mom wanted Heather and me to turn out just like Marilyn, who had no children of her own. Mom told us often, "Don't have kids, have dogs. If you don't like them, you can put them to sleep." She was mostly joking. The more we could model our lives after Marilyn, and the less we modeled them after the path she chose, the better. This was especially true for Heather, who was well-behaved with good grades. So, Mom saw Heather as the family's "ticket" to college. I was more of a long shot, if not a total lost cause, a premonition I picked up on with some degree of resentment. Marilyn never treated me as second-best, though. She never treated any of us as second-best, and I sometimes wonder if the adulation Mom heaped on her made her uncomfortable. However she felt about it, we all adored her. I credit much of what I've achieved to the fact that Marilyn always believed in me.

Mom reneged on her promise to Dad pretty quickly by allowing my sister to get a dog. By the time I was nine, I was desperate for a best friend of my own. So, what if Heather was more than two years older than me, more responsible, and never got in trouble? It wasn't fair, and I made sure to let everyone know.

"Please can I have a dog, Daddy?" I'd beg every day. "Please, please, pretty please, please…" Much to Heather's chagrin, he gave in, allowing me to get my own dog a full year younger than Heather had. But there was one condition: I had to pay for it myself. So, I started shoveling poop at dog shows, saving up my babysitting money, even stashing some of those dollars from Grandma Carter instead of buying candy. Eventually, I saved up enough to get Toby, a Sheltie, the only small dog in the family. Toby became my obsession. I worked with him in the yard, took him to classes three evenings a week, dressed him up in Cabbage Patch Doll clothes, and slept with him at the foot of my waterbed every night. (Remember when waterbeds were a thing? More on waterbeds later.)

The only money I didn't spend on Toby was spent on hot lunch at school. This may seem like an odd thing to prioritize, but trust me when I say it was of the utmost importance. You see, only nerds brought their lunch to school every day. Rather than enduring the embarrassment of skipping the lunch line, I developed a plan. Every day, I'd bring my ham sandwich to school along with not one but three sodas. These were readily available in the house thanks to Mom's unbreakable addiction to Pepsi. I'd sell my extra two sodas for fifty cents each, which would earn me enough money to buy "Sundance and Cheese." This culinary delicacy is prepared by opening a bag of spicy Fritos and ladling a large spoonful of hot nacho cheese on top. Best consumed with a spork. It was disgusting and gave me terrible gas, but it was a small price to pay for fitting in. This was only the beginning of my long career as a hustler.

After Toby, we added a Newfoundland to our family unit. Now, there were four dogs (we lost the lab mix to a canine virus), two cats, some hamsters and, of course, a fish tank I borrowed from my science teacher and never returned. The Newfie weighed about 130 pounds with long, droopy jowls and thick, shaggy fur, like the cuddliest, dopiest bear you ever saw. He was also a bit dumb and would, not infrequently, lock himself in the bathroom. Once inside, the space was too small to turn around, so he'd end up knocking the door shut with his body. Then, the desperate howling would begin.

"Get in the bathtub!" we'd shout from the hallway. "I Said Get. In. The. Bathtub!" Eventually, the well-trained horse of a dog would obey, and that would free up enough space for us to open the door to the three-by-four-foot space and let him out.

It may surprise you to hear that being a dog show fanatic did not help my popularity. It certainly surprised me. Elementary school wasn't so bad, but by the time I transitioned to the Sixth Grade Center (a failed social experiment by our district), where all the local schools combined for one hellish year of braces and BO, I was a certified loser. It didn't help that, in addition to being one of only two white girls in my homeroom, my teacher also happened to show Shelties. Of all the gin joints in all the towns...

I became an instant teacher's pet – no pun intended - which is precisely the opposite of what I wanted. I was supposed to be the troublemaker! Heather was the nerd, not me! But the thing about being in sixth grade, and the reason so many people hate it, is that how you perceive yourself matters a lot less than how others perceive you. Your peers get the final call, at least until high school. So, miserable at school, I did the only thing that made sense. I made dog shows my life.

Toby and I participated in all three categories: Obedience, Agility, and Conformation. Most people are familiar with the first two. Obedience is a show exhibiting how well-trained your dog is, while Agility involves a timed obstacle course. Conformation is what you see at Westminster from Madison Square Garden in New York City. To the untrained eye, it looks like people prancing around in a circle with their dogs. In reality, it's the strictest and most cut-throat contest in a dog show. In Conformation, your dog is being judged on how well it meets the standard for its breed. Basically, there's an Aristotelian Ideal for dog breeds. Dogs in Conformation are not judged in comparison with one another. (For example, it's not "I like the Pomeranian better than the Golden Retriever.") Instead, they're judged on how well they exemplify their own breed. (To continue my example, the Pomeranian is a better Pomeranian than the Retriever is a Retriever.) Toby was a Sheltie, sure, but was he the quintessential Sheltie?

Here are a few (although not nearly all) of the essential qualities of a Shetland Sheepdog according to The American Kennel Club, AKA The Word of God:

- Must stand between 13 and 16 inches from floor to shoulder.
- The head, when viewed in profile, "Should be a long, blunt wedge, tapering slightly from ears to nose."
- The top third of the ears should tip down – but only the top third.
- The tail must not be too short and must not tip up as the dog walks, but must rather stick straight out or straight down.
- Must not cross its feet while walking.
- "Neck must be muscular, arched, and of sufficient length to carry the head proudly."
- The mane should be "abundant" and "particularly impressive in males."

Naturally, there are all kinds of tricks for enhancing your dog's best features and obscuring others. You can mousse up that mane to make it extra fluffy. You weigh down the top third of their ears with liquid lead to train them to "tip." You can even brace the ears together to teach them to stand up. In something as high-stakes as a dog show, the line between cheating and competitiveness can be deceptively thin.

Now, Toby was a sable-colored Sheltie, which is a combination of tan, dark-brown, and white. It's important for sable shelties not to have any faded colors or gradual changes. Instead, they should have distinct patches of bold colors and a shock of white fur just around the nose. To help achieve this effect, I gave Toby a subtle rubbing of white chalk on his muzzle. As with any good makeover, the goal wasn't to change him, but rather to enhance his already stunning natural features. Now, when I tell you everyone did this, I mean everyone did this. Anything less would have been a disservice to Toby, and we can't have that, now, can we?

When I was 10, I made it to the final round of the Best of Breed Conformation competition. Dad was filming proudly from the audience, his 30-pound camera on his left shoulder and the separate VCR box in his right hand. The judge was known to not care much for children. After all, dog shows are a serious pursuit, best suited for adults. On the video, you can see the judge rubbing Toby's nose determinately, a big scowl on his face. He rubs and rubs until, finally, he lifts his thumb to his face, eyes wide in horror.

"This dog has been painted!" He exclaims, shoving his finger in my face. "You're excused, ma'am!" Oh, the shame!

I didn't even know what that meant. Other competitors in the ring had to inform me that I needed to exit the ring immediately. I was dismissed from that competition, but a fire had been lit within me. I had to come back and win it all.

After the horrors of the Sixth Grade Center, regular old middle school was a relief. I was still a dog-obsessed weirdo, but I started making some real friends. Most importantly, seventh grade is when I met Lisa, who sat next to me on the first day of homeroom. I immediately noticed her earrings, brightly colored bangles that complemented her perfectly smooth dark brown ponytail. Lisa had a coveted "caboodle" jewelry organizer, where she kept her vast collection of colorful earrings, which she changed out daily. My simple, tomboy-ish studs were no comparison. I was in awe.

Despite her impeccable fashion taste, Lisa also had a major impediment to being cool: her mom was the school secretary. Lisa became the yin to my yang. I was loud; she was quiet. I was built like a soccer player; she was built like a ballerina. I showed dogs; she danced tap. But we just "got" each other. With Lisa by my side, school was no longer a scary place. I always had someone to sit with in the cafeteria, to confide in, and to cheer me on when I finally got that blue ribbon.

At only eleven years old, I went back and won Best of Breed. Then, I received third place for the entire herding breed in the group competition. This is a Big Deal. I was also the youngest person in the Bi-State area to achieve the coveted Utility Dog title in Obedience. Toby, it was unanimously agreed, was a Very Good Boy. Dogs were really the center of my life in middle school, and I think things would have continued that way forever if it weren't for one minor distraction that got in my way: boys.

You know, the human kind.

It started with Ricky, the one boy who attended the after-school Arts & Crafts Club with Lisa and me. We never questioned his attendance at the club, although he wasn't particularly skilled at crafting. Ricky lived a couple blocks away from me in Glasgow Village, and we'd ride the same bus to school together every morning. He would sit next to me, three rows from the back, and we'd twist our legs together, like a pretzel, my right shin under his left calf, my ankle hooked behind his. We never mentioned this arrangement, never really made eye contact during this physical interaction, either. We certainly never did anything as terrifying as even hold hands or kiss. Molly and I decided to coin this the "twisty leg" during a recent girls' trip. In 7th grade, this was undoubtedly first base, right?

But it was just the beginning...

Middle School Craft Club – Circa 1994
That's me, back row, far left in my mom's oversized sweatshirt, with the curled under bangs. Lisa is front and center, bangled earrings on display and Ricky is to the right of Lisa in the white t-shirt with the coke can spectacles.

A Slice of Ham: *Dad's most cherished Christmas decoration was a 4-foot-tall mechanical Santa Claus that he received as a gift when he was 10. At the time, the Santa was the height of engineering progress. By the time I was in high school, the most impressive thing about Santa was that he was still working and hadn't caught the yard on fire. People from the neighborhood would drive by our house to watch Santa, in his own spotlight, slowly turn his head from side to side and wave. Dad was devoted to maintaining Santa, bringing him in every night to protect him from the elements. Santa went with him when my parents moved to Illinois, and later, when Dad moved into his villa.*

CHAPTER 3

GREG, STEVE, AND SANTA (THE BOYFRIENDS)

One day, I received an email from Dad with the subject line: "If I die." Alarmed, I clicked on the email only to see the following instructions: "Santa's head is in a trash bag in the garage. Do not throw away." The email was accompanied by photographic evidence that Santa's head was indeed in a white kitchen trash bag against the garage wall.

I honored Dad's wishes, until eventually Santa's legs fell off. Once he was officially in three pieces, my husband, Jason, finally convinced me to part with him.

All teenagers make mistakes. Many, like myself, make the same mistake multiple times. If we're lucky, we might learn a thing or two along the way. Sometimes, the best thing we can say about the adolescent years is that we got through them with our hearts and limbs intact. That's an accomplishment in itself. My years at Riverview Gardens Senior High can be neatly divided into three segments: Bad Greg, Good Steve, and Bad Greg II: The Return of Bad Greg.

During the summer after eighth grade, I swapped my glasses for contact lenses and started using Sun-In to lighten my hair. (My mom refused to let me dye it.) Most importantly, I quit dog shows. They had become a bit of an addiction, and if I wanted to hang out with someone other than Toby on the weekend, I had to make a change. I really wanted high school to be fun.

There was one major problem: Lisa and I were being separated. Her parents had chosen to send her to the Catholic High School. At the time, the decision seemed incomprehensibly cruel, but, in retrospect, there may have been some valid reasons for it. Riverview Gardens wasn't exactly what one would call an academic institute or center of excellence. Actually, Riverview lost its accreditation two years after I graduated. A typical graduation ceremony boasted more pregnancies than college scholarships, and the bathrooms always smelled like weed. Fights were a daily occurrence. None of this mattered to Lisa, though. She hated the Catholic school, with its ugly uniforms, strict rules, and cliques. All we wanted was to be together, weed bathrooms be damned. I felt an enormous sense of responsibility for both of us. There was no way Lisa was ever going to become close with those kids, so our social life was going to fall on my shoulders. I needed to make new friends, stat.

My first move was to attach myself to Susan, a peripheral friend of Lisa's and mine from middle school. Susan was a marginal replacement for Lisa in my daily life, but she came with a strategic advantage: she had a hot cousin who threw great parties.

I first laid eyes on Greg at a pool party at Susan's grandparents' house. Their backyard boasted one of the really nice above-ground pools – you know the type, with the little walkway around the rim and a wooden deck with an artificial turf covering. Greg was sitting on the side with his feet in the water, shirtless (naturally) to show off his ripped abs, smoking a cigarette like a sixteen-year-old pro. I thought back to all my attempts at smoking with Adam, usually resulting in gagging and coughing fits, and was immediately in awe. When he brushed his blond hair off his face and looked at me with those icy blue eyes, my knees went a little weak. He smiled at me, and I found my first real crush.

Greg was the type of bad boy all the good girls wanted. He was a star athlete at school, charming, and beloved by everyone, including his teachers, despite the fact that he was almost always in some kind of trouble. He had a penchant for petty crimes, such as stealing lawn ornaments from neighbors or workout equipment from school. He always managed to talk himself out of any serious consequences.

His mom birthed him at sixteen, so his parents were still very young and cool. They were happy to provide booze and cigarettes for all his friends. At one point, his mom gifted me with her expired ID. I used an X-acto knife to extract her picture and replace it with my own. Suddenly,

I was thirty-two and could buy myself beer, assuming, of course, that I had the guts.

"Wow, you look young for thirty-two..." observed the very astute gas-station cashier. "That's what my kids say," I responded, without missing a beat. I snatched the tall cans of Busch before he could question me further and was out the door, heart pumping loudly in my chest. After that, I stuck to buying cigarettes, which had a much lower penalty. But all that would come later.

For now, my relationship with Greg consisted mostly of passing notes back and forth in the hallway. If I saw him on the weekends, it was at the mall. Lisa and I used to swap clothes, attempting to be as sexy as possible. I'd smuggle her favorite white shirt with peekaboo shoulders in my purse – the one my mom thought was slutty – and change in the mall bathroom. Lisa's mom always bought her name-brand clothes with matching shoes, and her grandma took each grandkid shopping when they became a teenager. Oh, the envy! Fortunately, what was always tasteful on Lisa was short and sexy on me. I'd cram my feet into pumps two sizes too small, and we'd parade around the mall, hoping to run into Greg and his friends.

It was around that time that my sister Heather started complaining about irregular periods. When Mom took her to the doctor and she went on the pill, I saw a golden opportunity. Being the supportive sister that I was, I volunteered to go on the pill, as well. I'm not sure why my mom agreed. Maybe I complained of acne. Nevertheless, I got what I needed and was ready to take the next step with Greg.

I lost my virginity in the most '90s way possible: on a waterbed, looking up at a lava lamp. I was probably wearing a choker necklace.

Greg's bedroom was in the basement. The walls were teal blue and purple with a diagonal white stripe going down the middle. The headboard had shelves, one of which housed said lava lamp. The event itself was over fairly quickly. I'm pretty sure it was Greg's first time as well. Our budding romance – if you can even call it that – was pretty much over then, too.

As is so often the case with the very young, Greg and I hadn't exactly talked about our expectations going into this. I sort of expected it to be the beginning of something. For Greg, it was the end. Goal achieved. High fives all around. I can't say I was heartbroken when he stopped talking to me, but I was definitely disappointed. More than anything, I felt played. I was one of the countless naive girls that some guy used as a stepping-stone in his own coming-of-age story. How unoriginal. How dumb. It also sucked because it got me grounded from the homecoming dance.

Mom had a habit of listening in on my phone calls. In those days, you could pick up the landline and hear what was being talked about on the extension phone. It was a habit I was aware of, so I should have been more discerning when spilling the details about my tryst with Greg to Lisa. But I couldn't wait to tell her all about it and, in doing so, inadvertently told my mom. Needless to say, my mom was not as excited as Lisa was. There would be no homecoming dance for me.

Of course, it's one thing to forbid someone from doing something, but it's another thing to actually stop them. When the big night came, Mom and Dad weren't home. I'm not sure where they went, but as soon as their car pulled out of the driveway, I knew where I was going. I zipped down the street to a friend's house, borrowed a dress, and hitched a ride to the dance.

I still remember the look on Heather's face when I walked in: pure astonishment. Not only had I done the unthinkable (sex!), I'd also defied Mom and Dad's wishes and snuck out of the house. Everyone at school knew about it. They knew about the sex because Greg told them, and they knew about me being grounded because Heather had to field "where's your sister" questions. Some people might find this situation humiliating, but not me. This was my turning point. I was a goody two-shoes no longer. Now, I was a badass who no one – no one – could keep from the homecoming dance. Not my parents, not my sister, and definitely not stupid Greg. Newly cool, I set out to put Greg behind me as soon as humanly possible.

Wise women know that the best way to get revenge on a man is to upgrade. The second-best way is to sleep with his friend. Fortunately for me, I was able to accomplish both at once.

Steve was in Greg's class and was also his Riverview Rams soccer teammate. Coincidentally, Steve's grandparents lived right across the street from Greg. They were friendly in the way teammates are, but could not have been more different. While Greg was sexy, Steve was boyishly endearing. He was athletic, sure, but his short dark hair always stuck up in the back. Even in our Junior Prom photo, you can see that tuft of hair refusing to stay down. He drew me in with his lopsided grin, a dimple on one side, and beautiful blue eyes.

Steve drove a tiny gray Mercury Lynx hatchback. He used to swing by to pick me up, and he'd always come in to chat with my dad first. They'd talk about cars and sports, which delighted my dad. Then, we'd go frolic in the Lynx, and I'd be home by curfew. There wasn't a lot of room back there, but we figured it out. On one occasion, we were almost caught when a cop came upon us in the park with a flashlight. We managed to pull our clothes on at the last second, and Steve thought fast, explaining that he had lost his contact lens in the backseat. The cop, ever helpful, shone his light all around looking for it. We never found the contact. Imagine that.

With Steve, I felt safe and comfortable enough to be myself. He was someone I could trust and confide in, a real boyfriend, not a hookup. He used to come over for family dinners, and we attended one another's soccer games. He was the guy I did all my firsts with (aside from that one thing). I went to my first prom with him and had my first pregnancy scare. (After that, he committed to wearing two condoms, which I do not recommend.) Most importantly, he was the first person I said "I love you" to.

Your first love is always exactly like the songs and movies say it will be, yet nothing like them at all. It's both intense (I've never felt like this before) and mundane (everyone feels like this). With Steve, I knew it wasn't magic, but I really thought it might be everything there is to love. Steve and I were getting married someday. I believed it, and so did he.

My mom became concerned the relationship was too serious. "You're young!" she declared, "Play the field! Have fun!" This from the woman who was married at 19. I knew she was trying to live vicariously through me, urging me to make all the reckless and fun choices she abandoned after meeting my dad. Dad, on the other hand, was pretty comfortable with the idea of Steve and me ending up together. He thought we were destined to turn out just like he and Mom: two kids from Glasgow Village who fell in love, got married, and stayed right here in Glasgow Village.

Around this time same time, I became friends with a girl named Molly. We had known each other vaguely in middle school, but she was a year behind me. She recalls being confused on her first day at Riverview High. Sure, she recognized the name Amanda Carter. But I bore no resemblance to the dark-haired, dog-girl she remembered.

"Suddenly," she recalls, "Amanda was hot." Thanks, Molly. Queue the Sun-In commercials.

Molly played soccer with me, and I found in her the kindred spirit I had been missing at Riverview. While I did everything in my power to make myself cool, Molly just was cool. She had an effortless self-confidence, a nonchalant attitude that some might find intimidating. While I was trying to draw boys in, she was scaring them off. Molly was never mean, though. If boys were intimidated by her, it was only because she was funnier than they were and didn't try to hide it. She commanded a cafeteria table like an open mic night. Those of us lucky enough to sit in her orbit spent most of our time cracking up. I found myself spending more time with Molly and Lisa and less time with Steve.

I can't really tell you what changed for me and Steve. It was certainly nothing he did wrong. We were together for a year and a half, which is a lifetime in high school. To all our friends, we were the "It" couple. Molly and Lisa imagined themselves as bridesmaids at our wedding. Perhaps that's what scared me. Or perhaps it started at his soccer games. I looked out onto the field and saw Greg. Despite my previous experience, there was no question who I was more attracted to. Plus, I didn't want the life my parents had. Not yet at least. I wasn't the girl that Steve wanted me to be. I was a Bad Girl at heart.

So, one sunny day during Junior year, I blew it all up. I got back together with Greg.

At the time, Steve and I were working together at Finish Line shoe store. For some reason, I thought the best way to break the news to him would be at work. I figured things couldn't get too heated there. Instead, Steve broke down in the store, in front of customers, our boss, everyone. In the late 1990s, teenage boys were not supposed to cry, and I'm ashamed to admit I never saw this possibility coming. Steve was a wreck, and it was one hundred percent my fault. But I had to do what I had to do, and there's no good way to break a person's heart. Don't worry too much about Steve, though. I promise, he turns out all right.

My parents were very disappointed to see me get back together with Greg, especially now that we were older and the relationship could extend beyond parties in his basement. It didn't help that Heather's boyfriend was a perfect gentleman. He'd always come inside to chat with Dad while she was getting ready, and his parents took them to church every Sunday. Perfect Heather had managed to snag herself a fundamentalist boyfriend. Greg, on the other hand, was well on his way to becoming a full-blown teenage alcoholic. Very chic, very cool.

Finally freed of the expectations of my Good Boyfriend, one of the first things I did was get a tattoo. It was a generic heart-and-rose design I picked off a wall and paid $75 for it. When I got home, Dad was furious, and Mom was jealous. It remains to this day, reminiscent of a Guns-N-Roses album cover from the early 90s, albeit a faded one.

"You'll regret this when you're older!" Dad warned. (This was about as harsh as he was capable of being.) It turns out, the tattoo would be the least of my regrets.

My parents forbade me from smoking or drinking in the house, so I circumvented this problem by spending every waking moment at Greg's house. In addition to buying us booze, his parents would typically join in the party. Greg's behavior, while never unkind, became increasingly out of control. On more than one occasion, while completely drunk, he found his dad's shotgun and fired it into the sky. Everyone just laughed, including me. It never crossed my mind that he might need help.

To be clear, Greg wasn't all bad. For one thing, he was a great student. Perhaps this is the reason my parents never forbade me from dating him. That, and I don't think they wanted to create a Romeo-and-Juliet saga. Greg could ace any test, and his teachers all loved him. I also managed to keep my grades up and was even in the National Honor Society. My favorite subject was Chemistry. I loved it so much I skipped biology completely and went straight to Senior-level Chem. My parents had no idea where this affinity for science came from, especially since I had gotten a D in Algebra one quarter. They'd always considered Heather to be the college-bound kid.

My grades were so good, in fact, that I was able to turn my smarts into a profitable hustle. I charged people for the rights to copy my assignments. One guy paid me five dollars a week for the answers to our German homework. Wunderbar! I also sold Heather's English papers, without her knowing, of course. These were multi-page thesis essays on classics like The Scarlet Letter and The Great Gatsby. In the pre-computer years, I would have to sneak into her bedroom to do this. I'd wait until everyone was out of the house, pull up the paper on her personal word processor, and wait the painstaking thirty minutes for the papers to print. Later, I just made copies at Kinko's. I also became adept at editing photos on Adobe Photoshop, which allowed me to forge extra tickets to my high school graduation, gaining entry for all four of my grandparents and two aunts when each student was only allowed four total tickets. Despite the extra tickets being achieved by nefarious means, it was one of the few times in high school that I felt like I had impressed my Mom.

As for Greg, I often wonder what he could have achieved if his circumstances had been even slightly different. The question of nature versus nurture is one that I would meditate on much more later in life, but for now, I was only interested in the present. What I do know is that his parents did him no favors. The last time I saw Greg, I visited him in a rehab facility. I brought him magazines, and he showed me his full sleeve of tattoos. From the little I've heard, he turned out all right. But he could have been brilliant.

I once stayed at Greg's house for two whole weeks. I didn't so much run away as simply chose not to come home after the weekend. Dad called the house repeatedly, but we wouldn't answer. To this day, I don't know what kept him from marching over there and cursing out Greg's dad. Perhaps it was the guns and the fact you never saw Greg's dad without a Busch tall can in his hand. My parents weren't so much worried by my behavior as hurt. I had gone from being Daddy's little girl to choosing another family over my own.

A typical teenager, I hadn't thought much about how my actions impacted my family. I was only trying to have a good time. I was so oblivious that I still came home for Father's Day dinner at my parents' house, as if nothing was wrong. That's when Grandpa Carter pulled me aside to finally talk some sense into me. "You're breaking your dad's heart," he said. That was enough. I moved back home, where I belonged.

Eventually, my relationship with Greg would lead to my getting arrested. It wasn't a serious offense, but it was enough to wake me up.

I was working in the photo department at the Schnuck's grocery store, where my mom was a cashier. Back then, it cost around $10 to develop a roll of 20mm film. Whenever Greg's mom came in, I'd put all her photos into a single sleeve, so she'd only have to pay for one pack. I also allowed Greg's parents and all his friends to rent VHS videotapes for free. I didn't think of this as stealing – I was only doing them a favor.

My downfall was not paying attention to whether anyone bothered to return these free videos. They usually didn't. I also never considered that the value of a VHS tape was around $300-$400. This was because movies used to come out for rental before becoming available for sale. These tapes were the only accessible versions of these movies, and I was giving them away. When I was finally caught, I was arrested for over $2,000 of theft. The entire situation was extremely embarrassing for my mom, who determined that even her tough love was no longer enough. It was time to bring in the big guns: Aunt Ingrid.

Aunt Ingrid was a legendary figure in my eyes. She spent most of the year off doing feats of greatness, only to return home for one week a year, just in time to scare me straight. I was in the kitchen at Grandpa Louie's farm when she marched in, formidable and terrifying.

She put her hands on the table and leaned into me, looking me straight in the eye.

"If I ever hear of you doing something like that again, I'll pull your head through the phone," she whispered. And I believed her.

"I can be kind of hard," Ingrid admitted, recalling the event just a few weeks ago. It turns out, she took no pleasure in being the family disciplinarian. "I got in there, did my thing, and got out," she explains. She may as well have been talking about a military operation. Fortunately, the mission was successful. I was never arrested again.

I also started to seriously question my relationship with Greg. I was growing up, after all. And, while I'd definitely had a lot of fun in high school, graduation was upon me. I had to think about what I wanted to do next, and if marrying Steve wasn't an option, marrying Greg really wasn't an option.

Sometimes, as with Santa, you just have to throw out the whole man.

A Slice of Ham: *Dad firmly believed that the Amish owned Walgreens. Someone must have told him this fib as a child, and it wedged its way into his impressionable mind so deeply it could not be removed. Every time we passed a Walgreens, he would declare with full confidence, "You know, the Amish own Walgreens." We nodded along amiably, having given up on debating this long ago. Then, inexplicably, one day he changed his tune. Walgreens, he was now certain, was run by The Church of Jesus Christ of Latter-day Saints. (In case you're wondering, Walgreens was founded by Charles Rudolf Walgreen, a Methodist.)*

CHAPTER 4

MOLLY'S
INGROWN TOENAIL

D uring my senior year of high school, I drove a used 1985 maroon Escort Station Wagon dubbed The Shaggin' Wagon, a hand-me-down from a neighbor. It cost $800 and guzzled a quart of oil per week. While the wagon never saw any shaggin', it was the perfect car for hauling all your buddies around - and I mean ALL your buddies! That car was always rolling around the mean streets of North St. Louis County, loaded with no fewer than ten field hockey or soccer players. What can I say? It was the mid-1990s.

The fact that I went to college at all was somewhat serendipitous. I hadn't thought seriously about life after Riverview Gardens until I met an older guy, a student at Southern Illinois University at Edwardsville (SIUE). I'll call him Mark. We first met when we were working together in the photo department at Schnuck's. (He was not involved in any VHS-related crimes.) We connected over our shared fascination with technology and my desire to date a college hockey player. Mark helped me register my very first domain name, AmandaCarter.com. (I sold it a few years ago to a photographer.) For a high school senior, there's nothing more exciting than visiting a college campus with a hunky older man! But rather than take in all that the campus had to offer, we would mostly play on his computer, fool around on his twin bed, and ride around in his fake Iroc Camaro with the T-Tops off, me wearing nothing but jeans and a bra. It was no shaggin' wagon, but we were still the hottest nerds in town.

A whole new world opened up to me when I met Mark. Suddenly, I had no curfew, as my parents generally approved of me hanging out with someone who had a future. I also had a clear idea what I wanted from life, and that idea didn't include Greg. My future was the information technology field.

The break-up with Greg didn't go as smoothly as I or my parents would have liked. He, like Steve, was heartbroken. Unlike Steve, he did not take the news lying down. Greg started showing up at my house and waiting outside in his car. He threw rocks at my window until I relented and answered, then he would beg me to change my mind. At one point, he wrote me a five-page letter. I don't remember what it said, but it was certainly passionate. Things eventually got bad enough that Dad had to get involved. It's evidence of how happy Dad was about the breakup that my mild-mannered father would enter into such a confrontation. Naturally, though, he did it in the nicest way possible. Dad walked out into the driveway where Greg was sitting in his car and asked him to roll down the window.

"I know how hard this is," Dad told Greg gently, "but it's over now, and you have to move on. It's all going to be okay, young man. I promise." Incredibly, his mild-mannered approach worked. Greg never came around again.

Not long after that, I got the minimum score I required on the ACT to enroll at SIUE and moved into an apartment with a girl named Jessica. Oh, and I started dating Mark. Obviously. Not at all coincidentally, Jessica's boyfriend was Mark's roommate, also known as Hot Todd. (More on Hot Todd later.)

The first few months of college were full of new experiences. I paid rent for the first time ($210/month for my share of a two-bedroom), and Jessica convinced me to audition for a Jordache jeans commercial. I'd never done any modeling before, so I was pretty shocked when I got a call back and even more shocked when I was cast. You can still find the commercial on YouTube, which features me flying through the air, shaggy blonde bob bouncing and twirling, while a female voice moans a wordless melody over an electric guitar riff. I'm wearing loose-fitting pants and a three-quarter sleeve T-shirt with the number 55 on it. It's all black-and-white, very angsty skater-chic, very 1999. By the end of college freshmen year, I had a cool older boyfriend, a solid career path, a commercial on MTV, and my face in YM, Teen and Teen People Magazines, not to mention the posters all over Walmart (not nearly as exciting). The life of glamour suited me well.

I started driving the Shaggin' Wagon to frat parties at the American Legion Hall (that's some real Midwestern shit) all by myself. I didn't need to know a single soul, and I didn't need any drugs to have fun. I just wanted to dance. Alone in a sweaty basement, lost in a sea of bodies, I felt the way any young college kid is supposed to feel: unencumbered, unafraid, and free in my crop top and baggy pants.

I still felt this way in September of my sophomore year when I went to visit Molly at Northwest Missouri State University in Maryville. Other than drinking Tequila Rose Liqueur for the first time, I don't remember much about that visit, but Molly clearly recalls the nagging cough that plagued me throughout the weekend. Most likely, I don't remember it, because it didn't seem important. In college, colds are almost as frequent as hangovers. I powered right through it, carrying it along with me to bars and parties like the COVID of 1999. I didn't get to see my high school friends very often, and I wasn't about to let a pesky cough ruin a good time.

Once I returned home, though, the symptoms escalated. I had pain in my muscles and chest, swollen lymph nodes, exhaustion, and a horrible, phlegm-filled cough. There was only one possible explanation: the flu. Mom's solution was to take me to the neighborhood quack – let's call him Dr. Berlin – who was free and easy with the antibiotics, like an original "pill mill" doc before the opioid epidemic, pedaling bacterial resistance as a side gig. You'd walk into the tiny Glasgow Village clinic, tell him you weren't feeling so hot, and leave with a script. So, I loaded up on meds, and the symptoms subsided a bit. But try as I might, I couldn't shake that cough.

A few weeks later, I decided to go to the SIUE campus medical center. I was half expecting them to pull the typical "campus doctor" move and tell me I had gonorrhea or chlamydia while throwing some condoms at me. Instead, the doctor looked down my throat and promptly diagnosed me with bronchitis, prescribing more antibiotics and a boatload of cough syrup. It felt like a very reasonable treatment plan. This happened at least two more times.

"Yep. It's definitely bronchitis," he'd reassure me. Then, he'd give me still more antibiotics and send me back to class. The cough became part of my identity. I was no longer Amanda from the Jordache commercial with the cool boyfriend. I was Amanda from the Jordache commercial with the cool boyfriend and the ridiculous cough. Was this new glamorous life starting to slip?

The cough came with me to work at a local Edwardsville, Illinois, Internet Service Provider. If you recall the good-old-dial-up days of 1999, there was AOL and everyone else. I worked for one of the "everyone-else's," an ISP called Easy-Link. I was on the tech-support team, which meant I sat in a cubicle all day and took customer support calls. I coughed incessantly throughout my shifts. Not a dry cough, but a wet, productive cough with lots of gunk. My coworkers took to periodically yelling at me from across the room.

"Get a chest X-ray, Carter!" It was a joke, but it shouldn't have been.

By the time Christmas break rolled around, I had developed an ongoing earache and was pretty confident the antibiotics weren't working. Still, despite the teasing from coworkers and the stares from classmates, inertia kept me from doing anything about it. Fortunately, there was one person I would listen to: Marilyn.

My sister was supposed to dog-sit for her that weekend, but, for reasons none of us can recall, she had to cancel. So, the job fell on me. ("Oh no!" Marilyn remembers thinking, "You're totally irresponsible, but I'm desperate, so okay.") I came over to play fetch and get my marching orders, and that's when she noticed the cough. Marilyn was not impressed with my half-assed efforts to see doctors in my spare time and put her foot down.

"Get your butt to a real doctor," she demanded. "Not Dr. Berlin, not your campus health center. Someone who knows what the heck they're doing." I knew she was right and, finally, agreed.

Like a lot of college kids, I didn't have a primary care physician, evidence of just how confident I was of my invincibility. I tried to make an appointment with my parents' doctor, but he wasn't available. So, I went to Plan B: picking a doctor in the same practice with the funniest name. I flipped through the roster until I found a winner. You'd think, after months of misdiagnosis, I'd be more discerning about this process. Fortunately, Dr. Bean was a great choice. He was the first person to take my illness seriously.

The stethoscope felt ice cold on my chest as Dr. Bean asked me to breathe in deeply and breathe out. He frowned.

"There's wheezing in your chest," he explained succinctly. "You need a chest X-ray right away." My coworkers were right. I was surprised. Despite everything, I still fully expected him to tell me I had bronchitis. (Or chlamydia. Or a hangover.) Just to be safe, he prescribed me more antibiotics. Because really, what were the odds of it being anything serious?

After my X-ray, I headed straight to the financial capital of Amish Country (Walgreens...or was it the Mormons) to get my script filled. By the time I arrived back home, Mom was standing behind the plexiglass front door, waiting for me. I could tell by the ashen look on her face that something was very wrong. Dr. Bean had called and said he wanted me and my parents back in his office immediately. We got in the car and headed back. I still remember that quiet ride in the back seat of my parents' white Pontiac Grand Am. I was 19 years old at that point, but I felt like a scared child.

Dr. Bean had the chest X-ray in his hands when we arrived. I sat across from him at the desk, my parents on either side of me, as he pointed to the little white circles scattered across my lungs. Enlarged lymph nodes. Apparently, I was very lucky not to be gasping for breath. Dr. Bean reached across the desk to touch a bulge on the right side of my neck. This too was an enlarged node that no one had noticed.

"What have you had to eat so far today?" He asked me.

"What?" My head was in a fog, trying to process all this information. His question didn't make sense.

"For the CT scan, it's best if you don't have food in your stomach."

I racked my brain. Food? What was food, again? Then, I remembered the tube of Pringles I kept shoved between the Shaggin' center console and the Shaggin' seat. Oh yeah. Food. The perfect food, in fact, for when you must travel 30 miles back and forth to school. (I had already moved home because Jessica had dumped Hot Todd to run off with a new boyfriend, and secretly, I was a little homesick.)

"I've had some Pringles," I told him.

"That's fine," he responded. He scheduled the CT scan for that day, and we immediately proceeded to a dedicated imaging center a few miles away.

At this point, we were all pretty freaked out. If you've never seen a CT scan machine before, it looks like a white plastic version of the Stargate. You lie down on what's basically a conveyor belt, and you're passed through a big white circle: a real "donut of doom." Tony Soprano gets a CT scan in the pilot episode of The Sopranos after his panic attack involving ducks. Dad squeezed my hand before I went in, then I was alone.

"Breathe in, breathe out, hold it," the technician said. Then the machine would make a terribly loud noise and move ½ inch further. "Breathe in, breathe out, hold it." Repeat. CT scans took over an hour back in 1999. Now you can zip through in 10 minutes or less. I would know. I've been at this medical crap for a while.

Next up, three days later, the day before New Year's Eve, I went to Barnes Jewish Hospital for a core needle biopsy. It was a frigid December day. I can't recall which doctor performed the biopsy, but I do remember they took a lot of samples and inserted what looked like the internal ink tube piece of a ballpoint pen right into my chest during another CT scan. I had to wait until the following Monday for the results. In an effort to keep our mind off things, Mark and I attended a New Year's Eve party together. I wore a Band-Aid over my incision, and we both did our best to pretend like nothing was wrong. We kissed at midnight and rang in the year 2000. That party was one of our last happy nights together.

I got the call to return to Dr. Bean's office on January 3rd, Dad's birthday. It's funny how certain things stick in your mind and others don't. I don't remember him saying the words "Hodgkin Lymphoma," but I do remember the size of my tumor: 24cm long and 6cm wide. I couldn't believe something the size of a Blimpie sandwich was sitting in my chest, resting on my lungs. I remember my parents' distraught faces. I know my mom was thinking about my grandmother, the years spent bedridden and having to be fed from a tube, dying at only 59, but looking much older. I didn't cry. It's a strange aspect of being sick.

You try to take care of others. For me, that sense of responsibility was immediate. They might be my parents, but I was going to take care of them. I sat stone-still, trying to hold it together, and trying my best to understand how this could possibly be happening to me. Of course, nothing I could have done could make my parents less scared. Dad still cried – someone had to.

Later that week, Mark met my parents and me for my next appointment with the oncologist. I remember being fully awake, lying on my stomach, trying to turn my head so I could watch them grind down into my pelvis for a bone marrow biopsy. There was no pain, thanks to the amazing narcotics the nurse affectionately referred to as the "I don't give a shit" meds. I'm going to guess it was Dilaudid. While some patients would avert their eyes, I needed to know exactly what was happening to me. I watched, fascinated, as they slowly pulled up something long and pink, about the diameter of a #2 pencil and the color of the pink eraser. My bone marrow. Thankfully, this ended up testing negative. I would not need a bone marrow or stem cell transplant.

One thing people don't talk about with cancer is how weird it is breaking the news to others. I called Molly later that same day, still in shock. I started the phone call the same way I always did.

"What's up?"

What was up with Molly was an ingrown toenail. This was typical for her. She was always in a cast or suffering from some type of sports injury – an affliction that has followed her straight into adulthood. This particular malady was especially annoying because it was going to require a small procedure. Molly laid out, in detail, the trials and tribulations of life with an ingrown toenail. Her toe needed to be injected with an anesthetic before removing the nail. Then, she had to soak her foot in warm water for twenty minutes four times a day, a long and arduous process that left her bored and frustrated. Back in 2000, she didn't even have the luxury of a smartphone to play with while she sat around... some real tragic shit happening there! I let her go on about this for a full ten minutes before she finally stopped to inquire what was up with me.

"I have cancer," I said.

"You're a giant bitch," she replied.

And I laughed. It was a long, hard laugh that finally broke me out of the shock. I could still feel things, I realized. I was going to be okay. That night, Molly brought me a bouquet of flowers and a shit ton of balloons.

When you're diagnosed with cancer at nineteen, you figure out pretty quickly who your friends are. Molly and her mom went to Walgreens and bought every Get-Well card in the place. (Huge win for the Amish.) I received a card from them every week I was in treatment. Mark, on the other hand, became a ghost. Several days a week on his way to his fancy internship at IBM, he would drive past the exit to my house in that electric-blue two-door fake Iroc Camaro. I think I can count on two fingers the times he stopped to come in.

Dad knew this was happening. We never spoke about it on our long daily drives to the hospital, but I knew I could if I ever wanted to. I'm not sure why Mark and I didn't officially break up until well after treatment ended. I think there was too much on my plate to think about, and Mark was enjoying his senior year of college without me. He eventually moved away, met someone else and that was that.

It's one of the strange gifts of cancer: suddenly learning who people are in ways you never would have otherwise. I hadn't coined the phrase genuine human yet at this point in my life, but the concept was beginning to take shape.

Which brings me back to Steve. You know, the only decent boyfriend I'd ever had, who I dumped and left crying in the back of the shoe store? That Steve. Well, I promised you he'd turn out all right. Here's what happened:

After Steve and I broke up, he was so distraught that his parents started to worry about him. One day, his dad was ordering carry-out from a local Italian restaurant and noticed that the girl behind the counter was cute, friendly, and about his son's age.

"Will you go on a date with my son?" he asked, bringing out our old homecoming dance picture from his wallet. (The photo was carefully folded to hide my cursed face.)

"Sure, why not?" replied the cute girl.

That was Steve's future wife.

The new girlfriend's name was Mary, and she went to the local Catholic school. We were about as far from friends as you could imagine. To her, I was the girl who broke Steve's heart. I still remember giving one another the stink-eye on the dance floor at Steve and Greg's Senior Prom. Things got worse the summer after senior year when she and Steve were on a brief break. We may have had a small nostalgic fling, which may have involved some racy pictures. After they got back together, Mary discovered my nudies buried in Steve's closet. Her own senior portrait was in the background. Whoopsie. There aren't a lot of people in my life who I can legitimately say hated me, but Mary was one of them.

Although we had both chosen the same college, Mary and I did not expect to run into one another. So, you can imagine our mutual disgust when I walked into my sophomore history class at SIUE, and the only available desk was right next to her.

"You will not believe who I have to sit next to," she complained to Steve after class, "Amanda Carter. Ew." We spent the first part of that semester avoiding eye contact with each other. I had nothing to be sorry for, and she had no reason to forgive me.

All that changed when I was diagnosed with cancer. I knew I was going to have to miss some classes, and, although I didn't like it, I knew she was smart and took good notes. So, I got up the courage to ask Steve for her number. When it comes to cancer, you have to do what you have to do. Mary wasn't about to be a bitch to a girl with cancer, so she agreed to help me out. At first, it was just sharing notes. Then, she started checking in when I missed class to make sure I got everything I needed. Eventually, because she lived in the same neighborhood, she offered to give me rides to school, something my no-good boyfriend couldn't be bothered to do.

Those rides changed everything for us. It turns out Mary and I had a lot more in common than our taste in men. Little by little, we opened up to each other, talking about everything from music and TV shows to our dreams for the future. She was sweet, funny, and disarmingly sincere - exactly the type of person who would say yes to a date with the son of the guy at the Italian take-out counter. (Those were different times.)

Soon, Mary and I were spending lots of time together outside of class. She even invited me out to a few parties. She did everything in her power to help me feel normal. Eventually, Mary became one of my best friends. I stood by her side when she married Steve, heart glowing with the knowledge that everything worked out exactly the way it was supposed to. We've spent many great vacations together. Mary refers to me as her sixth sister, and, for fun, I frequently photoshop myself into their family photos. (With clothes on, of course.)

That genuine relationship would never have happened without cancer.

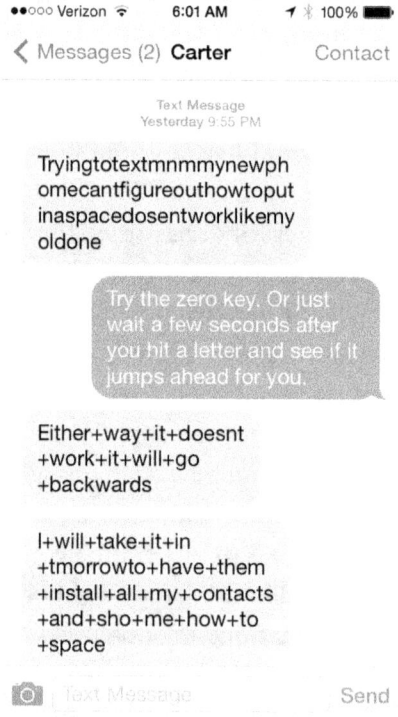

A simple example of the type of funny texts I'd receive from my dad. Originally I thought I'd be creating a coffee table book of these. I had no idea it would turn into a memoir

A Slice of Ham: *Proof that Santa's head was indeed in a trash bag. This is the exact photo dad emailed me.*

SQUAWK

Chemotherapy is like alcohol. There are many different types (think brands, flavors, proofs), and everyone gets their own signature cocktail. It's also like alcohol because it's basically poison.

Today, so-called chemo cocktails are mixed by machines in labs. In the '90s, they were mixed by hand. Mine was hand-crafted by the one and only Madonna. Okay, so Madonna was the name of my favorite chemo nurse. She was in her early forties with short, brown hair and a dark sense of humor that some might have found inappropriate for a cancer center, but not me. I was grateful for her blunt observations. "You're way too young to be in here," she'd proclaim, glancing around at a room full of patients in their sixties and seventies. "What the hell?" What the hell indeed.

Madonna wore thick, blue, plastic gloves that rose up past her elbows. Aside from making her look like she was about to appear in a music video or inseminate a cow, the gloves served to protect her from the chemotherapy chemicals. My particular recipe was called the Stanford V. That's a roman numeral five, although there are actually seven tasty ingredients. The most infamous is Adriamycin or Doxorubicin aka "The Red Devil." It's called that because it's bright red and absolutely brutal on your body. Madonna always inserted the IV in the same spot on the top of my hand, where she could easily see it. "I need to know immediately if it leaks," she explained, "because it will burn your skin off."

"Great!" I responded, "Inject that shit straight into my veins!" That got a good laugh out of her.

Eventually, the veins on my hand grew accustomed to the IV. My bladder, however, was a different story. I had to pee constantly while getting chemo. My IV pole and I would make the long trip down the hallway to the ladies' room and back at least a dozen times in the course of a single session. On the weeks when I received the Red Devil, my urine would be bright red. Scary, but also kind of cool.

Other fun ingredients in the Stanford V regimen include Bleomycin, an anti-tumor antibiotic which wreaks havoc on the lungs, Mechlorethamine, the primary ingredient in mustard gas, Vinblastine, an alkaloid cell toxin, Etoposide, a DNA toxin, Vincristine, another alkaloid cell toxin and Prednisone, a corticosteroid. With cures like that, who needs a disease?

Today, the Stanford V regimen is significantly less common or completely obsolete. Even if my doctors did want to use it on me again, they could not. I've maxed out my lifetime dosage of many of these drugs. This poses a serious challenge for patients with cancer the second time around, but I'll talk more about that later.

I showed up for the first day of spring semester, Sophomore year, knowing that I had cancer, and that before long, everyone would find out. I was determined to have as much fun as possible while I still could, including with my hair. I chopped off my bleach-blond bob in favor of a strawberry blond pixie cut. Next, my hair was bright green. When the Rams won the Super Bowl, it was blue and gold. If I was going to lose my hair, I would do it with style. "Yeah, I have cancer," my hairstyles seemed to say, "But I'm still fun!"

Before long, I knew my time had come. My hair started falling out in handfuls, and not just when I was brushing it. All I had to do was tug on a single strand, and an entire clump would come out. I could rip the hair out of my head like pulling a loose fiber on a string. It was a cool party trick, for about a day. But by the end, the little green tufts sticking out of my skull gave me the appearance of a poorly watered Chia pet. I took one look at myself in the bathroom mirror and thought...

"Nah."

I drove directly to the campus salon and told the unsuspecting woman to shave my head. "Did you lose a bet?" she asked incredulously. Yeah, I thought, with life.

"No bets," I said, trying to keep it cool. "I have cancer." I can't believe she still charged me for a full price hair cut for the five-minute buzz.

Losing my hair wasn't great for my relationship with Mark, which was coming up on two years at this point. I still loved him, and not just because he had pulled me out of my high school slump and introduced me to a whole world of opportunities. Over the past year and a half, we'd grown together. We shared friends and hobbies. He was a part of my identity, and yet I could feel him pulling away. Of course, he never critiqued my bald head or said anything demeaning. But he also didn't show me off the way he used to, and it was obvious he was struggling with attraction. Some of our mutual friends picked up on his attitude and followed suit. I still felt like me on the inside, but something about my appearance made them uncomfortable. No one, including me, had any idea how to address these changes. The space between Mark and me grew wider.

At the same time, other people were finding surprising ways to support me. I showed up to my shift at Easy-Link to discover one of my coworkers had shaved his head for me. I was stunned. "It's just hair," he said, shrugging off the gesture. "It will grow back quickly." But it wasn't just about the hair. He got a few other guys from work to join in, the same people who had been yelling at me about chest X-rays. Now I wasn't the only person at work with a shiny bald head. That made a huge difference. Work became an oasis, somewhere I could go and just be me, even for a few hours.

At the same time, Mary introduced me to a whole new group of friends who embraced me instantly. (Maybe they didn't realize I was the same Amanda she'd hated only months prior. I certainly didn't resemble the photos.) I went along with her to parties and even shared a beer or two. Madonna had given me permission, as long as I didn't overdo it. At one memorable party, the resident druggie even offered me some Molly (the drug kind). "I have cancer!" I protested. "Doesn't mean you should feel left out," he responded with a shrug. It was a nice sentiment, even if a little misguided. These new friends helped me navigate my new reality and reconsider not only who I surrounded myself with, but what kind of person I wanted to be. Repeatedly, the word genuine came to mind. The new friends liked me for who I genuinely was, not for what I looked like. When they asked how I was feeling, they wanted a sincere answer.

With so many new people invested in my recovery, it became challenging to keep everyone up-to-date. My thoughts turned to the website I had created with Mark during my senior year of high school. At the time, it was more about the novelty of making a website, and, since then, I mostly used it to display my graphic design portfolio. Now, I decided I would use it to document my cancer journey. The word blog didn't exist yet, but that's essentially what it was. Every day, no matter how I felt, I'd take the time to share a little about what I was experiencing. Sometimes, all I could manage was a couple sentences. Other times, I was able to share reflections and occasionally even surprise myself by saying something close to profound. The word spread through my family, friends, and friends of friends. Occasionally, I'd receive messages from complete strangers. The knowledge that there was a whole community out there rooting for me bolstered my spirits through the difficult days ahead.

Many people with cancer will tell you that the treatment is often worse than the disease. After losing my hair, the first major side effect I noticed was a tingling sensation in my fingers. Madonna informed me that neuropathy – nerve death – was common. Chemo is poison, after all. In addition to tingling and feeling numb, the tips of my fingers would turn white whenever they encountered something cold. There wasn't enough blood circulating in my fingers. I still hate the frozen food section at Publix to this day. My feet would tingle as well, especially if I tried to do something as ambitious as exercise. Of course, exercise wasn't really in the cards for me most days. I went from being a varsity athlete to someone who regularly struggled just to get out of bed.

The first time I was rushed to the hospital was the result of a high fever. Because of my weak immune system, we knew that any small infection could be deadly. I remember my mom watching from the window as Dad and I pulled out of the driveway. From the ashen look on her face, I could tell she was thinking about her mom and wondering if she would ever see me again. Ever since my grandmother's death, Mom had struggled with the idea of hospitals. She found it difficult to bring herself to visit me, saying that just stepping foot inside made her feel panicky.

At the hospital, the nurses ran a blood test and discovered that I had barely any white blood cells. I was basically walking around without an immune system. I stayed in quarantine for four full days, during which time a hot male nurse had the unenviable job of testing everything that came out of my body. That's pee, poop, snot – you name it. He took cultures of all the fluids, looking for anything that might be trying to kill me. I tried not to die of embarrassment.

To his credit, Mark made an effort to visit me in the hospital. He brought a deck of cards, and we passed the time learning to play Texas Hold 'em, (Rounders, starring Matt Damon, was a big hit at the time.) When it was just the two of us, we really did have fun together. If only this stinking cancer wasn't getting in the way. But when Hot Nurse popped in to tell us it was time for him to go, Mark looked at me like he might never see me again. In some ways, he might have been even more afraid than I was. Honestly, I found that annoying.

Because I was 19, legally an adult, my parents weren't entitled to any information about my condition unless I approved it. If I wanted to, I could withhold the results of every test. This was bizarre to me because I had never felt more like a child in my entire life. I was Daddy's little girl, and I needed his advice, now more than ever. I insisted that my parents know everything that I knew, but the hospital's perseveration on obtaining consent with every conversation did nothing to ease Mom's discomfort with hospitals. It pushed her further away.

Eventually, my white blood cell count rebounded to something closer to normal. Friends sent flowers and cards, filling my room with color. I was even able to update my website by calling a co-worker and dictating exactly what I wanted publicized. About a week later, I was finally allowed to go home, with the caveat that I would now have to receive weekly injections to stimulate my bone marrow and encourage the production of white blood cells.

During my brief stint at the hospital, Mom found a new hobby: collecting exotic birds. You know, typical Sonja stuff. There was a giant blue-and-gold Macaw, a Quaker Parrot, and an African Grey Parrot. Each bird had its own cage, occupying the entire floor plan of what had once been Heather's bedroom. (Heather was away at college by this point, having transferred schools to be closer to her boyfriend.) The Macaw cage was so enormous, a grown person could crawl inside and stand up straight. Although I have no idea why you'd want to. Initially, during chemo, Mom had taken a leave of absence from work to care for me, but maintenance of the birds became a full-time job and an obsession. The birds had their own grocery list, consisting of fresh fruits and vegetables that needed to be cut into bite-sized pieces. She was constantly cleaning their cages and attempting to train them. Despite her Herculean efforts, the dumb birds never learned to talk, instead mimicking the sounds of our cordless home phone ringing and the dial-up computer modem. Ba-dum-ba-dum-ba-dum SQUACK!

One of many weird and unfortunate side effects of chemo is that everything tastes different. Foods I used to love, like popcorn and peanut butter, were inedible now. But I craved hard-salami roll-ups with cream cheese. On one particular evening, when I was scouring the fridge desperate for my cream cheese fix, I realized, to my horror, that all we had were endless containers of fresh fruit and raw veggies. From that moment on, the birds became my sworn enemies. Meanwhile, Mom was struggling with my new injection regimen. The needles were large and had to be injected deep into my arm or leg, and she hated giving the injections as much as I hated receiving them. Possibly more. She'd often lose her nerve right when she was about to prick me, meaning she'd have to try multiple times. I'd clench my teeth, trying not to complain, but she could tell by my expression that I was miserable. This made her more nervous; her hands would start shaking, and we'd both end up frustrated and angry. Sometimes, when I knew it was time for a shot, I'd strategically make sure I was around someone else who might volunteer to do it. There was a nurse who lived down the street, and a couple friends had moms who were nurses. When Dad gave me the shot, however, she'd retreat to the bird-room to sulk. I'd frequently hear them arguing through the walls. It would go something like this:

Dad: "You need to pull yourself together!"
Mom: "I don't understand how this is so easy for you!"
Dad: "How dare you say this is easy?"
"Squawk!"
(That was the parrot.)

In addition to emotional stress, overstimulated bone marrow caused intense joint pain. For me, it was especially bad in my jaw region. I'd take copious amounts of Percocet, but it was never enough to combat the constant, gnawing ache. My mom was at her wits' end. "I mean, what do you even do for your kid when they say their jaw hurts?" I overheard her complain to Marilyn, exasperated. I felt the heavy weight of guilt on my shoulders. I felt awful that she felt awful, and she felt awful because I felt awful. Dad felt awful because Mom and I couldn't get along, and nothing we tried could break us from this cycle.

One morning, I woke up and realized I didn't have the strength to get out of bed. The moment I stood up, the breath rushed out of my lungs. I felt like I had just run up six flights of stairs. I don't remember how I managed to call for my parents, but when they finally came running, they found me on the floor with my face paper white. "I can't stand up," I panted. "I can't breathe."

This time, the problem was my red blood cells. The bone marrow stimulation had caused an inverse reaction, which led to those numbers plummeting. I ended up being transfused with four pints of blood during a two-day hospital stay. Now, there was a second set of shots I would have to take on the off weeks between the white blood cell shots. That meant more uncomfortable injections and more pain.

It's important to note here that, if it weren't for the excellent insurance Dad had through the union, my treatment likely would have bankrupted my parents. The shots alone were a thousand dollars per injection, and that doesn't even touch the cost of chemotherapy and radiation. We weren't wealthy people, and it's easy to understand how someone else in our situation could become crushed by these costs. As it was, our copays were never more than a couple of dollars. I don't think it's an exaggeration to say Dad's union membership saved my life.

As much as I wanted to spend time with Mary, or with Molly and Lisa when they were in town, I couldn't always drum up the energy. With little motivation to get dressed, I started wearing the same set of ultra-comfortable clothes each day. This uniform consisted of Mark's old hockey t-shirt (number 22) and a pair of baggy black windbreaker pants with red Adidas stripes down the side. The t-shirt made me feel close to him, yet we rarely saw each other or communicated aside from sporadic phone calls. He'd ask how I was doing, and I'd put on my bravest voice. "I'm doing great!" I lied. "I feel really good." He never really pressed further.

Unable to get ahead of the pain or the tiredness, I ended up taking incompletes in both the classes I kept that semester (I had dropped the majority of my course load back when I was diagnosed). This was a huge disappointment, because I really wanted to graduate on time. Fortunately, my history professor made my passing a priority. He decided to become my private tutor, meeting with me every Tuesday the following summer until I passed the final exam. I ended up getting full credit for the history course. To this day, I'm not sure if he'll ever know just how much that meant to me.

There's a saying I read on Instagram recently that brought me right back to this period in my life. It was one of those floral-background images with cursive text that read simply "Breathe in confidence and exhale fear." There was a lot to be afraid of during that time and a lot to be bitter about. But it's a privilege to be able to witness the best in people. Sometimes, it takes hard times for loved ones to really expose their hearts to you. These positive experiences, like with my history professor, are what I try to breathe in. I breathe in the friends with the bald heads and the ones who drove hours out of their way to see me. I breathe in Madonna and all the nurses and doctors who took care of me. I try to let go of the Red Devil, and the illness, and the people who never knew what to say.

I also breathe in the memory of my hats. Believe it or not, the hats were Mom's idea, one thing she got very right. When a few friends from the dog show community wanted to know what they could do to help, she suggested sending hats to cheer me up. It worked. Before long, she was soliciting hats from everyone I'd ever met, and even a few I'd never met. They were a great addition to my website. Every time I received a new hat, I'd take a picture of myself wearing it and post it online. Digital cameras were new. I would download the photos from the camera and upload them manually. I didn't use a website editor; it was all my own code in HTML. Of course, by today's standards, none of this is impressive, but at the time, it was exciting, and I really thought I was a badass programmer. People got a kick out of seeing me wearing their hats on the website. The more photos I posted, the more hats I received. There were definitely more hats than I could ever dream of wearing, but I loved each and every one of them.

After twelve weeks of chemo that felt more like twelve years, I had a two-week break, then moved right on to radiation treatment. Meanwhile, I had to wean myself off painkillers. It's incredible how quickly the brain becomes adjusted to those substances and will actually manufacture pain to convince you to take more. It's not at all surprising to me that so many cancer patients wind up with addictions.

Because of Mom's aversion to hospitals, responsibility for my daily radiation fell squarely on Dad's shoulders. Now, it was his turn to take off work, which was a much better arrangement for everyone. Mom needed the distraction of work to feel normal; Dad wanted to be with me as much as possible. Aside from a few occasions where Molly or another friend stepped in, radiation became a strange form of father-daughter bonding. He drove me there and back every day and sat with me throughout my treatment.

The big problem with radiation is that, in addition to curing cancer, it also causes cancer. Because of where my tumors were located, my doctors knew that treating me with radiation would significantly increase my risk of breast cancer and cardiovascular issues. But future problems only matter if you actually have a future in the first place. So, in an effort to mitigate potential harm, every patient is given a personalized lead block adhered to plexiglass to protect from excess rays. Mine looked like a big M, with a handle on the side for convenient transportation. The resulting burns were the inverse of this shape, an enormous angry W across my entire front chest. I was slammed with so much radiation that I will never have a normal chest X-ray for the rest of my life, nor a normal hairline at the base of my neck.

On top of all this, I still wanted to save my relationship. I sensed that Mark wasn't as attracted to me as he once was, and, rather than talking it out, I took it upon myself to fix it. Channeling my inner Madonna, I went into one of those year-round Halloween stores and bought myself a sexy nurse costume and adorned my long blonde wig. I drove to Mark's apartment in this get-up, and, when he answered the door, I proceeded to perform a striptease. I'm going to admit, doing a striptease is a lot of fun, and, if you haven't done one, you should try it. But the gesture didn't change much between us. When the sexy nurse costume came off, that big red burn was still the only thing he could look at. He was still too immature to recognize my gorgeous vulnerability. How deeply unfortunate for him.

As a young person, you experience life at the speed of light. School, sex, work, fun, repeat. Because everything is fast and easy, it's also a bit cheap. Cancer changed all of that for me. Suddenly, almost nothing was easy. When spending time takes effort, you think more deeply about who you want to spend time with. You realize that the attention and awareness you put into your relationships is just as important, if not more so, than what you do to pass the time. I spent hours sitting around the hospital with my dad, just learning to be patient. Waiting in that bland basement waiting room, flipping through outdated magazines, I realized that even the dullest moments can be gifts and promised myself that I would live all of them with profound gratitude. I envisioned myself slowing down, reaching out, being as genuine as humanly possible, and not wasting another second, because every second is precious.

Then, of course, I'd take a deep breath and go have a few beers with my friends. You can't be profound all the time.

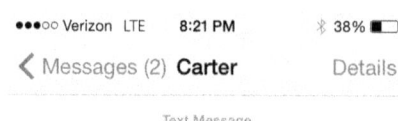

Text Message
Today 8:05 PM

Don ' t Worry It an 't over
until the Fat Lady
Sings,the2nd Base
umpire is Ron Kopa he
lives past Ofallon MO he
goes to the same Barber
IDo love Dad

📷   Text Message   Send

A Slice of Ham: *Whenever Dad had to drive anywhere new, he'd make a "dry run" first. He'd roll by the location a few days ahead of time and report back to us. "I took a dry run by their house last week," he'd announce, "It's pretty nice, but someone has to mow that lawn!" We all teased him about this, but deep down, I got it. He liked knowing what was coming up around the corner. Unfortunately, life doesn't always give you a dry run. You have to get pretty comfortable with surprises, both good and bad. For those of us with cancer, it's more like driving without any directions at all.*

CHAPTER 6

IT'S A WIG, OKAY?

Midway through my chemo treatment, around February of 2000, I had a second CT scan. I had to go to the film imaging center in person to pick up all my images and bring them to my doctor. Naturally, I wasn't going to wait for my appointment to find out what was going on in my chest. I had to look at them myself first (a dry run, you might say). This was the first time I really saw and comprehended the measurements for my original tumor, and I was shocked to realize there had been something the size and shape of a rolling pin sitting in my chest (24cm long by 6cm wide). But this new scan held good news: the tumor had shrunk significantly. I was responding well to treatment. By the end of radiation, the news was even better. I was in remission.

My first feeling upon hearing the news was elation. I had a new lease on life! The second was abject fear. When would this lease expire? Based on the size of my original tumor and stage of my cancer, I still had a 20% chance of dying before the age of 35. For the next two years, I would wake up every morning with my heart racing, convinced my cancer had returned. I dreaded my regular check-ups and the fatal news they might bring. On the outside, however, I was the ultimate optimist. I'd kicked cancer's butt, and I was ready to take on the world. I wanted to do everything right away. Whether this sense of urgency was based on genuine positivity or veiled panic varied from day to day. The important thing was that I refused to allow fear to paralyze me. If I was going to be afraid, it had to be a motivating fear. Whether I had another eight years or another eighty years ahead of me, I had a lot of shit to get done.

Two days after my final radiation treatment, I showed up for the first day of my internship at IBM Global Services. Mark had been interning there for years and, after graduation, had landed a coveted full-time job. He put in a good word with his boss for me, and I'd shown up for the interview while I was still in treatment. This was only the third time I'd donned a wig, the first being the strip tease and the second, Mark's commencement ceremony. I didn't want him to face uncomfortable questions about his sickly girlfriend on such an important day. The problem with disguises, though, is that you have to either keep wearing them forever or admit the truth. They're also really itchy. (That is, if the disguise involves a wig.) I showed up for my second day of work with my bald head gleaming.

"No, I haven't joined a protest movement," I assured my stunned boss, "I had cancer for a little bit, but I'm feeling better now. This chia head should fill in by the end of the summer." And that was that.

IBM Global Services placed me on a rotation at Boeing, which meant I was able to obtain a Secret Security Clearance. Not Top-Secret, just regular secret, but still pretty cool for a college kid. The pay was even cooler, a decadent $16.25 per hour. For the first time in my life, I had actual savings. The first thing I did was move out of my parents' house and away from those dang birds. Mark's good friend Dusty and I had become close, and he was also interning at IBM, so we moved in together. We were one big happy family, almost as if I'd never gotten sick. Only now Mark was living in North Carolina for work, meaning we were long-distance. Fortunately, my hefty paycheck allowed me to fly out to see him once a month. After being unable to drive myself around for months, these solo flights felt like the ultimate freedom.

As much as I would have liked to shove my experience with cancer into a metaphorical box and lock it in a closet somewhere, I couldn't. For one thing, there was the persistent worry that it would return. That was unpleasant, but at least it made sense. It was much harder to explain my sense of undefined loss. I didn't for a second miss cancer treatment, but I felt like something was unresolved inside me. It's hard to describe the feeling of something so massive and all-consuming, suddenly just being over. I'd had cancer, and now I didn't. What the heck do I do now?

The answer was service. Marilyn had been participating in Relay for

Life since her brother-in-law was diagnosed with Hodgkin Lymphoma at age 24. Relay is an all-night event in which participants raise money and walk around a track continuously for twelve hours straight. There are musical performances, games, and entertainment throughout the evening to keep participants motivated, and all the proceeds go to the American Cancer Society. Marilyn invited me to join her team, and I quickly agreed. Survivors aren't required to raise money for Relay for Life, but Dad suggested I write a few personal letters to family and friends. I still remember sitting at the kitchen table with him, handwriting those letters. In the end, I raised about $100 in donations. It wasn't much, but it was something.

My parents and I showed up for my first North St. Louis County Relay for Life on a disgustingly hot, sticky, St. Louis summer night. I immediately wondered if this had been a mistake, especially for Dad, who was already dripping with sweat before we even started walking. I stood in a line of fellow survivors, anxiously awaiting our opportunity to introduce ourselves and walk the opening lap. To my surprise, there was a young woman nearly my age ahead of me in line. She introduced herself as Jenny Steinman.

When it was my turn to approach the microphone, I noticed, to my great surprise, that my hands were trembling slightly. I'm not usually uncomfortable with public speaking, but this was different. I looked out at the sea of purple, green, and blue shirts (each color with its own unique significance) and was suddenly keenly aware of the fact that my newly-sprouted hair was matted to my scalp with sweat. Everyone was looking at me.

"My name is Amanda Carter, and I'm twenty years old. I had Hodgkin Lymphoma, and I'm three months cancer free."

The crowd erupted in applause. For a moment, I felt like I was floating on air as the colors blurred together and spun around me. Was it an out-of-body experience, or just my eyes watering? My parents met me on the track and supported me, one on each arm. As we walked the oval together, the tears flowed freely for the first time since I'd learned the good news. I was alive. Alive. Alive. Alive.

Fortunately, the temperature dropped as the sun set, painting the sky pink and purple, and a cool breeze dried the sweat from our skin. I caught up with Jenny on the track, and we chatted for much of the night. I knew I'd met a kindred spirit, someone who understood exactly what I'd gone through. We put one foot in front of the other and kept it up all night long.

That night, I learned about a $1000 annual scholarship for survivors who were diagnosed under the age of 21. Never one to pass up an opportunity, I dashed off an essay as soon as I got home and soon found out I had received the scholarship. Recipients of the scholarship were encouraged to do twenty-five hours a year of volunteer work for ACS, but this wasn't going to be enough for me. I had caught the bug. I didn't just want to do a bunch of shit anymore; I wanted to do a bunch of shit that helped people. I was determined, in recognition of my annual scholarship, to raise at least $1000 for Relay in the following year.

This higher goal made my original strategy of handwritten letters less feasible. Fortunately, Relay digitized their fundraising platform, allowing me to raise money online. This turned out to be a game-changer. I sent email requests to every person who had visited my website, left a note, or sent me a hat. I also emailed local businesses, asking them to donate $500 for a sponsorship sign at the event. I never let a "no" discourage me, and there were a lot more yesses than nos. I raised $1200 for my second Relay, barely surpassing my goal. That year, I received two shirts in the mail, one purple and one green. Purple was for survivors, and green was for everyone who raised over $1000. I ripped both shirts in half and sewed them together. I'd earned them both, after all.

Meanwhile, my long-distance relationship with Mark was at a turning point. While he never explicitly asked me to, I'd started the process of going through RCIA to become a Catholic. No, I didn't have a dramatic post-cancer religious conversion. I mostly just adored Mark's mom, and I knew how important it was to her. There was also something appealing to me about the visual beauty of Catholicism. I could easily picture a wedding in a Catholic Church, with my dad walking me down a long aisle with stained-glass windows on either side. Unfortunately, it was becoming harder to imagine Mark waiting for me at the other end.

I was still flying to North Carolina on a monthly basis, but the trips no longer felt like mini-adventures. Mark wasn't able to return the favor, or so he claimed. He had a real job, and I was still a student and an intern. I sensed a growing distance between us. Our happy family of college friends weren't his primary friends anymore, and I didn't know the new people he hung around with. Our phone calls became briefer and farther apart. I realized I didn't miss him nearly as much as I should. Honestly, I don't remember which of us finally had the guts to call it quits, but I know we were both relieved when it finally happened. After five years of ups and downs, I was more heartbroken over the prospect of losing his family than I was over losing him. That's how you know it isn't right. Fortunately, I was able to remain close with Mark's family. They still donated to Relay, even after I quit RCIA. Years later, they would attend my wedding when I married Jason.

After the breakup with Mark, I swore off boys for two whole months. (I know, I know.) I had intended for it to be a bit longer, but when I found myself locked in a kiss with my childhood best friend, I realized I should probably give that a try. Adam, of stolen-car fame, had stuck by my side through a string of guys, some of whom tolerated his special place in my heart and others who were less easy-going. He had stepped away quietly when asked but was always there to fall back on when heartbreak reared its ugly head yet again. Being with Adam was like pulling on your favorite cozy sweatshirt: warm, cozy, and comforting. We had the same dry sense of humor, the same sense of mischievousness. What we didn't have was a magnetic attraction to one another. Everything was perfect, except the physical connection, which was rather absent. In retrospect, it might seem a bit odd that I never considered that Adam might be gay. But in fairness, I don't think he had considered it yet either. Whatever reasons we used to justify it, we were better off as friends. Years later, at a friend's birthday party, his mother confessed that she was still heartbroken over our breakup. While it could have made another sweet Glasgow Village love story, it obviously wasn't in the cards.

Sometime during my third year of college, I started feeling restless again. I was still waking up every morning with my heart pounding and the dreaded sensation that my time was running out. Neither my fancy internship nor my relentless fundraising could suffice. I needed to see the world and soon. I went to my school's study abroad office and picked up a brochure, scanning for programs in English-speaking countries. (I'd given up on German back in high school.) They offered two programs in England: Newcastle and Sheffield. I wasn't familiar with either place, but I'd at least heard of Newcastle before, thanks to the copious amounts of brown liquids sloshed around at frat parties via the American Legion hall. This decision-making process wasn't too far off from how I'd chosen Dr. Bean, and that had worked out all right. I registered for the program before even mentioning it to my parents.

"I'm not sure that's the best idea," Dad mused, pushing food around his dinner plate. It was his way of saying he hated it. This was only a few months after 9/11, and the idea of me boarding an airplane and flying off to an unknown land was close to unthinkable.

"You're not going," was Mom's matter-of-fact response. "What if you have a relapse while you're over there?"

"I won't," I responded, willing myself to believe it. I had to, or risk cancer controlling the rest of my life. "Anyway, it's not up to you," I insisted," I'm paying for it myself." I had saved up enough money at IBM to cover the entire trip, including room and board in the campus dormitory.

This was an important turning point in my relationship with my parents. I'd gone from an irresponsible rebel to a sickly kid dependent on them for everything. Finally, I was an independent adult capable of making my own decisions. Of course, it was hard for Dad to let go of thinking of me as a little girl. Wanderlust wasn't an emotion he could relate to; he was happy to live his entire life in Glasgow Village. Mom, on the other hand, saw me living the life she always wanted. I was a self-sufficient, career-minded woman. She gradually shifted to becoming more supportive of my trip. Dad accepted it mostly because he had to.

"Whatever you do," he told me, "Just stay safe." I promised that I would.

When I arrived in Newcastle, my gut feeling was that I had made a huge mistake. First off, it was sleeting. My fingers, which never recovered from neuropathy, started to ache and turn purple in the cold. There was also no one to pick me up. All I had was an address in my pocket and an enormous, unwieldy green suitcase (the kind that rolled longways on tiny wheels). I didn't even know how to hail a cab. I ended up walking two miles to the address, dragging my massive suitcase behind me along with a pile of heavy tech equipment. Like any Computer Information Systems nerd, I'd brought with me a laptop, digital camera, camcorder and multiple spare hard drives for downloading movies from Napster.

When I finally arrived at what turned out to be an old English castle, they were completely baffled by my presence. Somehow, no one from school had informed them that I would be arriving. I collapsed on a bench in the front lobby, sweating despite the cold, and tried to think of how to tell Dad that he had been right all along.

"We're going to put you in the first-floor suite," the program manager told me. It turned out to be my lucky day. Unlike the standard dorms upstairs, the suite had its own kitchen and bathroom with an enormous soaking tub. I would fill that tub with hot scalding water and submerge myself completely, sometimes twice a day. It was the only cure for my aching hands and frozen feet.

Aside from the icy cold, my time in Newcastle was everything I could have imagined and more. I travelled by train with new friends, staying in crappy hostels in cities I'd never heard of. I was able to cement my popularity with the other students by my ability to hack into the (off-limits) campus network and download full-feature movies from Napster. We'd watch movies before going out, usually on weekdays when we could afford it. Our favorite disco was named the Tuxedo Princess, a retired cruise ship along the River Tyne. We'd dance the night away until the wee hours of the morning to a European genre all of its own on a rotating dance floor.

I found myself a local boyfriend, a British hunk who took me to visit his family in a remote town on the English/Scottish border. We looked over the edge of a cliff, feeling the icy spray from crashing waves, like something out of a cheesy romance novel. The relationship wasn't anything serious, a typical European fling, but it felt great just to be Amanda again, not "the girl with cancer." Of course, I told him about my cancer, but it was just another distant fact about me, like living in St. Louis, having a sister, or cohabitating with giant birds.

While I was in England, Boeing ended their contract with IBM, abruptly terminating my internship along with it. While this was disappointing, I didn't lose sleep over it. I knew that I'd need to find a new paying gig as soon as I got back to the US. (I had already blown through all those fabulous savings on trips to discos and late-night munchies.) While abroad, I managed to land a phone interview with Anheuser-Busch's Information Security department, which happens to be based in St. Louis. The basic hacking skills I had honed while in England secured me an internship with them before even returning home. Unfortunately, the rate was a measly $14.35 per hour. Eventually, my time in England ended, and I was forced to give a bittersweet farewell to the British hunk. But that semester healed me in a way chemo never could. I returned home refreshed and ready to take on the world.

Back in the US, I hit the ground running in two directions: my internship at Anheuser-Busch and Relay for Life. I opted for a work schedule that was as close to full-time as they could legally allow, shifting most of my classes to evenings. (By now, the traditional four-year schedule had gone out the window.) Whatever free time I had was devoted to building a Relay for Life Super Team.

The Relay Rejuvenators was a massive team with over 100 members, led by Marilyn, her friends Liz, Debbie and me. If you want to get something done, call my friend Marilyn. She was a master recruiter; no one in the dog show community was safe. I wrote to every businessperson I'd ever come in contact with. If you cut my hair or cleaned my teeth, you could expect an email from me.

The Rejuvenators became known for creative fundraising strategies. We brought in student massage therapists to offer chair massages, for a donation, to exhausted and aching walkers. We also sold root beer floats, a huge hit because the July North County Relay was always sickeningly hot. We'd sell light-up mugs, necklaces, whatever it took to garner a couple more bucks for the cause. The Rejuvenators averaged $20,000 in donations annually, which drew a lot of attention – and attention to me personally. I was often asked to speak during Relay events, honing my story over and over for crowds of strangers. One year, in honor of the Summer Olympics, I lit a torch and ran it around the track for the opening lap.

My parents always came to watch me do my survivor lap, but it was Marilyn who stayed by my side for the entire night. By this point, Dad's weight and hip replacement made it difficult for him to make it around the track, but he always managed to finish just one lap with me. Mom began a tradition of bringing me roses -one rose for every year I was cancer-free. After the opening ceremony, they'd stay for a couple hours, enjoying the crowds and festivities. But once Dad ran out of willing audiences for dad jokes, they'd head home. They were clearly proud of me, but this was my thing. My way of taking ownership of my life, my way of being a grown-up.

After everything I'd been through, I'd finally come into my own.

Dad, me, Grandpa Louie, and Mom North St. Louis County Relay for Life 2004

Southern Illinois University
Edwardsville
May 10, 2003

A Slice of Ham: *Dad never shared my sense of wanderlust, but he did love sightseeing around his own town. He would drive people around on guided tours of Glasgow Village. "That's where I wash my car!" he'd point out excitedly. "That's where I had my first job!" Or, if you were really lucky, "That's where the guy who cuts my hair's brother lives." He was the ultimate homebody, but not because he lacked a sense of wonder. In his icy blue eyes, the commonplace turned extraordinary.*

CHAPTER 7

10 GUYS TO DO
(BEFORE YOU SAY "I DO")

I showed up to my college graduation stark naked. Under my graduation gown, that is. I don't remember what gave me the idea, but I went to great lengths to conceal the fact that I was rocking my birthday suit. First, I cut the front out of an old sweater so only the collar remained. Back in the '80s, these false collars, known as "dickeys," were all the rage. I pinned the dickey to the top of my graduation gown, threw on a pair of heels and some earrings, and voila: the perfect disguise. My parents had no idea what I was up to, but my boyfriend at the time, a musician at a ducling piano bar, was in on the fun. I met him in a gas station parking lot before the ceremony, waited until no one was looking, then lifted up my gown and said "Weeee!"

"That," he observed, "is pretty awesome." It felt awesome. Not only was I finally graduating after everything I'd been through, but I was doing it while being authentically me. After all, there's nothing more authentic than being naked.

I met Mike the Piano Man at a happy hour at the Big Bang on Laclede's Landing. I dropped my phone number, along with a nerdy drawing of two sets of parentheses and two dots forming a pair of boobs, into the tip jar. I was absolutely surprised and tickled when he called me several weeks later. Mike fit in well with the work-hard-play-hard lifestyle I'd built for myself in my later years of college. I was interning and doing community service during the day while finishing my classes at night. My friends and I would show up for his sets at the Big Bang at 10 PM, then finish the night off at late-night sketchy establishments in East St.

Louis. Deja-Vu had become a favorite among us after going there on a lark for my 21st birthday and realizing, to our delight, that beers were only $2. Beggars can't be choosers.

Dating Mike was a blast. He not only played at the piano bar, he regularly had gigs with other bands, cementing my status as his groupie and "leggy blonde love interest," as described by the Riverfront Times in one article in which he appeared. He was seven years my senior, taught me how to bake chicken and opened my eyes to a more mature way of life.

I was still two months out from graduation when I started my first big girl job at the consulting firm PricewaterhouseCoopers. PwC had been the IT security auditor for Anheuser Busch, so I'd worked with their team before and thought the transition would be fairly seamless. It turned out to be an enormous step up in terms of workload. At only 23, I was flying all over the country, conducting IT security audits for dozens of enterprise organizations, catching a few hours of sleep in a hotel before taking off again. PwC expected its consultants to be 100% billable. More, if it were possible, and you were one of the super nerds who could script their work. I regularly left town on Sunday night and didn't arrive home until Friday evening.

After Mike moved to Phoenix to pursue his dreams of being a rock star, I arranged my flight itineraries so I could drop in and visit. My boss was fine with this, probably thinking these sexy layovers would be seen as a perk of the job. But really, it only made me more exhausted. I was used to running on all cylinders, but all this travel meant that other important things, such as my family and my service work, were falling by the wayside. Plus, Mike wanted more than a fly-by-night girlfriend. When a mutual friend informed me that a college girl in a Phoenix bar had introduced herself as Mike's girlfriend, I wasn't particularly upset. Building a relationship around connecting flight routes probably wasn't a recipe for success, and I'd had enough experience by this point to know when a moment had passed. Mike and I parted amicably and went our separate ways. But every time I see a picture of myself on graduation day, I think about him and that gas station parking lot. Weee!

Love leaves a mark more enduring than any radiation burn or dark spot on an X-ray. I'm proud of all my scars, but especially those left by love. Throughout high school and college, I considered myself an equal opportunity girlfriend. I firmly believed – and still do - that everyone has something to offer, a unique story, a sacred something worthy of being discovered and cherished. I'm glad I allowed myself to fall in love again and again, whether a relationship lasted a few weeks or a few years. What's there to regret in caring for another person?

After healing from cancer, I committed myself to loving my body as much as possible. It helped that I was raised without cumbersome shame around sex. Aside from that one very necessary instance with Greg, Dad never gave my boyfriends a scary talking-to. He wasn't the gun-polishing type. Mom all but encouraged me to date around. "You have to play the field!" she insisted, "Have fun! See what's out there!" As happy as my parents were together, I could tell she regretted not having that opportunity herself. It was the only advice she gave me that I really took to heart. So, my dating history read something like the Cosmo article "Ten Guys to Do Before You Say I Do." There was the amateur golfer with Tourette's, the sculptor/art student at Lisa's college, Mark, the hockey-playing IT Guy, Good Steve, Bad Greg, the Gay Boyfriend, the European Hunk, and Mike the Rockstar. But nothing prepared me for Jason.

After only thirteen months at PwC, I was feeling burnt out. A friend of Mary's, who we would often party with, was working at an up-and-coming company called World Wide Technology and offered to pass my resume along. (He may or may not have been the guy throwing the party where I was offered ecstasy during chemo.) I'd never heard of WWT, but I knew it was based in St. Louis and wouldn't require me to fly all over the United States, so I sent in my resume and received a request for an interview within the week. I spent the morning prepping myself in the bathroom mirror, trying to think of every possible interview question they might ask. I put on my best power suit and marched into the office, determined to nail it.

As soon as I saw Jason, my stomach did a backflip. He was sitting by himself at the conference table, slightly balding, sure, but exuding a masculine energy that would have been intimidating if it wasn't for his very kind blue-green eyes. He smiled at me with a charming smile, and suddenly, all my preparation flew out the window. I stammered something like an introduction, focusing all my might on getting my name right.

At 27, Jason was already leading a team of seven engineers. Originally from Mississippi, he'd joined the Navy in the hope of seeing the world and ended up stationed at Scott Air Force Base near St. Louis working for DISA (the Defense Information Systems Agency). This wasn't exactly what he'd had in mind, but he ended up liking the city. After his tour, he decided not to re-enlist and took a job at WWT. If that hadn't happened, we never would have met. It was even more of a stroke of fortune, I'd find out later, because I hadn't exactly been a shoo-in for this interview. Out of a pile of nearly identical resumes, mine stood out for being the only one with a woman's name at the top and an email address that demonstrated I owned my own domain name. When Jason went to amandacarter.com, he discovered, to his great surprise, that the two of us had a mutual friend. There was a photo of me drinking beers with a buddy of Jason's from the Air Force Base and the caption "Me and Larry!" Unfortunately, Jason's friend wasn't named Larry. He was Gary, but everyone at Anheuser-Busch called him Larry as a nickname. No idea why. Doesn't even seem remotely funny 20 years later.

After calling Gary to confirm that he did not, in fact, have a secret twin, Jason asked if he should interview me. "Go for it!" Gary said, "She's hot and a lot of fun!" Those were different times. But back to the interview.

At one point, Jason left the conference room and was replaced with another team leader who stared me down with deadly seriousness.

"If you were a tree, what kind of tree would you be?" He intoned. From the look on his face, he must have thought this was the most profound interview question of all time. I struggled not to laugh.

"I'd be a dogwood tree, because there was a dogwood in my front yard growing up, and I like dogs." I responded, saying the first thing that popped into my head. Without so much as a response, the coworker stood up and left the conference room, leaving me bewildered and sure I'd just blown the whole thing. "Why hadn't I thought about that question this morning?" I asked myself. "Because it's stupid!" What about Jason? Would my stupid answer to a stupid question be the thing that prevents me from ever seeing him again? Was there any professional way to get his number before walking out of there for good?

My mind was still running on a hamster wheel when Jason reentered the conference room and announced that the job was mine, presenting me with an offer letter on the spot. I stood up, gave my most professional smile and firmest handshake, and strode out of the office, calm, cool and collected. I saved my celebratory dancing for the sidewalk. My days at PwC were coming to an end, and the future was looking very good.

I tiptoed delicately and discreetly around my crush on Jason for the first two months at my new job. That is, if you consider inviting him to a bikini car-wash fundraiser discreet. Hey, it was for a good cause! Besides, I figured, I invited everyone I knew to the Relay Rejuvenators' events. There was absolutely no way that anyone could tell that I had a crush on my boss.

"You have a CRUSH on your BOSS!?!" Marilyn exclaimed with horror the first time she saw us together. She quickly rushed into damage control. "Do not, under any circumstances whatsoever, try to date him." I guess I was being less discreet than I originally thought. Trusting in Marilyn's advice, I vowed to push my feelings for Jason aside. If I just ignored him really hard, maybe I'd stop thinking about him.

Unfortunately, Jason and I seemed to run into each other everywhere. I saw him at the gym, local bars, even at my regular car wash. If it were anyone other than Jason, I might suspect that he was using GPS to track me. He jokingly accused me of stalking him. I wasn't stalking, but I was thrilled every time I ran into him. Whether it was the professional thing to do or not, I decided to go after what I really wanted. We started out slowly, hanging out with groups of friends. Then, we went to a coworker's wedding together. We had a blast dancing that night and kept the party going on the way home, rocking out to Jet's "Are You Gonna Be My Girl?" in his Nissan Altima. I caught his eye for a moment during the song and knew he was asking the question for real. That night sealed the deal. (No, I didn't sleep with him... Surprisingly, I actually made him wait a while.) We decided we could try to pull this relationship thing off, provided we kept it out of the office. We were a couple by summer.

Jason started joining me for all my Relay events, not just the ones that involved bikinis. His easy-going attitude and sense of humor won over my girlfriends fast. He was the perfect addition to the pub-crawl team I joined with Molly, the Hodgkin's Haters Lymphomanators, going shot-for-shot and joke-for-joke with one of the funniest people I know. Even Marilyn had to admit that maybe, just maybe, it was okay to bend the rules for him. Some things are just too real to deny.

Not long before the start of my relationship with Jason, my parents moved out of my childhood home and into a doublewide in Brighton, Illinois. There was over an acre of land for Mom's menagerie and Dad's hoarding habit. The place was a cross between a zoo and a pet rescue, with three birds, three dogs, one cat, and sheds...so many sheds. They were filled with storage, everything from old family photos, to broken tools, and more Christmas decorations than you could ever imagine. Santa was living there as well, of course. The dog-mobile, which finally retired after over 200,000 miles, was essentially serving as yet another shed. I was less than eager to introduce Jason to this sight, but I wasn't about to embark on another serious relationship without Dad's approval. It was a strange feeling because I'd never really bothered to get his approval before. It wasn't an expectation in our family. But then again, I'd never been with someone who felt so much like family.

I took Jason to meet my parents at a KFC in Brighton. (My parents were both huge KFC fans. In fact, Mom had a habit of passing KFC coleslaw off as her own. She'd buy up several containers, dump it into a Tupperware, and bring it with her to potluck gatherings.) While going through the buffet line (yes, it was indeed a KFC buffet Jason recalls), Mom gave Jason all the ins and outs of caring for a giant macaw. Dad grilled him about his time in the military. The two of them hit it off right away. Dad saw Jason as a brother-in-arms, and Jason paid Dad the same respect. This immediately struck me as something special. Few people looked at my dad and saw a hero, but I sure did. And so did Jason. Past boyfriends tended to get a little bored with Dad's endless stories. I could tell by their body language, the way they'd shift in their seats and look to me, hoping to find a way out of the conversations. But not Jason. He was comfortably munching on fried chicken and laughing at every cheesy joke. It warmed my heart.

Not long after meeting my parents, Jason joined me for his first official Relay for Life, where he met my extended family, including Grandpa Louie, and even more friends. He got Grandpa Louie's approval right away, when he immediately shot back to one of Grandpa Louie's sarcastic comments with an even drier zinger. Grandpa Louie turned to me and made a check mark in the air, signaling to everyone that Jason got a point, a sure sign of approval. Jason fit into my life like a hand into a glove.

That year, I personally raised $4,000 for Relay for Life, and the St. Louis Business Journal decided they wanted to feature my story in a two-page spread. Harkening back to my Jordache days, I met a photographer for a photo shoot in the WWT data center. The article was all about my battle with cancer and what it's like to be a woman in tech. It came out great, but the executive suite at WWT was pretty perplexed. At that point, I'd been at the company less than four months, and I was garnering press with the company name attached to my personal story.

"Who the heck is this random girl in IT, and why is she all over the Business Journal about our company?" one executive asked Jason. Trying to bite back his annoyance, Jason calmly explained that I had raised thousands of dollars for cancer research. "How do you know?" the executive asked sharply. "I read the article," Jason responded. The executive dropped the subject, but Jason's strong defense of me was the first clue that the two of us were more than just coworkers. Thankfully, at 650 employees, WWT was no stranger to interoffice dating.

There would be more hints over time. Once, we took a business trip together to do a server install in Plano, Texas, and we only expensed one hotel room. Oops, rookie move there. The biggest giveaway, however, was my cat. I kept a photograph of my orange and white tabby pinned to the side of my cubicle, where some people might put a picture of their wife or kids.

Most people knew that Jason was deathly allergic to cats. The first time he stayed the night at my place was a weeknight, and when he woke up the next morning, one of his eyes was swollen shut. The other eye was a slit that barely opened, and he had red splotches up and down his arms. I'm not exactly sure how he drove himself to work that morning, but we were at least smart enough not to ride together or arrive at the same time.

"What happened to you?" laughed our coworker. "You get in a fight?"
"Yeah," Jason admitted, "With a cat." The coworker raised an eyebrow.
"...Amanda's cat?"

The cat, as they say, was out of the bag.

SATURDAY
28

SUNDAY *LIVING RM LOVE SEAT + COUSH 9YRS OLD (2006)*
29

November						2015		December						2015
S	M	T	W	T	F	S		S	M	T	W	T	F	S
1	2	3	4	5	6	7				1	2	3	4	5
8	9	10	11	12	13	14		6	7	8	9	10	11	12
15	16	17	18	19	20	21		13	14	15	16	17	18	19
22	23	24	25	26	27	28		20	21	22	23	24	25	26

A Slice of Ham: *Dad was obsessed with record-keeping. He meticulously wrote down the number of every check he wrote and the date of each bill he received in the mail. He had file folders full of the paperwork for every medical procedure he'd ever received. His personal calendars were filled with birthdays, anniversaries, and anything he saw fit to record. Once, when cleaning out his belongings, we found a planner where he'd written, in huge block letters, "Living room love seat and couch nine years old" Happy Birthday couch!*

CHAPTER 8

THERE'S NO
PREPARING FOR THIS

𝄆 You'll be fine!" I intoned, focusing my eyes on my pink toenails poking through the white foam bubbles. My phone was precariously balanced on the bathtub's porcelain edge. "This is a very routine procedure." Mom had spent the past two weeks agonizing over her upcoming tonsil removal, and I was having some trouble empathizing. It's not like she was getting injected with the Red Devil.

"There's always a risk with anesthesia," she reminded me, her voice strained, "sometimes people don't wake up!" It was a good thing she couldn't hear me rolling my eyes.

"Mom, it will be over before you know it," I promise. "Whoops, look at the time. Got to go!" I hung up with a deep sigh of relief and sank more deeply into the warm bubbles.

A few months prior, in summer 2005, Jason and I bought our first home together, a large, gray two-story with four bedrooms, a two-car garage, a huge lawn, and a finished basement. The crowning glory was the in-ground pool in the backyard. This, more than anything, was proof that I had made it. We threw a pool party for the Fourth of July, the first of many such flings, and the first thing Mom did was plop her butt on the concrete and stick her feet in the water. She said she couldn't wait to do it, and that it wouldn't feel real until her feet were wet. I'd finally lived up to the dreams she had for me.

The best part of the house for me, though, was that Jason lived there. I was madly, blissfully, in love, and extremely certain that I had found my person. Goodbye boyfriend parade, hello future husband! Between my perfect relationship, our beautiful new house, and my successful career at World Wide Technology, it was impossible to imagine anything going wrong for me now. The hard days were officially behind me, and the future was so bright it was blinding.

If I had anything to be concerned about, it was Dad's worsening health. Despite being on Metformin for his Type 2 Diabetes since his early 40s, he never bothered to monitor his sugar levels or give a second thought to his diet. He was on medication, so why bother? One day, Mom came home from fishing (her latest hobby) to find Dad standing in the middle of the kitchen, mumbling to himself. When she tried to ask him what he was doing, he shouted at her. "Get away from me!" Mom was shocked; Dad never yelled. Ever.

Certain he was having a stroke, Mom called 911 immediately. By the time the paramedics arrived, his blood sugar had dropped below 40, and he had grown even more aggressive. He shouted profanities at the paramedics and physically resisted them as they tried to place him on the stretcher. Dad was well above 300 lbs., and it took four able-bodied men to finally wrestle him down and inject him with insulin. He eventually stabilized, but he had to remain in the hospital for several days while doctors monitored his blood sugar around the clock.

After this incident, the doctors insisted that Dad be much more careful about his health and diet. Diabetes isn't something you can just fix with a pill, they explained. You must work at it yourself. This was advice that Mom took straight to heart, and Dad absolutely did not. Caring for his health became a daily battle for her. He complained about not having ketchup, gravy, or butter on his food. He complained about her attempts to replace soda with unsweetened tea. He complained about exercising. Eventually, Mom gave up. He was an adult, she reasoned, and could make his own decisions. She, however, stuck with the new habits. She cut back on smoking (for the most part) and became a step-aerobics fanatic. Aside from one incident where she fell off her stepper and broke her big toe, Mom was in the best shape of her life.

She was also the happiest I'd ever seen her. No longer crammed into that 900-square-foot-house, she was finally free to let her many hobbies blossom at their new property in Brighton, Illinois. She was working in the garden, tending to her birds, and fishing almost daily in the new

John Boat dad bought her. She woke up each morning at 5:45 to drink her cup of coffee and sneak a cigarette while watching the sunrise, then headed out to the lake, where she'd spend long, solitary, and luxurious hours playing catch-and-release to her heart's content. For the first time in her life, she seemed genuinely at peace with all her choices, including her decision to marry young. This contentment rubbed off on Dad, who always adored her, but no doubt sensed her restlessness. He had renewed confidence. They were in the middle of their lives, and Sonja was happy to have chosen him.

She even convinced him to travel with her to Germany. A full decade after my first adventure abroad, which she envied and he adamantly opposed, Dad finally felt comfortable enough to venture outside the United States. It helped that they were going to visit my sister and that I had made the trip first. Heather's husband Tom was stationed at Ramstein Air Force Base in southwestern Germany. Jason and I had gone to stay with them over Thanksgiving and had fallen in love with the castles, Christmas markets, and my five-year-old nephew, Micah. I found myself bonding more with Heather than we ever had as kids. Now that we lived half a world apart, we realized we liked each other. Isn't it funny how that happens?

I relayed every detail of my trip to Mom, as I always did when I traveled, and she reveled in them. This time, however, she wasn't satisfied with hearing the stories from me. She put her foot down and insisted to Dad that they go to Germany themselves. Reluctantly, Dad agreed. Prior to this, Dad's travels were confined to a handful of states via his military enlistment, the dog show circuit, and one family vacation to Biloxi, Mississippi. But I'd survived Europe twice now, so he figured he probably would too. On the day of their flight, he insisted they arrive at the airport four hours early. Mom told me that he double-checked their paper tickets no less than twenty times. Despite his nerves, he did get on that plane.

It was high summer, and Mom delighted in long walks through the winding streets of little German towns and the steep hikes up to ruined castles. She also asked Heather to score her a pack of cigarettes with a ration card, a task Heather was less than enthused about doing. But aside from the smoking, Mom was the picture of health. She could practically run up the cliffs. Dad, being the recipient of two hip replacements, struggled to keep up, but he made up for it by taking hundreds of photos. We have albums full of photos of Mom from that trip. She's tan, smiling with the sun in her hair, toned legs in shorts fit for a teenager, smiling with her arms outstretched as if to say, "Look at me! I'm finally here on the trip of a lifetime!"

The one place they didn't visit was Bayreuth, Germany, where Grandma Giraud had grown up. I was surprised, and a little disappointed, by this decision, but it was a three-and-a-half-hour drive from where my sister lived, and Dad was already exhausted by the end of the week. Mom was certain she'd have another chance. Heather lived in Germany, after all, and they'd had such a great time they were sure to come back one day. Once more, the future was dazzlingly bright.

This brings us back to Mom's tonsils and that fateful conversation in the bathtub in December of 2005. Mom had never had a health crisis of any sort, but she had spent plenty of time garnering sympathy for herself over mine. Although our relationship was much better now, I still held slightly bitter memories of the times she'd made herself the center of attention during my cancer treatment, and I couldn't help but suspect she was milking this tonsillectomy for all it was worth. I wasn't about to give her that satisfaction, so she turned to her old friend Vera.

Vera had lived across the street from Mom growing up, and then was our next door neighbor when Heather and I were kids. She was a sort of proxy mother figure to Mom. I remember Vera as a sun goddess, oiled up in her lawn chair in the backyard and sucking back endless packs of Benson and Hedges. Not at all coincidentally, Mom smoked the same brand. Vera had smoked 2-3 packs a day for most of her life, and she had the voice to show for it. Her tonsils were a distant memory, and she didn't miss them at all.

"I know you love to be dramatic, honey," she said while blowing out a long train of smoke, "But no one gives two shits about this."

Mom's tonsil surgery was scheduled for a Monday morning. The Friday before, she complained about cramping in her calves while strolling the small-town Illinois Walmart. Dad told her to lay off the step aerobics.

Over the weekend, she noticed blood in her stools. Sunday afternoon, she decided to lie down for a nap on the living room couch. Dad thought nothing of this; Mom was a big napper, given her years of early rising for dog shows and shifts at Schnucks supermarket. An hour later, when he came back to check on her, it was clear something was very wrong. Mom was mumbling incoherently and struggling to lift her head. Frantic, Dad knelt to help her up and saw that the entire right side of her face had gone completely slack. Now, it was his turn to call 911.

Meanwhile, I was just powering off my phone. Jason and I had decided to catch a Sunday matinee of the Johnny Cash biopic, I Walk the Line, starring Joaquin Phoenix and Reese Witherspoon. I remember enjoying it. After the movie, we went to Fazoli's "Real Italian." It's basically a blue-collar Olive Garden, somewhere to go if you're a real sucker for garlic breadsticks (which I am). I didn't bother to turn my phone back on until midway through dinner and was surprised to discover I had several missed calls and multiple voicemails from my dad. My heart quickened. That's never a good sign, especially on a Sunday evening.

"Mandy, Mom's really sick." Dad's voice sounded scared, shaky. "They think she had a stroke. The ambulance is taking her to St. Anthony's in Alton." Next voicemail. "Mandy, the doctors say Mom's white blood cell count is through the roof and her red blood cells are super low." Third voicemail. "Mandy, we are at the ER at St. Anthony's, and they are airlifting your mom to Barnes Jewish to prep her for brain surgery. Call me back as soon as you can."

My skin felt cold, and the restaurant seemed to spin around me. All those people and their damn breadsticks. What was I doing here? Why hadn't I checked my phone earlier? I struggled to swallow. Somehow, I must have managed to explain to Jason what was happening. He must have stopped at the counter to pay the bill, or maybe we just walked out. The next thing I remember is racing toward the hospital in the car, apologizing to Dad profusely for not answering, for not being there, for everything. Dad told me not to beat myself up; there's nothing we could have done to change anything. It was meant to be a comfort, but my stomach twisted. I'd never felt so helpless in my life, even when I'd had cancer. When we pulled into the ER, I could hear a helicopter hovering above us. Jason and I didn't speak, but we were both thinking the same thing: that must be Mom.

We piled into the emergency room, where Mom lay unconscious and intubated on the bed. I was stunned by how small and frail she looked, and by the amount of dried blood on her earlobes and pillowcase. Someone should clean her ears, I thought. It's strange, the things you notice when you're in shock. We were only in there for a few minutes before the doctors ushered us out into a private waiting room.

The doctors explained they had rushed in from on call to save Mom's life, but she appeared to already be too far gone. They were going to perform a series of tests to determine how severe her brain injury was, and we were promptly ushered into the cold and stale waiting room. By that time, I had already lost hope that there was any saving going to take place that night.

When diagnosing brain death, doctors must run several tests to ensure symptoms aren't being caused by other factors, such as overdose, abnormal body temperature, or severe underactivity of the thyroid gland. Doctors shine a light in a patient's eyes, tickle their feet with feathers, and even pinch them to try to stimulate a reaction. A thin plastic tube is pushed down the windpipe in the hopes of prompting choking or gagging. As a last resort, a patient is removed from the ventilator for a few minutes to see if they make any attempt to breathe on their own.

This entire process took somewhere between 30 minutes to an hour. During that time, we were sitting silently in the waiting room, unable to talk or read the outdated magazines scattered on the tables. (Imagine reading Better Housekeeping at a time like this.) A few friends arrived, including a former neighbor from Glasgow, my dad's friend Joe. Grandpa Louie and Ruth had to make the long drive from Bowling Green, MO, and still hadn't arrived when the attending physician emerged through the double-swinging doors. We all rose to our feet; the look on the doctor's face told us everything we needed to know.

In a kind, steady, but sorrowful voice, the doctor explained that his team had been fully prepared to conduct life-saving brain surgery to relieve the pressure caused by the aneurysm. The entire team had dropped what they were doing on a Sunday night and assembled to save my mom.

But it was too late. She was brain-dead before she arrived at Barnes. None of us questioned this assessment; we'd seen the way she looked in that hospital bed.

When Grandpa and Ruth arrived at the hospital, Joe met them in the parking lot. "She's already gone," he told them before they could get inside. When Grandpa walked in, clearly already knowing the news, I saw red. It wasn't Joe's right to tell him. I could tell by the hurt on Dad's face that he felt the same way. I took a step toward Joe, ready to tell him off, but I felt a gentle hand on my shoulder. "Not now," Jason whispered. And he was right.

Thankfully, the doctors had cleaned Mom up before allowing us to return. The blood was gone from her ears and pillow. The family gathered around her bed. Jason held my hand while I told her I loved her and would miss her. Grandpa Louie didn't say much, which was out of character for him but seemed fitting. Dad promised Mom he would take care of her animals, listing each of her dogs and birds by name. Eventually, we were out of words, and all we could hear was the sound of the machines. The doctors again ushered us out of the room, and suddenly it was over.

Jason and I agreed that I should go home with my dad and stay the night with him in Brighton. Grandpa Louie and Ruth would stay with Jason at our house. From the moment I stepped into Dad's car and he turned on the engine, something flipped in my brain. Amanda the project manager took over, and I was in crisis management mode. As Dad drove up the highway, my mind raced a million miles an hour. Who's going to call Ingrid? How can we contact Heather in Germany? Who's going to take care of Dad now? The answer to that final question, I immediately knew, was me. But there was no time to dwell on that yet. It was a long, quiet, fifty-mile ride home.

When we arrived at the house, Mom's shoes were still by the door. The couch pillow was on the floor, where Dad had thrown it off only hours before. You told her she'd be fine. The cruel thought appeared in my head, unbidden, and I immediately pushed it away. Dad was moving in slow motion around the kitchen, touching everything, as if reminding himself that the objects were real and that the last person to touch them had been my mother.

"We have to make some calls," I said matter-of-factly and took a seat at the kitchen table.

I called Ingrid first. She took the news with military-like detachment and a statement that may as well have come from me: "How can I help?" Typical Ingrid. It turns out, we did need her help. Heather and Tom didn't have cell phones, and it was a Monday morning in Germany, which meant they were both at work. Ingrid, who worked in the Air Force Personnel Office, was able to track down Tom's work number on Ramstein Air Force Base. I told him what had happened, half hoping he would relay the news to Heather himself, but he said it should be me. I knew he was right.

I had to wait over forty-five painful minutes for Tom to drive to the early childhood education school on base where Heather worked, get the director to pull her out of the class she was teaching, and put her on the phone. I don't remember how I got the words out or what exactly I said, only that it was the hardest conversation I've ever had with my sister. And I remember the tears.

I slept in my parents' bed that night, on my mom's side with my head resting on her pillow. Despite being exhausted, I stared at the ceiling with my eyes wide open. The thoughts I'd been avoiding ever since the hospital came flooding in. Could all of this have been prevented? How could it possibly have gone so wrong? Didn't she have preop blood work for her surgery? If I slept at all that night, it was only briefly, and never long enough to forget.

A few months later, we received Mom's autopsy report. She had AML Leukemia in every major organ, most likely linked to her 40-year smoking habit, her one vice. Ingrid immediately believed that Mom knew about the cancer and chose not to tell us. My first instinct was to doubt that. After all, she'd been so dramatic about my cancer, I couldn't believe she'd keep hers a secret. Then again, the thought of illness had always horrified her. Maybe she didn't want to put us through the same suffering she had gone through, all the worry and stress. Maybe she wasn't nearly as attention-seeking as I always thought. Now, I can never ask.

It snowed the night of Mom's wake, and she hated the snow. It seemed fitting, though, like she was giving the middle finger to the whole damn situation. Heather and her family flew in from Germany, and Ingrid flew in from San Antonio with my then seven-year-old cousin Tre'von, who'd never seen snow before. At least one of us was happy.

When someone dies as young as my mom, all their friends are still around. So the wake was packed. Not to mention all my ex-boyfriends who showed up: Steve, Mark, and Hot Todd were all in attendance. I held Grandpa Louie's hand the whole time. I remember staring at it so I wouldn't have to look at my mom. I hate open caskets and so did she. People always say how nice the body looks, how great a job the mortician did, but it's never true. A dead body always looks dead. In Mom's case, we'd given them a photo to show how she liked to style her hair, but they curled it like an old lady. I suppose they weren't used to doing a young person's hair. "I loved doing people's hair at the morgue," I remembered mom saying while recalling her beautician days, "You don't worry about the back, and the customer never complains!" As the memory floated through my mind, I bit back my lip to keep from laughing.

We buried Mom in the dress she wore to Heather's wedding. It was a light pink mauve and had looked great on her about eight years prior. Now, it seemed like an odd choice. Should have put her in her dog show outfit, I thought to myself. An old sweatshirt and a pair of black jeans covered in dog hair were always her go-to for competition. Too late now, I sighed, shaking my head.

One thing we did get right: we buried Mom with all her deceased dogs. Well, the boxes of their ashes that formerly adorned our fireplace mantle, that is. There was Brandon, her obedience champion Golden Retriever, Ben, the first enormous Newfoundland that took up the bathroom, and Splash, the Newfie who passed away young from a seizure condition. We placed their ashes near the front of her casket on a table, and when it came time to close up, we placed them inside. It was just what she always wanted and had repeatedly told Dad.

The last memory I have of the funeral is of leaving the cemetery. Everyone was hurrying to their cars to get out of the snow, eager to warm up, and I caught sight of Marilyn. She was in a heap of tears, trying to maintain her composure, but weeping beside her car. She was wearing a black pantsuit and looked amazing, as expected. Somehow, that comforted me, knowing how much my mom was loved.

After the funeral ended and the many guests drove off, there was a brief moment of quiet. I allowed myself about half a breath before returning to the next piece of business. Now, it was my turn to take care of Dad.

A Slice of Ham: *An (incomplete) list of odd things I found while cleaning out my parents' Brighton, IL home: A "dipstick heater" from Grandpa Pigeons in the shed. (Don't ask me what that is.) Several one-gallon ice cream containers of years-old frozen spaghetti sauce. Ostomy supplies. A raised toilet seat. A walker. Enough dog hair behind the fridge to knit a baby blanket. A coffee cup that read "I'd walk a million miles for one of your smiles, and even farther for that thing you do with your tongue." (Omg!)*

CHAPTER 9

GET RID OF THE BIRDS

In the whirlwind months after Mom's death, I was almost too busy to grieve. There was the funeral to plan, and family coming in from out of town. Heather and her family stayed in the States for several weeks. There were friends to inform and errands to run. (Why death has to involve so many errands I'll never understand.) I think I preferred it this way, on some level. I think I convinced myself that if I ran in place fast enough, I could get the Earth to stop turning. As long as I stayed busy, I wouldn't have to feel anything. But time has a stubborn way of moving forward. Eventually, I looked around and realized all the extended family had gone home. Heather was back in Germany, Ingrid in San Antonio. My world became hauntingly quiet, and in that quiet, grief crept up on me.

It started with the dreams. Each night, Mom would walk into my room, as natural as you could imagine. With a rush of relief, I'd realize that it was all a horrible mistake. Mom wasn't dead. She's merely gone on a trip, and now she was back. How could I be so silly as to think she was dead? Then, we'd take the dogs on a walk or head to the park. I'd be blissfully happy until, suddenly, I found myself back in my bed. It always took a few moments to figure out what had happened and where I was. It would take a few more moments to realize, with fresh sadness, that Mom was really gone. I relived this discovery each night until I didn't want to sleep. Insomnia gave way to exhaustion, which gave way to dreams. Sometimes, I would cry quietly in bed, trying not to wake Jason. I rolled away from him, hoping that he wouldn't hear me but also longing for him to comfort me. I didn't know how to tell him what I needed.

I sublimated my grief by stepping into my new role as Dad's caretaker.

It turned out that he needed a lot of care. Up to this point, I'd thought I understood his health situation, but I had no idea how much of his daily functioning was handled by Mom. Dad agonized over tiny decisions, like whether he should get a haircut. He once spent weeks pondering whether he should go back to his flat top, inquiring about my opinion on a daily basis before finally deciding to do nothing. I suppose Mom always told him what to do with his hair. He also had a strong aversion to waste that prevented him from throwing anything out, especially food. He once gave himself food poisoning from eating two-week-old KFC. Mom must have been the one to tell him when food had gone bad, or maybe she cleaned out the fridge when he wasn't looking. The more I learned about my dad, the more I understood my mom. Her various neuroses, her restlessness, maybe even her fishing habit made a lot more sense when coupled with the fact that her husband couldn't pick out his own pair of shoes. Then again, it was quite possible that some of this was learned helplessness. Dad helped Mom feel needed, and she helped him feel cared for. That was all well and good for her, but I had a full-time job.

If Mom's death was hard for me, it was almost unbearable for Dad. She had been the one worrying about him, after all. He was the one with the health problems. For her to die first was inconceivable. The tenor of Dad's random conversations with strangers took a morbid turn. Where the first sentence out of his mouth used to be "Thank you for buying an American car," now it was "my wife died." He talked about it constantly, regardless of the appropriateness of the situation. Whether you were bagging his groceries or getting your car fixed, you were certain to find out about Sonja's sudden passing. Maybe Dad thought that if he said it often enough, he would come to understand it. Maybe he was having bad dreams too.

Dad sublimated his grief by stepping into his new role as caretaker for Mom's menagerie. It was a near-impossible task for someone in his physical condition. His diabetes was out of control, and his cholesterol through the roof. On a family trip to San Antonio that summer, he struggled for breath with every few steps. That's when Jason pulled me aside.

"I think your dad should move closer to us," he said, "so we can look after him." We. If it wasn't clear before that this is the man for me, it was undeniable now. Despite the hard times, there were bright things on the horizon. I was ready to get engaged. But first, we had to figure out what to do about Dad.

The house in Brighton was way too much responsibility for Dad. Plus, it was extremely far from the best hospitals. We'd already learned that the hard way with Mom. What if something happened to him and no one was around to call 911? But Dad would hear none of it. He'd made a vow to Mom to take care of her animals, and nothing else mattered. Never mind that the house was on an acre of land and quickly becoming overrun with weeds. It took him an entire day just to mow the grass and properly tend to the three birds, two dogs, and one cat (not to mention the strays that roamed the property).

Dad had a rather unusual understanding of his own health. If he was taking pills for something, he considered it cured. Once, I went with him to a doctor's appointment, and the doctor asked if he had high blood pressure, to which he replied, "No."

"Yes, you do!" I reminded him, shocked. "No, Mandy. I take a pill for that!" For a big softie, he was about as stubborn as could be.

There were some good times in those years. Three days a week, Dad would drive over an hour each way from Brighton to St. Louis for his job at Classic Auto Trim. Jason joked that it was good he got so much out of the job, because his salary didn't cover his gas. But Dad loved sitting for hours in the breakroom talking with his friends Denny and Mel. All three of them had worked together on the line at GM, and they'd known my mom when she was young. His friend Russ, who lived in the same house Mom grew up in, also shared his memories of the good old days. Dad and his friends had a seemingly endless capacity for shooting the shit. After a long day at the garage, he'd call Russ from the car and talk the whole way home. On the weekends, the guys would watch baseball games "together" on the phone. Dad would set up his speaker phone in the living room, and they'd talk for the whole game.

Dad's love of chitchat could occasionally interfere with major life events. Once, Jason took Dad and I out to lunch with the intention of asking his blessing to propose to me. He waited patiently for me to get up to go to the bathroom so he could broach the topic. But as soon as I left the table, Dad pulled out his cellphone and called Russ. Jason watched, aghast, as Dad carried on the most pointless, inane conversation possible. "Hey Russ, how are you doing? I'm out to lunch with Mandy and Jason. Mandy just went to the bathroom. I'm having chicken. Have you had lunch today?" Needless to say, I returned before Jason had a chance to pop the question.

The first Father's Day after Mom died, I rented Dad a classic car. I knew the day might be hard for him, and I wanted to get him something he'd never think of for himself, much less spend money on. Jason just happened to be flying out of the city for work, so I dropped him off at the airport then dropped my car off at the classic car rental. I got a call from my dad at that point. He knew we were planning on going to the Cardinals game, and he was at my place early, of course.

"I'm on your porch!" he told me. "I'm pulling up in a second," I responded. I pulled into the driveway and revved the engine of the 1965 cherry red Chevelle Super Sport. Dad's jaw just about hit the floor. I got out of the car, tossed him the keys, and said, "It's yours," then paused for a minute, "for the day." He was in Heaven.

I took him to the WWT baseball suite, where he was astounded by all the complimentary food. Thankfully, we got there before anyone else, so none of my coworkers could witness him raving to Russ on the phone about the toasted ravioli. ("It's all free!") Later, we drove the car over to Russ' house so Dad could pretend I had bought it for him. We took several glamour shots outside the house, all of which ended up in a personalized album Dad made for me. He loved making photo albums. Looking back on those photos, it's great to see him genuinely smiling. For just a day, the old Ed was back.

Our worries about the Brighton house being unsafe were well-founded, though. We had our first major health scare almost two years to the day after Mom died. Dad hadn't been able to, you know, go in about four days, and his stomach became hugely protruded and hard to the touch. Rather than letting anyone know about this development, he continued mowing the grass and feeding the birds as if nothing was wrong, hoping whatever it was would just go away. When it didn't, and when the pain was too great to ignore, he drove himself to the nearest hospital. He called me from the emergency room to say he had some kind of mass in his colon.

"It's cancer." The thought came into my head unbidden as I felt my entire body go cold. At this point, I'd lost both my mom and my grandma, not to mention my own traumatic experience. Would cancer ever leave us alone? My fears only worsened when I arrived at the hospital. Sitting in the waiting room by myself, live chatting Jason updates over AOL instant messenger, I overheard one surgeon say to another that he was about to operate on "a guy with a colon the size of Massachusetts."

It turns out that Massachusetts is a giant pile of shit. I mean that in the clinical sense. Dad didn't have cancer at all, thank God. He had diverticulitis, which is a fancy way of saying he had a terrible blockage and was so constipated he had damaged his colon. Dad was going to need to have a large section of his colon removed, which meant he'd have to wear a colostomy bag for several months. As the doctor explained the intricacies of changing the bag, emptying it, and keeping it clean, I realized I was going to need to set some serious boundaries.

"I'll help you practice as much as you need," I promised, "but when it comes to the real thing, you're on your own." Dad rolled over on the hospital bed and sighed heavily. "I think I have to get rid of the birds," he admitted. Hallelujah! Sweet baby Jesus!

Within the hour, I had those fuckers posted on Craigslist. A few hours later, I received a response from a lovely gay couple who – for reasons that will forever remain a mystery – desperately wanted the birds. While Dad and I watched more videos about the art and craft of changing colostomy bags, Jason raced back to the doublewide in Brighton. He helped those guys pack the birds into giant dog crates and waved as they gleefully drove off in a truck, never to be seen again. Jason returned to the hospital and smacked $400 cash into Dad's hand. Just like that, the birds were gone. Next in line: the whole house.

After the diverticulitis incident, Dad finally accepted that it was time to move. Jason and I were engaged by then (don't worry, I'll get to that later) and thought it best that he live near us. We took dad to tour a villa near our neighborhood and told him we were going to buy the house so he could rent it. He was elated. The next step in simplifying his life necessitated getting rid of the two dogs and the cat that were still living with him in Brighton. I assured Dad that by finding new and more suitable homes for the animals, he was still fulfilling his promise to Mom to care for them. Privately, I prayed to Mom, if she could hear me, to let this arrangement go. Aside from his medical needs, Dad needed to move on. We all did.

One of Mom's dog show friends took the big Newfoundland, Truman. Russ's daughter took the hyperactive Golden Retriever, Player. I can't for the life of me remember who took Queen Elizabeth (the cat, not the person), but I know she went to a good home. Jason was allergic to cats anyway. Sorry Queeny!

After rehoming the pets, we sent Dad to stay with Heather for a week in Oklahoma (she was back in the States by then), so we could clean out the Brighton house without him hovering over us. We knew the place was a museum to Mom's memory, but we had no idea what we were really getting into. As soon as we started cleaning, we realized we were going to need major reinforcements.

The double-wide modular home was surprisingly large: three bedrooms, an office, and a large family room. The bedroom set, which Mom splurged on back when I was in high school, was enormous and classic 90's, gold frame bed and all. I shuddered looking at it, thinking of the night she passed. Then there were the three huge sheds filled with junk, not to mention the dog-mobile, which was functioning as shed number four.

Every time you embark on a major cleaning project, it's a sort of excavation. You tell yourself you don't need all the old junk in your closet, for example, but then you find your favorite dress from freshman year in high school, a love note from your first boyfriend, or a trophy from your first soccer game. All of a sudden, you're asking yourself if you really need to part with this, or if there might be some reason to keep it. So, you put it back in the closet and forget. For Dad, every object in his home was something like this. It might have emotional value, or it might turn out to be "useful" in some way. (Please explain to me how supplies from dad's original C-PAP machine that didn't fit his current model would be useful. But I digress.)

Thankfully, we were able to call in some reinforcements. Jason's best friend. Greg and my best friend, Lisa came to assist. It was certainly an effort best tackled with a five-man team.

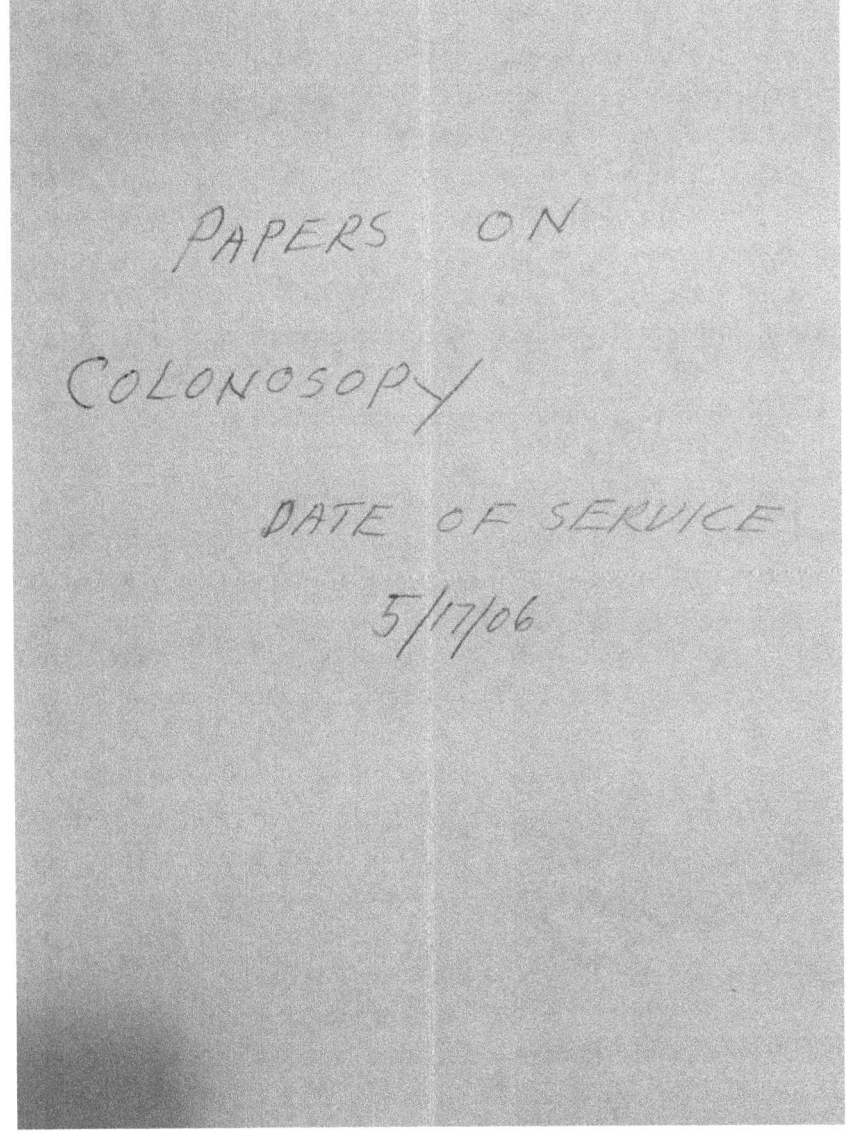

There was silverware from 1975 that still hadn't been used. There were envelopes for every colonoscopy he'd ever had. They were all marked with the "date of service," like he was a car and his ass was the transmission. He had multiple drawers full of nothing but scotch tape and stray batteries. A fridge covered with pushpin magnets. Multiple pieces of paper taped to the fridge with his own address on them. Just in case, I suppose. All of Mom's old credit cards were still there, and seemingly every bill he'd ever been sent labeled with the check number he used to pay it and the date it was mailed. We realized he'd been paying $25/month over the years for the internet, despite the fact that he didn't know how to turn on the computer. At one point, Greg screamed that there was a small dog behind the fridge. It turned out to be only an enormous (and extremely gross) pile of dog hair. There was also expired food in the fridge. There were broken kitchen appliances, old Christmas decorations (Santa was there of course, still in good working order), and every free souvenir from every Relay for Life he'd ever attended. That one really struck me.

Aside from that fabulous '90s bedroom set, which I knew Dad would never part with, all the furniture had to go. It was all mauve. Everything from the curtains to the wallpaper to the enormous sofa. I took photos of all that mauve furniture, plus all Dad's tools and lawn equipment, and posted it all on Craigslist. I only made one mistake. I sold his super comfortable, extra-wide Coleman camping chair, his favorite. I ended up buying him another one.

There were a few things in the house that were meaningful. My mom had two pillar candles that smelled like fresh cut grass. We both loved that smell. I found those candles while we were cleaning out the living room and decided to light one, in the hopes of making the endless cleaning a little more pleasant. Smell, they say, is the sense most tied to memory. As soon as that candle was lit, the memories began to wash over me. Mom, drinking her coffee at the kitchen table. Mom with her dogs on the front lawn. Mom, leaning in eagerly, peppering me with questions about my latest trip. If only I'd taken more time. If only I'd taken her with me a few times...

No, I told myself, it's not about feeling guilty. Guilt is an unpleasant feeling, but as a means to avoid grief, it's excellent. Cleaning out that house unlocked a cascade of memories and, for the first time, I let them run freely through my head without judging them, without trying to hide. I even shed a few tears without turning away from Jason. It was okay for him to know. He already knew anyway.

Mom didn't have a lot of extravagant jewelry, but she did have these very thin gold hoop earrings that she wore every day. I even remember her wearing them when I was a little girl. I kept the earrings as well as her wedding and engagement rings. I gave the engagement ring to Heather and kept the band for myself. I still wear it along with my own wedding band to this day.

Speaking of which, I bet you want to know how Jason proposed...

Photo by Chris Croy

A Slice of Ham: *Dad had a knack for calling his friends (on speaker phone of course) as soon as he had new details to share about his day. I recall the Father's Day after mom died, I took him to the company suite at the St. Louis Cardinals game. As soon as we arrived, he proceeded to describe, in full detail, every appetizer and meal item to a handful of his friends he could get a hold of. "It's all free", he boasted! I always enjoyed showing him the perks I was fortunate to enjoy.*

CHAPTER 10

ON THE CAN

For Christmas 2005, Jason presented me with cruise tickets. The cruise would be over Valentine's Day, and everyone, including me, believed I was about to get engaged. A friend of ours even made one of those hyper-organized wedding planning binders with little tabs for the venue, the menu, and the guests. She wasn't the only one super disappointed with the outcome. Jason was the only person who understood that two months after my mom's death was probably the wrong time to get engaged. I slept most of that cruise, exhausted from a combination of grief and the new task of caring for Dad. What I needed was rest, not a massive party to plan.

A full year later, however, I was feeling pretty antsy. I wanted a ring by Christmas 2006, and I confessed as much to Lisa, who decided to do some detective work on my behalf. With no context whatsoever, she called Jason up. "What are you getting Amanda for Christmas?" she inquired in what she surely thought was a sly manner. "Are you going to propose?"

"No," Jason replied. "I got her a bike." Lisa couldn't believe her ears. "A bike?" she asked. "Yeah," he confirmed. "It's in the basement. I already got it." Lisa shared the bad news with me later that day, and we both shook our heads at just how dense men could be. But, in case Jason might be pulling one over on Lisa, I decided to go looking in the basement for said bike. I didn't find it. I called Lisa back that night.

"There's no bike in the basement!" I chirped happily. We both squealed with excitement. Jason had lied about my Christmas gift. That could only mean one thing...

Christmas 2006 was our year to spend with Jason's family down in

Memphis. Dad was spending it with Heather, who had moved back to the States with her family to Oklahoma. Because Memphis was a relatively short drive from St. Louis, Jason and I were planning on driving down Christmas day. Christmas morning would be just the two of us. In my mind, it was perfect: I'd come downstairs to find a ring under the tree or dangling daintily from a branch. We'd share a special moment together, then we'd drive down to share the good news with his family, who would scream and hug us while we toasted to the future.

So, you can imagine my disappointment on Christmas morning when I went downstairs to find a shiny new women's bicycle under the tree.

"But...but..." I stammered, "Where did you hide it?" Jason told me it had been in the basement bathroom for weeks, so big that it stuck out through the doorway. He had no idea how I'd missed it. I guess I didn't want to see it. Furious, I texted both Lisa and Molly to let them know the devastating news: "I got a fucking bike for Christmas." Molly replied that Jason was dead to her.

I tried my best to put on a brave face during the ensuing four-hour drive to Memphis. Outside, I was calm and relaxed, the cool, no-pressure girlfriend I'd always been. Inside, my mind was reeling. Does Jason expect me to be a forever girlfriend? Is he having doubts about our relationship? A new thought entered my head: Is he expecting me to propose to him? Then so be it! I don't need a man to make all the decisions in this relationship, I mused angrily. I'll do it myself, just like I do everything myself-

"You all right?" Jason asked innocently. "Sure. Fine," I smiled sweetly. "I love the bicycle." Jason nodded, giving me a satisfied smile. Inside, I was seething.

I calmed down a bit by the time we got to his family's house and started opening presents. I was excited about the gift I'd gotten his mother, Sharon. It was two side-by-side frames, one with a classic photo of Jason and his two brothers as kids on that day of her wedding to Jason's stepdad, Mark. Jason is standing on a step, wearing a mischievous smirk next to his brother Jeremy, who is leaning against the railing. At the end of the line, the oldest brother, Steven, crosses his arms like he's about to conduct some business. In the second frame, the three boys had recreated the photo at Jeremy's wedding. Unfortunately, I can't locate that version. Sharon's eyes lit up when she saw the frame.

"Oh, there's one more," Jason said, and passed her another frame. I was a bit confused, as I didn't remember there being a third picture. She unwrapped it, then looked up at me with her mouth agape.

"You guys didn't already-" I was completely perplexed. Do what, I wondered? She turned around the frame and it was empty with no picture but it had "She said Yes!" engraved across it.

Then I saw Jason on one knee.

"You're doing this here?!" In the full year I'd had to plan this engagement out in my head, I'd never once imagined it happening in front of his whole family. Plus, giving his mom a frame with the words "She said Yes!" before I actually said yes was more than a little presumptuous. Of course, I did want to say yes.

Little did I know Jason had been trying desperately for the better part of a year to get the ball rolling on this engagement. The main barrier had been my dad. Not that Dad had turned him down; he loved Jason. It was simply that Jason couldn't get the five minutes alone with him necessary to ask for his blessing. That ill-fated lunch in Brighton was only the beginning of a prolonged comedy of errors in which every time I left the room, Dad proceeded to call someone, ask Jason to replace a lightbulb, or – and this happened more than once – proceeded to make a fart joke, which wasn't exactly the mood Jason was going for. It was, however, a pretty good preview of what was to come.

By Christmas Eve, Jason had resigned himself to the fact that his important conversation would have to be a phone call. Jason didn't regularly call Dad on the phone to chat (one of the few people who didn't, I suppose), but Dad was unfazed when he saw Jason's number.

"Jason!" He exclaimed happily. "What's going on?!"

"Hi Ed, there's something I'd like to talk about. Do you have a few minutes?" Jason asked in a tone that conveyed seriousness and gravitas.

"Sure, this is a great time," Dad assured him, "Anything for you!"

Jason then launched into an eloquent speech about love, commitment, and family. He thanked Dad for sharing his daughter with the world and with him. He ended in the most traditional way possible: "I'd like to ask you for your daughter's hand in marriage." It was truly the whole spiel.

Dad was elated. "Absolutely!" He exclaimed with a smile so big it was almost audible. "I'm so proud to have you as a son. Welcome to the family." It was a beautiful, heartfelt moment between the two of them, and Jason hung up feeling closer than ever to my dad.

After the proposal, I called up everyone I knew to share the good news. Lisa was overjoyed but also slightly annoyed that Jason had so masterfully duped her. ("She wasn't exactly being subtle," Jason told me later.) Molly insisted she never doubted. Marilyn said it was about time. But when I called up my sister, Heather, there was no screaming or jumping to be had.

"Oh," she said, "we already know." "How?" I asked, somewhat disappointed, feeling like the air was just let out of my balloon.

"Dad came out of the bathroom yesterday and was like 'you'll never believe who I just talked to...'" That heartfelt conversation had taken place while Dad was on the shitter. Typical Ed.

I had never been the type of girl to fantasize about my future wedding, so I was surprised to discover how much I already had planned out in my mind. One thing I'd definitely pictured: my mom being there. I felt her absence acutely. It wasn't so much that I wanted her help planning the big day. Honestly, we probably would have butted heads at every step. I just wanted her around.

Fortunately, I had Marilyn. Although she would never claim to fill the role of my mom, she did step into many of the jobs that a mom would traditionally have done. She came with me to my dress fittings and threw my bridal shower. She even helped maintain my enormous spreadsheet with its copious number of accurately labeled tabs. Fortunately, Marilyn and I have similar styles when it comes to organization. We both consider the word "anal" to be a compliment. She also managed some of that inevitable family drama and came along with us to sample food from the caterer and pick our menu. Dad came to that event too, but he wasn't much help. He just kept raving over how delicious everything was. As someone who drowned everything he ever ate in ketchup or gravy, his invite was more symbolic than assistive.

I spent the night before my wedding with Lisa, who was my Maid of Honor. (Molly, Heather, and my good friend Sara from WWT were also bridesmaids.) We stayed up that whole night talking, despite the fact that Lisa insisted I should try to get to bed early. We'd both agree it was time for sleep, then just go right on talking. It didn't matter what we were talking about. There was only that mutual understanding that, after so many sleepovers over so many years, this one was different. So, we kept talking until, eventually, we fell asleep.

Jason and I were married at Webster Groves Presbyterian Church. It was 65 degrees in late November; Fall had decided to linger for us. There were still red and yellow leaves on the trees as Jason and I posed for photos in front of the church's gigantic arched red doors. My wedding veil was about eight feet long, my "something borrowed" from Lisa.

Before walking down the aisle, Dad put a penny in my shoe (Sketchers, of course) for good luck. Grandpa Louie had done the same thing for Mom some thirty-seven years prior. I straightened Dad's corsage, which kept wanting to flop to one side. As we walked slowly down the aisle, I felt him grip my arm tightly. He was leaning on me for support, eyes watering, trying not to look into the crowd where he knew he wouldn't see Mom. Instead, he kept his gaze focused on the altar, where a white candle burned next to a framed photo of her that said, "In Loving Memory of Sonja Carter." I had another tiny photo of her hanging from my bouquet of 25 red roses.

Mom had always disliked sitting through church services, not because she didn't believe in God, but because she always felt like she was about to either be scolded or struck by lightning. So, when the tiny, framed photo fell off my bouquet during the middle of the ceremony, we took it as a sign that she was there.

Dad intended to give a welcoming speech at the reception, but kept putting it off. He allowed the best man and Lisa to speak first. Finally, Jason told Dad that it was now or never. Dad couldn't do it. Every time he thought about what he might want to say, he got choked up. He knew if he tried to speak, he would break down in tears. He couldn't stop thinking about Mom and how much he wished she were there.

After the wedding, Dad pulled Marilyn aside to thank her for being there for me when Mom couldn't. Specifically, he thanked her for coming with us to the caterer and helping plan the menu. "Choosing between all that delicious food was just so hard!" he told her. Marilyn laughed and told him that was one of the easier parts, and she was happy to help.

Jason and I spent our wedding night at Harrah's Casino, where earlier he won thousands of dollars at the craps table, or so he claims. He and all the groomsmen were actually late boarding the bus to the reception because he was on a heater. Every time he tells that story, the amount of money seems to grow. A thousand, two thousand, five thousand. I'm not sure exactly how much it was, but I know it went a long way toward our honeymoon at Sandals St. Lucia!

My favorite memory from the wedding was watching Dad dancing with my nephew, Micah. There is truly nothing more exuberant than a seven-year-old dancing. Just before self-consciousness kicks in, before they start worrying about being cool or looking funny, that's when kids are the most fun. It was also the only moment all day that Dad seemed to really allow himself to let go. Seeing them together took me by surprise. Up to that point, I'd never felt strongly about having kids. I was always on the fence and had even said on several occasions that I didn't think I wanted a family. Now, something was tugging ever so gently at my heart. Before I knew it, that pull would become a current so strong that nothing on Earth could hold it back.

Above: Yes, that's a post-it note that reads "Sonja called this lady her grandma but she wasn't." There were dozens of post-it notes all over Dad's photo albums, including his wedding album, pictured here, which we displayed at his wake. I have so many questions!

A Slice of Ham: *The only thing Dad loved more than striking up conversations with strangers was taking photos of random things. He carried his Kodak Easy Share Digital Camera with the automatic telescoping zoom lens wherever he went. If something struck his fancy, he'd make everyone stop in their tracks so he could "take a pitcher" of it (that's how he pronounced picture). The camera made a painful zip-zip-zip sound as it struggled to focus. He took photos of palm trees in a McDonald's parking lot, of a stranger's car or boat and – his personal favorite – the headstones of deceased relatives. He normally took between five and six photos of a single headstone. It's unclear what he thought was going to change. He loved giving us Shutterfly photo albums as gifts, but the really special photos might end up screen printed on hats, mugs, or other souvenirs. One Christmas, everyone in the family received a T-shirt depicting Dad holding up the Cardinals World Series trophy. Stylish!*

CHAPTER 11

THERE'S HAM
IN THE FRIDGE

Dad called Jason and me a lot when he was living in the villa. It seemed like every day brought some minor catastrophe, an injury, cooking mishap, or broken appliance. I checked in regularly to make sure he was attending his various doctors' appointments and brought him healthy pre-made meals, in the vague hope that he might attempt to keep his diabetes in check through more means than just pills. My efforts, however, were futile and completely counteracted by Dad's absolute determination to overfeed Jason and me. It wasn't his fault; his mother had been the same way. The entire Italian side of the family loved to eat and serve others food, which isn't much of a surprise.

The moment Jason and I stepped into the house, Dad would start offering us food. Mostaccioli, hard-boiled eggs, granola bars, and – his ultimate go-to – sliced ham. Jason and I started betting on how long it would take after we arrived for Dad to offer us ham. The average was about five minutes. Even if we had just arrived from the biggest dinner date and complained of being stuffed, there was ham in the fridge, and we'd better be prepared to decline some.

Life for Dad was about food, so maybe I should have accepted that I was fighting a losing battle with his health. Instead, because I'm a glutton for punishment, I made an appointment for him with a nutritional counselor (2-3 hours per year is covered by Medicare), and everything went in one ear and out the other. I'm not sure why I wouldn't give up and let the man enjoy his processed deli meats.

In the meantime, I was starting to feel a bit restless at work. I loved

World Wide Technology, especially the many close friendships I had, but it was by far the longest amount of time I'd worked anywhere, and my nature had never been to sit still. Plus, I was coming off a very large project and feeling exhausted. Considering everything that had changed for me in the past two years, it's probably not surprising that I was looking for a transition. It was at a business conference in Boston that I met some fun guys who were working for a small Florida-based competitor to WWT. They were very eager to grow their team and practically forced their business card into my purse. I told myself I would ignore it, but of course I didn't.

Only a few months later, a friend of ours let us know that he was running a triathlon in my honor for the Lymphoma and Leukemia Society in St. Petersburg, Florida. Desperate for a break, Jason and I took the opportunity for a vacation, and I gave in to the temptation to let the Florida-based company know that I was going to be in town. They pulled out all the stops. Their VP of Sales bought us baseball tickets and took us out to dinner. He boasted about the company's rapid growth, how we'd have the opportunity to get in on the ground floor and make our own destiny. We'd have the chance to lead the company through explosive growth. That sounded good to me, but I still wasn't ready to commit.

We continued to receive texts throughout the entire weekend, and on the Monday morning when we were about to fly out, they invited us to breakfast. This is when they put on the hard sell. I can't remember exactly what was said that made me truly change my mind, but by the time we caught our flight that day, I was thinking about how nice it would be to live in Florida. Jason and I both hated the cold St. Louis weather. And wasn't it Heather's turn to take care of Dad? I desperately wanted to escape the level of responsibility I had gotten myself into, both personally and professionally. It was exciting for us both to start something new.

"Are you shittin' me?" Dad asked incredulously when we finally broke the news a few months later, after hours of back-and-forth deliberation. We were sitting in the living room of his villa – the one we owned, which we'd convinced him to move into so he could be closer to us – explaining that we were moving eighteen hours away. He wasn't angry exactly, more shocked, and extremely disappointed. I tried to make the case that this would encourage him to visit Heather more often. After all, Oklahoma was an easy driving distance from St. Louis, and his only grandson was there. But we both knew that Heather didn't have the capacity to do everything for Dad that I'd been doing. He hadn't truly lived on his own in a very long time, and now I was forcing the issue.

He wasn't the only person who was shocked by our decision. Everyone at WWT assumed that we were lifers, including my boss, Matt. Nearly half of all our wedding guests were WWT employees, for crying out loud! The rest of our teammates were equally flummoxed, so much so that rumors began to swirl around Jason's and my departure. Maybe Matt and I were having an affair, and I was having his baby. Or maybe Jason and I were nudists. (Those were my personal favorites!) Deep down, some of the rumors bothered me a little, but I guess people need to make up stories when they don't understand the situation.

Still, Jason and I stuck to our guns. We sold our home, packed up our lives, and moved to Tampa in September of 2008. In terms of the city itself, it was wonderful. We loved the warm weather, the slower pace, and the palm trees. Without the memory of Mom lingering everywhere I looked, I felt my spirits truly starting to lift. Bits of grief I didn't even realize I was still carrying began to melt away. We loved Tampa.

Unfortunately, we didn't love the Florida-based company. It wasn't long after we arrived that we realized something was seriously amiss with the organization. It started when I noticed the sales team had a habit of delaying booking maintenance on products they sold. If a client called and said, "Hey, I thought this was under warranty," then they would start the process of putting in a maintenance order with the manufacturer. If no call was made, no order would be placed, and more margin would be realized. I pointed this out on several occasions; it certainly wasn't how we did things at WWT. Excuses were made, but nothing ever changed. Jason, in his role as a sales leader, tried to issue an ultimatum on some counterfeit equipment that was being sold, but he was ignored.

Next, it was the partying. Now, I'd been a bit of a wild child back in my day, so far be it from me to consider myself a prude. However, during company offsite meetings, I started to feel like I was working in a fraternity house. These guys were working for a small tech firm in Tampa and living like they worked at Stratton Oakmont in the '90s. It wasn't cute and not something I wanted to be associated with.

The breaking point for me came when I saw some emails (security wasn't exactly tight) alluding to why the company would be a great acquisition. I realized that Jason and I had been courted so hard, not because they wanted us to be leaders and masters of our own destinies, but because they saw us as responsible adults who could get the place in enough order to be sold. Eight months into my new job, I called my former boss Matt in tears and begged to return to WWT. Having left them with two weeks' notice and little explanation, I had low expectations. I was willing to come back at any level, but Matt didn't miss a beat. He had a few options he thought might work, and suggested I meet with the head of Federal Southeast Sales. The WWT Federal team had recently opened an office in Tampa, not far from our downtown condo. Eventually, Matt suggested Jason and I get on a flight back to St. Louis and discuss things in person. Two days later, we quit our jobs and were inbound on a non-stop Southwest route. I didn't take it for granted how liberating it was to be in a financial position to make that decision.

Although I was eager to go back to my previous company, Jason was unusually quiet on the trip. At first, I thought that he was feeling regretful. It wasn't like us to come crawling back with our tails between our legs. Then again, shit happens. I encouraged Jason to talk to me about what was going on inside his head. He took a deep breath.

"I want to start my own company," he said. "If I don't do it now, I probably never will." We spent the rest of the flight talking about what that company would look like, how it would operate, and what we needed to do to get it started. He developed the idea for a consulting company that would be the exact opposite of where we just left. It would be honest, reliable, and consistent. He'd start right away full-time, while also finishing up his bachelor's at the University of Tampa. Meanwhile, I'd try my hand at sales with WWT. What was a short detour for me ended up being a major crossroads for him. Life is like that sometimes, and I was excited to support him.

The new sales role was perfect. I would be able to continue living in Tampa, provided I worked from the new office they opened and visited

WWT HQ regularly. It was a perfect arrangement, really. My trips to St. Louis would allow me to see Dad frequently while keeping my life in the sunshine. I accepted WWT's offer on the spot and immediately went looking for old friends in one of the newly renovated buildings. While I was surprising my friend Brian Ortbals in his office, the co-founder and chairman, Dave Steward, walked by. He immediately came over to me, a huge smile on his face and gave me a hug. "Welcome back," Dave said without missing a beat. "Let me know if there is anything I can ever do for you. How's Jason?" I was astonished Dave was so in touch with the business and knew I was returning. This was home for me professionally, and I was going to work like hell not to mess it up. Unsurprisingly, two months after our decision to leave, the Florida company was acquired by a large global integrator.

After settling back in at WWT, life in Florida got much better. Dad visited us frequently, which turned out to be great for him. Every time he came down, he'd take enough "pitchers" to fill a whole Shutterfly book. He took these albums with him everywhere he went, showing them off to the guys at the garage, his barber, cashiers at the grocery store, and really anyone he could get to look at them.

One person he couldn't convince to look at them: Heather. When Dad wasn't staying with us in Florida or working, he was spending time with Heather in Oklahoma. It was great for him to get lots of quality time with his now three grandsons. Yet there was a strange tension there. Heather seemed to resent the photo albums, the constant waxing poetic about the beaches and plastic palm trees of Florida while she was living near a military base in what was essentially the middle of nowhere. Although Heather and I had grown closer since Mom's death, there was still some distance between us. There was a bitterness that, despite my rule-breaking and wild ways, I had ended up being the golden child. Mom never really forgave Heather for the alleged grave sin of getting pregnant at twenty-three. (A completely normal age! She was even married, for goodness sake!) Even though Tampa isn't exactly an exotic and glamorous city, it seemed that way to my family. Thus, Heather couldn't bring herself to be interested in the photo albums, and this hurt Dad. Eventually, Heather and her family would head back to Germany. Dad was crushed that his grandsons would be moving overseas, but I think it was a bit of a relief to my sister. Fortunately, Dad had plenty to distract him, including some compelling personal drama.

By that time, Dad was checking in with his diabetes doctor, an endocrinologist, on a monthly basis. He went so frequently that he developed a friendship with a front office worker named Donna. She was one of the few people who seemed genuinely interested in his Shutterfly albums. After every trip to Florida, he'd stop in for a checkup and bring his pitchers. Donna knew our entire family by name, as well as our professions, hobbies, and life stories, before we ever knew a thing about her. Dad genuinely enjoyed chatting with Donna and found himself feeling that special spark for the first time in a very long time. Eventually, he got up the nerve to ask Donna out on a date. Even better, she agreed enthusiastically. There was only one problem: Dad already had a girlfriend.

Sally was an old friend from high school. She and her ex-husband had been good friends of my parents, part of the old weekend boating and water skiing crew. It seemed natural for the two of them to spend time together now that they were both single. Sally had been there for Dad when Mom died, and they had a lot of shared history. But Sally didn't like looking at Shutterfly photo albums. In fact, she seemed pretty bored around Dad. He wasn't thrilled about her either, but he wasn't sure how to break up with someone who had essentially been a good friend his whole life. She wasn't sure how to break up with him because she felt bad for him. It had been a very long time since either of them had dealt with anything like this, naturally. Rather than addressing the issue head-on (or asking me about it), Dad decided to send a Facebook message to Russ to ask for his input. To this day, I do not know why Dad chose Facebook to communicate with a guy he spoke to on the phone every single day, especially when he didn't have a clear idea how Facebook worked. So, I found out my dad was caught up in a love triangle when it scrolled across my public newsfeed. Dad had posted on Russ's Facebook wall that he was dating two women at once. Whoopsie!

After a frantic phone call, I managed to acquire Dad's password (it took three or four attempts before he could remember the right one) and deleted the post for him. I'm not sure if Sally ever saw it, but thankfully, their relationship ended amicably. I did not anticipate that I would be managing my dad's dating situations from Tampa!

Donna ended up being a real blessing in Dad's life. She took good care of him, and they got serious enough that when he moved down to Florida, she eventually joined him. It was nice to have someone else in the picture dedicated to taking care of Dad, especially as his health would continue to decline. He was hesitant at first to open his heart to someone new. Mom had been the love of his life, and moving on felt like betrayal. (Although I'm sure Mom would have undoubtedly moved on if the roles were reversed). Slowly but surely, though, he and Donna built a partnership. They enjoyed each other's company immensely during his first two years in Florida, which were his best since Mom had passed. Additionally, her support would become invaluable when his health eventually took a turn for the worse.

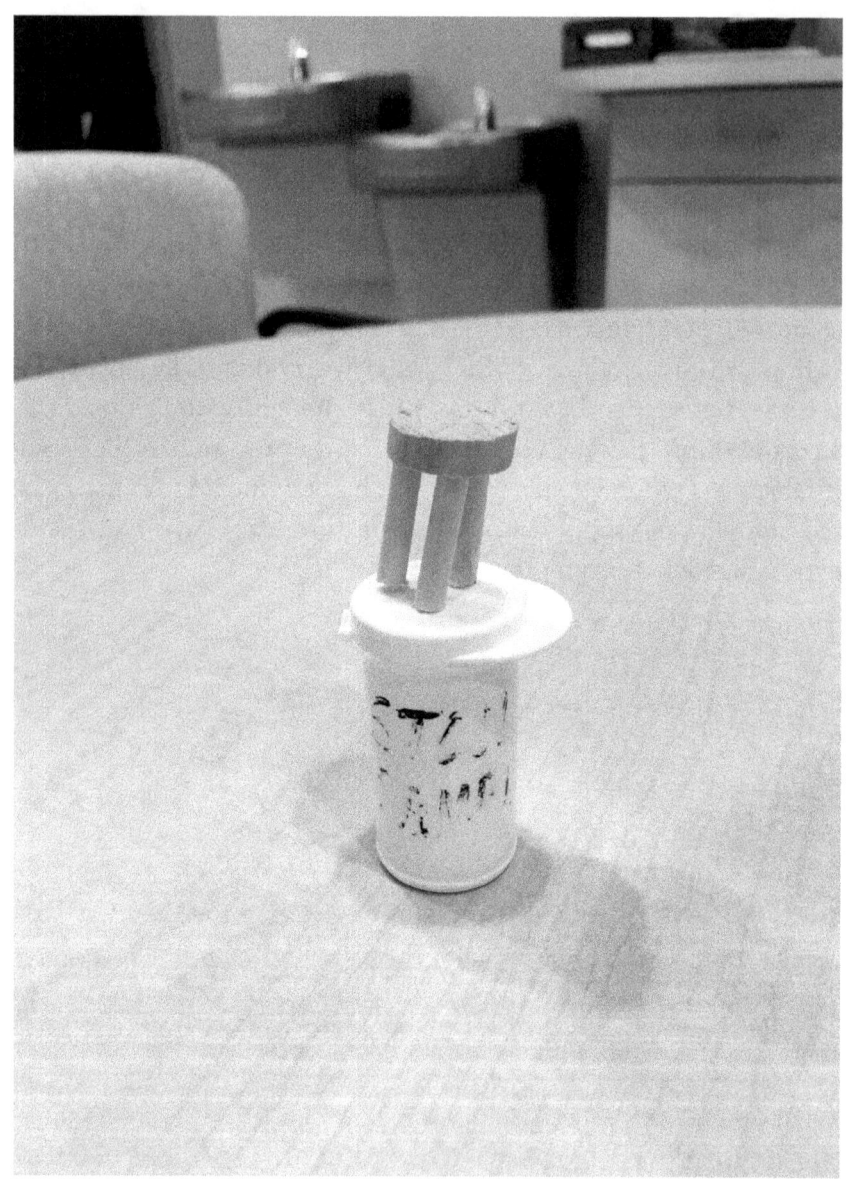

A Slice of Ham: *Whenever we visited a new physician – which was often – Dad would announce that he had brought along a stool sample. To the doctor's horror, Dad would then open up a small 20mm film container and dump the contents into his hand. There was, quite literally, a small wooden stool in the container.*

CHAPTER 12

THE EAR SCAB
(AND OTHER MALADIES)

Dad's early days in Florida were some of the best times we spent together. We moved him into a senior apartment called The Fountains of Boca Ciega Bay, not too far from our St. Petersburg home. Every Sunday night, Jason and I would come over for the big Bingo extravaganza. (I'd come a long way from Saturdays at Deja-Vu.) It took a little encouragement on our part, but eventually Dad put himself out there and made some good friends who he could chat and trade complaints with. More than anything, though, he loved spending his time with us.

After failing to control his diabetes by myself, I set him up with a dietitian, an employee of Jason's who was working towards earning her dietitian certification through a local community college. Elinor met with Dad on a weekly basis to review the log of his blood sugar numbers and discuss his meals for the week. In return, I think I PayPal'd her $30 a week. Incredibly, he listened to her. In six months, his diabetes was under control, and he was taking far less insulin. He was doing so well that his doctor asked me how he could replicate these results in other patients. I modestly told him it was all the student dietitian's doing, but privately I accepted the praise. I'd done it! I'd taken control of Dad's health and staved off any future disasters. One might think that by now I would have learned that such control is an illusion, but I can be pretty stubborn. It was going to take a few more hard lessons before I'd really accept life's unpredictability.

The first setback came when this brilliant dietitian informed us that she was pregnant and moving out of state. I was disappointed, but I thought surely Dad and I could keep the good habits going. Unfortunately, Dad's aversion to change threw a pall over the transition. He trusted her advice more than he trusted mine, or maybe I just didn't have the same knack for motivation. Or, perhaps the power of inertia was just too strong. Whatever the reason, Dad gradually went back to his old ways, and his sugar levels spiraled out of control quickly. He went back to taking a gargantuan amount of insulin, eventually needing such a large dosage that a nurse once confessed to me that she was nervous about administering that much at one time. Although I rationally understood Dad's failing health wasn't my fault, it was a humbling moment. Circumstances can change so fast.

The next major setback happened during a two-week visit from Dad's now serious girlfriend, Donna. Jason and I invited the two of them to go out on a pontoon boat, one of those eco tours out of John's Pass. John's Pass Village is a waterfront area located in Madeira Beach near St. Petersburg. Known for its quaint atmosphere, the "pass" was created by a hurricane in 1848. It was a great place to rent a fishing charter, jet ski, or even go on a nice booze cruise. While absolutely a tourist trap, it was also the best place to find all the souvenirs needed to take home to her grandkids.

By this time, Dad was seriously overweight again, to the point that stepping down from the dock onto the wobbly seat cushion of a floating pontoon was a perilous proposition. His doctor had advised that he try stepping backwards in situations of unsteadiness like this. So, that was his first plan of action on one fateful sunny day at John's Pass.

As he slowly stepped backward, the guide noticed his shakiness and shouted, "Wait a second, I'll help you!" Hearing this, Dad turned his head quickly and stumbled back, getting his leg caught between the bobbing boat and the dock. After a few seconds, we pulled him up, but not before a huge chunk of skin was scraped off his shin. The wound stretched all the way from his knee to his ankle. The tour guide provided Dad with a wad of paper towels to press on the wound. Dad kept the gash completely covered throughout the entire tour, so none of us realized just how deep it was. I think he was too embarrassed to end the trip. We didn't understand the extent of the damage until we got him home and cleaned the wound. When the gash had barely begun to heal a few days later, we took him to a doctor.

Dad had started taking Metformin for his diabetes when he was in his late forties and always assumed the pill would take care of the medical condition. If his A1C was off, his physicians would simply increase the Metformin. Back in the late nineties, they didn't have a fancy fool-proof way to administer insulin. Patients had to be educated on how to count carbohydrates, calculate how many units of insulin they'd need to offset, draw that up into a syringe and administer the shot themselves. This was far too complicated for Dad, so they continued to increase his oral medications to compensate for his worsening situation.

Unfortunately, he never kept his blood sugar under control (aside from the brief period when he was working with the nutritionist), so his diabetes continued to worsen. High blood sugar levels prevent nutrients and oxygen from energizing cells, which in turn prevents your immune system from functioning properly, leading to increased inflammation and difficulty with healing. So, Dad's scrape turned into an ulcer, which led to a string of wound care nurses revolving through the door for nearly ten weeks.

During his prolonged healing period, Dad began to agonize over the state of his relationship with Donna. She was making huge efforts to travel down to see him, even spending extra time with him while he was recovering. It was clear that she wanted to move to Florida and had started dropping hints about rings and weddings. Whenever she did this, Dad would suddenly find something very interesting to take a pitcher of. ("Look! A plastic flamingo wearing a hat!")

When Dad wasn't picking up on her hints, Donna began dropping them in front of Jason and me, surely in the hopes that we would step in on her behalf. I began to gently nudge Dad about it. He and Donna were great together, and she obviously made him happy. Plus, she was the only person I knew who loved looking through his photo albums. What was the holdup?

Dad admitted that dating was one thing, but he couldn't shake the feeling that getting married felt like a betrayal of Mom. There was just no way Donna could ever replace her.

"Donna doesn't want to replace Mom," I reminded him, "She'd never expect that." Donna understood how much Mom had meant to my father. She even got him a card every year on the anniversary of Mom's death. All Donna wanted was to be around for the next chapter. After a lot of gentle prodding, I finally convinced Dad to take the big step. We went ring shopping together at the mall and found the perfect, simple, second-hand diamond ring. Something about it just felt right. Both Dad and the ring were getting a second life.

Dad proposed to Donna in the exact same way Jason proposed to me. (I'm pretty sure he asked Jason what to do, which wasn't necessarily the best choice considering I didn't love my proposal.) We were all visiting Jason's parents' house for Christmas, as we did every year. Dad gifted Donna a framed photo with the words "Will You Marry Me?" Fortunately, Donna loved it. She cried happy tears and hugged all of us. I could tell by the look on Dad's face that all his doubts were wiped away. He knew he'd made the right choice. Once again, things were looking up.

Next on the road to chaos came the infamous ear scab incident. I was away at a World Wide Technology sales conference over my birthday week in Austin when the drama unfolded. Jason was about to head into a meeting at our nascent IT consulting company, DGR Systems, when he received an unexpected call from Dad.

"Hi, Ed!" Jason said. "What's going on?"

"My ear's bleeding and I don't know what to do," Dad replied. Jason's mind immediately went to a scab on Dad's ear, which he'd been picking at for some time. "Have you tried applying pressure to it?" Jason asked in the same tone in which one asks, "Have you turned it off and on again?"

"Yes," Dad confirmed, "but it's still bleeding." "How about a band-aid?" Jason suggested. "I tried to put a few band-aids on it, but it didn't really work," Dad replied. A few band-aids? That was certainly odd, but Jason didn't have any more time to devote to this discussion. He told Dad that he was about to go into a meeting, but he could come over after work. Did Dad think he could wait that long?

"Sure, no problem!" Dad agreed.

"In the meantime, keep applying pressure," Jason advised. He went into his meeting fully expecting the issue to be resolved before he was done. Unfortunately, this was not so. Somewhat annoyed, Jason took his time packing up his things before the hour-long drive to The Fountains senior living apartments. He was hungry, so he stopped at a deli along the way and had a BLT. By the time he reached Dad's place, a full two and a half hours had passed since the original call. Still, Jason wasn't concerned. It's not like this was an emergency.

When Jason opened the door to Dad's apartment, the place looked like a murder scene. A large bloodstain had spread over the tan carpet and, bizarrely, there was a sizable smear on the wall. "You made it," Dad said nonchalantly from his seat in his recliner. His formerly white t-shirt was now crimson, and blood was gushing from his left ear down to his shorts. Jason, not normally a squeamish person, started to feel a bit dizzy. "Ed! How long have you been bleeding like this?" He asked. Dad paused for a second to look at the clock before answering. "Well, since about an hour before I called you."

Jason's first instinct was to call 911, but Dad insisted the situation "wasn't that serious." Apparently, he didn't want to inconvenience the "ambulance guys," or take away a spot in the ER from someone who "really needed it." Jason, who was in a bit of a daze at this point, accepted Dad's request not to go to the hospital. He made Dad change his shirt and wrapped his head in a large towel. Then, the two of them got into Jason's car and drove to urgent care.

The nurse at urgent care took one look at Dad's ear and said it would have to be cauterized. Unfortunately, all the clinics with that ability were closed by then. She suggested they go home and try again the next day. "Do you see this guy!" Jason exclaimed, "He looks like he's been to war!" The receptionist locked eyes with Dad, whose head was still wrapped in what looked like a bloody turban. She suggested they try an emergency room. Dad categorically refused. "That's too much of a fuss!" he insisted.

Jason spent the next two hours driving around St. Petersburg, calling every doctor and urgent care he could find who might be able to help them. Finally, he found an open clinic with the tools to cauterize Dad's ear. "We'll be there in ten minutes," Jason promised. "If it's not too much trouble!" Dad shouted from the passenger seat.

Eventually, Dad got the cauterization, and they headed back to The

Fountains. Jason collapsed on the couch three feet from a pool of blood that could easily have been part of the set of Halloween. The incident would become one of our favorite stories to tell, the kind you laugh about at every family gathering. Typical Ed, always finding the most obtrusive way possible to be unobtrusive.

Unfortunately, the long-term prognosis wasn't so funny. After the cauterization, we took Dad in for an examination. The doctor discovered two additional concerning growths, one on his arm and one that looked like the top of a pencil eraser on his neck. Fortunately, they were removed easily and without complication by a plastic surgeon. This plastic surgeon and I really connected. He was a very kind and patient physician who had many geriatric patients. I felt my dad was in good hands, and he needed to be. About a week later, that doctor called to tell me the growths were actually Merkel Cell Carcinoma, a very rare and often fatal form of skin cancer. My heart raced. I really hadn't prepared myself for that call and had pretty much forgotten the growths were even sent out for biopsy. Immediately, I Googled this type of skin cancer and learned it was not "one of the good cancers." Five-year survival rates: 30-50% for Stage 1.

What followed was an endless revolving door of surgeries, radiation, and medications. Dad's unholy trinity of cancer, diabetes, and heart disease meant that treating one issue would invariably aggravate another. I kept a running list of his medications, which I brought along to every appointment. Whenever a doctor wanted to prescribe something new (just about every time we visited), we'd check it against the list to make sure there weren't any adverse reactions. It became apparent that all these doctors were operating in a silo, each responsible for one particular aspect of Dad's health and none for the whole. That responsibility fell on me alone, but if I'm honest, I liked it that way. My experience with surviving cancer felt like boot camp for caring for Dad. I knew how to do the research, how to compare medications, even how to deal with the side effects of radiation. For everything else, there was Molly, who was now a Nurse Practitioner. Again, the more knowledge I had, the more in control I felt. But, try as I might, I couldn't control for Dad's own special brand of chaos.

In January of 2017, Dad backed into another car in the parking lot of the standalone radiation oncology center. A month later, while walking out of that same radiation center, he tripped and fell. He sustained minor injuries, which, of course, turned into major wound care complications and more visits from home health care nurses.

It was around this time that, on a whim, I decided to take a 23andMe DNA test and made a fascinating discovery. To my absolute shock, I was 25% Ashkenazi Jewish! I knew there was no way that the Jewish ancestry came from my dad's side. He was Italian through and through, and there was definitely Italian reflected in my DNA. With Mom no longer around, I took my discovery to Aunt Ingrid. She confessed that she had always suspected that her grandmother was a German Jew and never told anyone about it. My DNA results appeared to confirm that suspicion, and we decided to do some more investigating. I started badgering everyone in the family to take a DNA test. Unfortunately, Heather was in Germany by then and not particularly curious about Mom's potential secret family history. When I told Dad about my newfound fascination, he showed some interest, but I never really pressed it. This was fair enough, as he had enough doctors to visit and tests to undergo. Consequently, I set aside the noteworthy results and did not pursue them any further.

On the day of Dad's final radiation appointment, I was flying back from yet another World Wide Technology sales conference. My plane was delayed slightly, and I landed in Tampa only an hour before his appointment was scheduled to begin. Still, I was determined to make it to his grand finale. A friend of mine, Nathan, had a Porsche Boxster convertible, essentially a racecar, and offered to drive me there. Let me tell you – we flew! Nathan took this as a rare excuse to push that car to its limit, cruising at over 100 mph with my heart going at the same velocity. We looked like we were filming a high-speed chase scene in a James Bond movie. I kept my eyes off the speed gauge and just prayed that we'd get there in time and in one piece. I think my friend enjoyed that drive a lot more than I did. Fortunately, I waltzed into the radiation clinic with five minutes to spare, calm, cool, and collected just like they do in the movies. (Actually, I may have looked like a total sweaty mess at that point, but I didn't care. I made it for dad's last treatment, and he couldn't have been happier.)

The one bright spot in all this mess was Dad's marriage to Donna in the summer of 2017. They waited until the end of his first rounds of radiation to host a small, simple ceremony at our house on the water in St. Petersburg. It was a very hot July day in Florida. Even though it was strange to see my dad with someone other than Mom, it was good to see him genuinely smiling again. Donna's daughter and two granddaughters came for the occasion, and a friend of a friend married the happy couple in our living room. Afterwards, we ventured to downtown St. Petersburg to take photos and then out to Harold Seltzer's Steakhouse for dinner, Dad and Donna's favorite restaurant.

Since we can't have happiness without chaos, it pains me to report that two weeks after the wedding, Dad had a heart attack. He was home with Donna at their ocean-view condo (they'd moved out of The Fountains). He started having chest pains in the middle of the night, was rushed to the hospital and had an emergency stent implanted. I couldn't believe it. Diabetes, cancer, and now this? Now, I had even more medicines to keep track of and still more treatments that could potentially interfere with one another. What else could possibly go wrong? (The answer: plenty.)

After that, everything went to shit. Dad's primary care doctor made what we thought was a routine visit to the condo and discovered a lump on his neck. Upon further examination and a chest X-ray, the doctor confirmed that Dad's cancer had returned, and it had metastasized to his lymph nodes and lungs. The survival rate for metastasized Merkel Cell Carcinoma is less than 20%. I knew this right away, of course, because I Googled it as soon as news of his relapse came through. But knowing something and accepting it are two very different things.

He first tried an immunotherapy agent that was approved for advanced Merkel Cell, but twenty minutes into the first infusion Dad went into cardiac arrest and was unable to breathe. They rushed him to the hospital, which thankfully, was down the street from the cancer center. Of course, I was in Orlando at the time, attending a coworker's wedding. Jason was in town and was able to meet Dad and Donna at the emergency room. I remember Jason keeping me updated via text as I drove home and telling me things didn't look good. Thankfully, Dad pulled through after a couple days in the ICU. Dad's follow-up appointment with his oncologist, however, was pretty grim. Any available treatment options would be too hard on his body. That's when I first heard the term "palliative care" used in reference to my dad.

Palliative care meant that Dad would not be getting better. There would be no second remission. It was only a matter of time. Palliative care is different from hospice in that they did hope to prolong Dad's life as much as possible, and he could still receive medications and treatment. They determined subsequent rounds of chemo or immunotherapy wouldn't be something he could tolerate. He had far too many comorbidities.

That August, Jason and I went for one of our regular visits to the condo. When Dad opened the door, he had a black eye that was red and swollen up like a balloon.

"Who punched you?" Jason asked, incredulously. Dad gave him a puzzled look, then shrugged. "No one," he said, "I just woke up this way." "Does it hurt?" I asked. The answer should have been obvious. "Oh yeah, it hurts," Dad responded casually. We went straight to the doctor.

It turned out, the situation was even more serious than it looked and completely unrelated to the cancer. Dad had been diagnosed with glaucoma as a young adult and had an artificial lens implanted in his left eye decades prior to relieve the pressure. Over the years, the lens had deteriorated, resulting in a severe infection. The doctor informed us grimly that, if they couldn't stop the infection, Dad may lose his eye. Fortunately, the antibiotics worked well enough that the eye was able to be saved, but Dad lost his vision on that side permanently. Yet another long-term ailment we'd have to manage.

By now, I was in desperate need of a break. Instead, I got hurricane Irma.

A Slice of Ham: *Nothing prepares you for the chaos of coordinating the safety for multiple individuals (Dad and Donna, Trev'on, and nervous coworkers who just moved to Florida) during a hurricane. Hurricane Irma was no exception.*

CHAPTER 13

IRMA ARRIVES

rma formed as a tropical storm on August 30, 2017, just west of the Cape Verde Islands and rapidly intensified into a major hurricane within 30 hours. She quickly strengthened into a Category 5 storm headed straight for Florida. The one good thing about hurricanes is you (usually) receive a lengthy heads-up that they are headed your way. The bad thing is the "cone of uncertainty" can encompass the entire state of Florida, and at the last minute head west towards Texas and Louisiana—or even U-turn out into the gulf, hitting absolutely no one.

Jason and I wavered daily over whether we should evacuate, and where to go, or if we should simply hunker down. On September 5, I decided to fill up some sandbags and put them on the back porch. Our pool was known to overflow and back up water all the way to our sliding glass kitchen door. While the Tampa Bay water in the canal behind our home had never come over our seawall, forecasts predicted some very high tides. As the storm drenched South Florida, Bay News 9 filled the Tampa Bay area with extreme anxiety. Even so, as the storm crept closer to Tampa, we remained on the fence. Dad was a major factor in our considerations because he was in no shape to travel for a long car ride. He was calling us three times a day, filled with anxiety over what he should do. Eventually, he and Donna decided to go to a shelter, freeing Jason and me from responsibility. Or, so we thought.

Aunt Ingrid called me the following day to ask if my eighteen-year-old cousin, Tre'von, could come to stay with us. Tre'von had graduated high school earlier that year in San Antonio and scored a job at Disney World. He is on the Autism Spectrum, but has never allowed it to hold him back. Only a few months after graduation, he was thriving on his own, and we were all incredibly proud of him. But a hurricane is a different story. Ingrid was pretty freaked out that the storm was barreling towards Florida. It didn't help that when Tre'von arrived at the hotel she booked for him, along with his pets and hurricane supplies, he was quickly turned away for not being of age to rent a room. Since he was of legal age, I'm confident the hotel was just making an excuse. Whatever the reason, I assured Ingrid that Tre'von was welcome here. "Sure," I said, "three's company!"

Tre'von drove himself in Grandpa Louie's old VW bug down to our home in St. Petersburg from Orlando. I knew Tre'von had a dog, Cookie, and a tiny pet turtle, named Chance. What I did not realize is that he also had a brand new 8-week-old puppy and a bit of a hoarding problem. Tre'von arrived at our house with his car packed to the gills. We put Barley, our Vizsla, out back and Cookie in the living room while I ventured out to the car to assess the situation. The turtle, about the size of a computer mouse, was housed in a 30-quart plastic Tupperware bin fit for about eight pairs of adult shoes. It also happened to be filled with water and had dozens of holes poked in the top, so the water sloshed and splashed from side to side when jostled. As I carried this precarious habitat into the house, I encountered Cookie conveniently taking a dump on the hardwood floors of our living room. Allll-righty then...we'll just clean that up real quick and pretend it didn't happen.

Tre'von's "go bags" consisted of a large duffle bag packed with nothing but clothes and dog food and a second clear zip-up bag that obviously once contained a new king-sized comforter. Inside this clear "comforter bag" were various kitchen staples: a few cans of soup, various spices such as cinnamon and nutmeg, a super sharp kitchen knife, a book, ramen, grenadine, some Sharpies, battery-operated touch lights, and several cans of Bruce's yams in various sizes (15-ounce and 40-ounce). In addition to the duffle and comforter bags, Tre'von carried in a mysterious plain brown Amazon box, about half the size of a shoe box. I decided not to ask any questions about the third box and just focus on keeping the dogs separated. Both Cookie and the puppy, Tot (yes, Tot...as in Tater Tot), were infested with fleas.

For the rest of the day, we were glued to the television while I fielded multiple phone calls and text messages from Dad and Ingrid. Dad had initially been impressed by the shelter, a community center near the center of St. Petersburg, because it boasted cots for them to sleep on, a free spaghetti dinner, and plenty of electricity. The following night, when local nursing homes and patients from the department of mental health showed up, it was a different story and quickly lost its luster.

As the storm continued to get closer and gain strength, Jason and I

finally made the decision to drive north. We decided that six hours towards South Carolina should put us out of harm's way. The following morning, we loaded up three adults, three dogs and one turtle into my Infiniti QX60 SUV. (We actually had Tre'von drive his VW bug behind us for a short time before dropping it off in a Landry's parking lot off Interstate 4.) No sense in having him drive all the way back to St. Pete after this debacle was over.

Once we got to the car drop lot, I convinced Tre'von to consolidate his bags into one duffle and leave behind the non-essentials. (You know, maybe only bring one can of yams, a little dog food, and zero steak knives, and spices.) I placed the comforter bag and the half-sized shoe box in his trunk, sure I had seen the last of them. It wasn't until two hours later that I realized the shoe box had reappeared. Tre'von had surreptitiously placed it back in our car when no one was looking.

I discreetly snapped a photo of the mystery box and texted it to Aunt Ingrid. "WTF is in this box? It's following us everywhere!" I typed with a winky face at the end.

"That's Lulu," replied Ingrid. "Well, Lulu's cremated remains." Oh my God! I tried to stifle my laughter, which ended up coming out as more of a snort. Still, it was sweet that Tre'von didn't want to leave behind his precious deceased dog. I didn't attempt to disturb his box again, and Tre'von and I continue to laugh about it to this day.

Our six-hour trek to South Carolina had turned into an eight-hour drive, and we were still barely to Jacksonville. I frantically refreshed the Hilton app over and over again, trying to score us hotel rooms. I finally found an Embassy Suites in Jacksonville Beach, and Jason was very happy to stop driving. The storm was about 36 hours away by this point and had already taken out the Florida Keys. I got Tre'von and his petting zoo their own room and reminded him about every two hours to take the dogs out to potty. I scored a new umbrella, four beers, a deck of cards and a couple of peanut butter sandwiches from the hotel lobby while we waited. Tre'von was less than thrilled about the $1 sandwiches and was wishing for more yams.

We stayed at the Embassy Suites for two nights until the storm finally blew through (yep, it basically followed the exact path we drove, lucky us!), pouring biblical amounts of rain into the Jacksonville area. While Irma initially hit Florida as a Category 4 hurricane, by the time it got to Jacksonville Beach, it was a weakening tropical storm. We got very little sleep, but wanted to get back to Tampa ASAP to see if there was any damage to our home. Word on our street was that we were out of electricity, yet Dad and Donna's condo never lost power. The news proclaimed the Jacksonville River was starting to flood the streets, so we packed up the car quickly. Because of the rising tide, they were closing the bridge from Jacksonville Beach into Jacksonville. We were the last car to make it over. Jason saw in the rearview mirror that no other cars made it through the police, who were then blocking traffic. Score! A rare Dugger win! We'll take it.

We got to Orlando within a couple of hours and dropped Tre'von off at his car, making sure he'd text us when he arrived back at his place. He was without electricity yet completely unfazed and going with the flow. He's such a resilient young man. We survived! Jason and I made it back to St. Petersburg and, while the streets were riddled with downed tree limbs and an occasional uprooted tree, everything was mostly intact. Jason immediately pulled a (previously) frozen pizza from the freezer and threw it on the grill. We ate dinner by candlelight and went to bed both physically and mentally exhausted. The following day, our electricity returned, Dad and Donna were back safe in their condo, and all was well with the world.

The stress of that evacuation hit all of us hard, but it was especially tough on Dad. On September 14, less than a week after the ordeal, the stent in his heart collapsed. When the paramedics arrived at the condo, they greeted him like an old friend. "He's the most popular guy on our route," one of the paramedics informed me happily. I couldn't help but laugh, despite the situation. Dad was once again rushed to the hospital.

The surgery was long and arduous, but they successfully replaced his defibrillator with a dual-function pacemaker/defibrillator combo device. When he came out from under anesthesia, I was there to see him wake up. "I've got an idea," he said, smiling, "let's take it easy for the rest of the year." "Now, there's an idea," I said, smiling. "Let's do that."

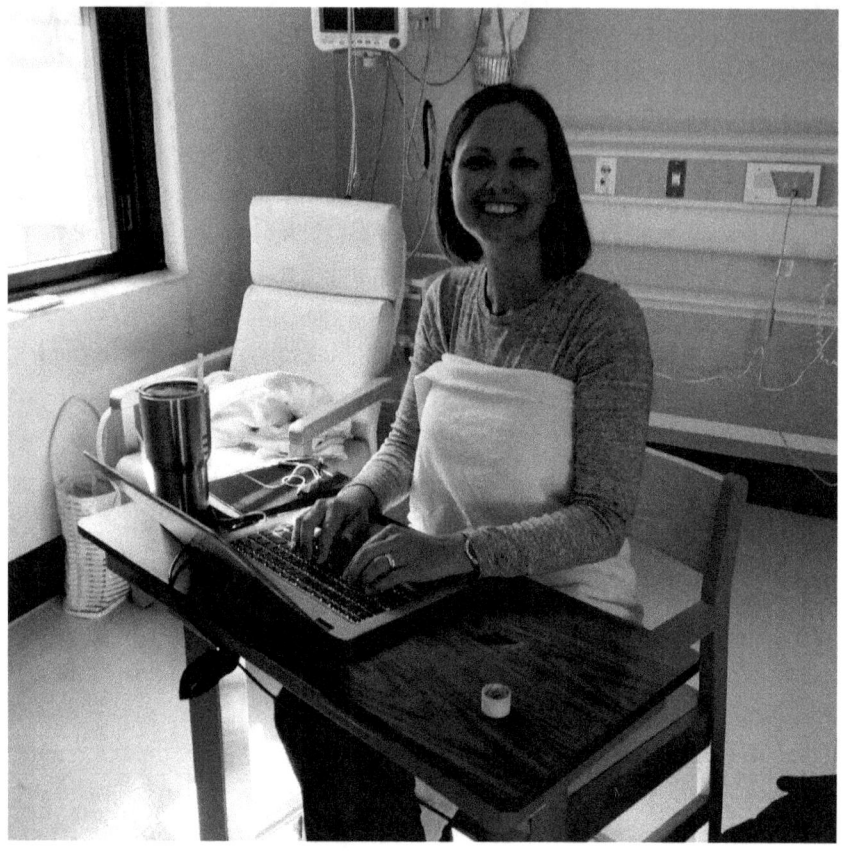

Me working from dad's hospital room while he's in surgery.

On October 26, 2017, I shared the following message on Facebook: "I am so proud of and incredibly happy for this man, Ed Carter! He's had one hell of a year: radiation for Merkel Cell Carcinoma, two heart events (including one heart attack with stent procedures and two defibrillator/pacemakers implanted), and a severe eye infection leaving him blind in one eye...oh, and he got married in July!

He's on the road to recovery, has lost an incredible amount of weight and has been eating well and exercising so much that they took him off three out of four blood pressure meds and decreased his insulin quite a bit! Join me in telling him how awesome he is!!!"

It had truly been an unbelievable year. What I hadn't shared in this message, and didn't share with anyone really, was that through it all,

Jason and I had been desperately trying to get pregnant, struggling with a multi-year-long battle with infertility. I'd carefully tucked this part of my life away, not wanting to cause additional stress for Dad. Sounds familiar, doesn't it? But that's a story for another chapter.

In the meantime, things did seem to settle down after that second heart surgery. Dad's diabetes improved, as he once again made an effort to eat better. Still, the combination of his wounds and weight made mobility difficult. Whenever we talked about going out somewhere, Dad would ask how many steps were involved and how far he'd have to walk. If there were more than three steps, he'd refuse to go. The memories of his pontoon accident and the fall in the radiation parking lot loomed large for him. He never wanted to inconvenience anyone or slow anyone down, and he knew the effort required to get him up the steps would cause him embarrassment. As a result, he and Donna stayed home most of the time. They enjoyed their quiet time together and their view, from the balcony, of the Gulf of Mexico. It made me sad to think of him stuck there day in and day out.

By the time Christmas 2017 came around, I realized this year had been one of the most difficult of our lives. And that was saying a lot. I wanted to do something to make this Christmas special, to make all our efforts feel worthwhile.

Every year around the holidays, the Tampa Zoo hosts a light show. The entire place is decked out with thousands of twinkling lights, dazzling light tunnels, and fountains of lights. I knew this was exactly the type of thing Dad would love. (Think of all the "pitchers" he could take!)

The only problem was the walking. When I first brought it up to Dad, he dismissed the idea outright.

"No way," he said, shaking his head, "I'm not getting in the way of all those people. What about the kids?" But I had a plan. I contacted the zoo ahead of time and reserved an electric scooter, which would allow Dad to easily maneuver through crowds. I promised him that he wouldn't have to do any walking and that he'd have a great time. Dad was highly skeptical, but once I put my mind to something, I don't let it go. Fortunately, I also had Donna to make the case for me. I told her about my plan and why I thought it would be good for Dad to get out of the house. She wholeheartedly agreed. Personally, I think she also wanted any excuse to get out. It's not easy being a caretaker 24/7. Finally, Dad agreed to go on the condition that, if there were any problems, we'd turn around and go home right away. I accepted the challenge eagerly, and we all made plans to go to the zoo.

That day was a Christmas memory to last a lifetime. It dawned sunny and mild, the perfect winter day in Florida. When we arrived at the zoo, the electric scooter was waiting for us right beside the entrance. Dad barely had to walk ten yards before he was comfortably situated on the scooter. Wearing a grin from ear to ear, he drove the scooter into the park, zipping around corners and laughing as he cruised past all of us. "Come on, slow pokes!" he called back, "Try to keep up!" When I looked over to Donna, she was wiping a tear from her eye.

We saw it all that day: the dramatic light show, timed to the music of Trans-Siberian Orchestra, the animatronic penguins waving to us from the roof of the penguin house, Santa's Workshop, covered in twinkle lights and fake snow. Dad's favorite part was the live manger. The sheep and goats from the petting zoo cuddled up against the actors playing Mary and Joseph as everyone sang "Silent Night." We stayed at the zoo until closing time, when the exhausted staff in elf hats cheerfully but sternly insisted we make our way to the exit. Christmas music still played softly as Dad steered himself one last time past all of his favorite displays, marveling again at the sheer number of lights. ("Think of how long it took them to put those up!") When we finally got to the exit, we stopped for one final picture in front of the enormous tree. At the end of a long, hard year, the brightest lights were the ones glowing in our hearts.

A Slice of Ham: *Dad was obsessed with hats. One of his favorites was an Army Veteran cap, commemorating his time in the service. Compared to his other hats, it was downright stylish. The first time Jason saw it, he made a point to give Dad a big compliment, which turned out to be a mistake. That very same day, Dad went out and bought Jason the ugliest Navy Veteran hat you could ever imagine. It looked like a boat sitting on top of his head, but Dad was so proud. "Now we match!" he declared. Jason wore it in the house every time Dad came over, and not a moment more.*

OPENING WEEKEND

Christmas was always a big deal in Jason's family. His mom, Sharon, didn't grow up with much, and neither did Jason and his brothers, so she loved showering everyone with the joys she didn't have and couldn't provide as a single mom. Over the years, Jason and I watched his nieces stampede down the stairs to ostentatious piles of presents that filled up the whole living room. The sound of the delighted squeals tugged at a place in my heart I didn't know existed. I'd always been career-focused; some might say career-obsessed. Although I loved being an aunt to my nephews and enjoyed watching my dad with his grandchildren, I'd never thought parenthood was the path for me. But, as the wrapping paper flew through the air, and the happy, weary parents shared looks of exhausted satisfaction, a thought passed through my head, unbidden: *I want that.* My first instinct was to push it down, but as the years went by, I started noticing the longing on Jason's face as well. We had changed our minds. We wanted to be parents.

Backing up a bit, on our sixth anniversary, in October of 2013, we planned a trip to Napa. I ceremoniously tossed my birth control into the garbage, bought my first pack of ovulation strips, and declared it "opening weekend." We thought it would happen right away. We were young, healthy, and how hard could this be? If the sex comes easy, pregnancy should come easy too, right?

When we weren't pregnant after that first trip, we didn't think much of it. After four months of trying pretty (um) *diligently,* I still wasn't pregnant. I confessed my concerns to a few friends, but they assured me that this was normal. Four months wasn't that long, really. The most important thing for me to do was relax. Relax? Me? I wasn't sure I knew how.

By six months, I was sitting, legs spread wide, in an examination chair at my gynecologist's office while she roamed around my uterus with an ultrasound wand, looking for anything that seemed off. "Everything looks normal," she said nonchalantly. By this time, I'd been through too much to accept being dismissed by doctors. I had a persistent, nagging certainty that something was off. "Aren't there any more tests we can do?" I asked. "What if my estrogen is low? Can we try Clomid?" Naturally, I'd done my research and knew what I wanted. The doctor gave me a sweet, sympathetic, but unwavering smile and spoke to me like I was a small child upset about getting a B+ on a math quiz.

"You just have to keep trying," she assured me. "Let's give it another six months." My skin prickled. "And, try to relax," she cooed. Damn, I hate that phrase.

Well, forget that. I dove headfirst into Pregnancy Acquisition Mode. I started going to an acupuncturist who specialized in fertility. In addition to the typical ovulation tests, I started taking my basal body temperature every morning, tracking my cycle so I could pinpoint the *exact moment* of ovulation. Then, I'd call Jason up at work and demand he come home. "It's time," I'd declare, morphing into a terrifying combination of mad scientist and sexual drill sergeant.

None of it worked. Six months later, I was spread-eagle at the doctor's office again, feeling both smug and worried. "There's a medication called Clomid we can try," she helpfully informed me. No shit, lady. We should rewind back twenty-four precious weeks, when that was my idea. But I let it go.

After three unsuccessful rounds of Clomid, we knew something was seriously not right. (I already knew, but by now other people were starting to catch up.) There was a high chance that the harsh chemotherapy I'd had as a teenager had impacted my fertility. They informed me, back in those days, that infertility was a potential risk, but I hadn't given it much thought. There were so many potential risks, and none of them really mattered when measured against saving my life. Plus, I wasn't thinking about kids at nineteen. Now, nearing the age of 34, the alarm bells were going off.

At the same time as our parental quest was commencing, I started to receive pushback from my oncologist about the prospect of receiving any fertility treatment at all. I was still seeing a Hodgkin Lymphoma specialist annually, but the dread of relapse had faded years ago. However, this fear came roaring back when the doctor warned me against fertility drugs. "They can cause breast cancer," she said. Simple as that. I'd already had a lump removed from my left breast in April 2012. That all-important Napa trip had actually been delayed by the pesky intruder making an appearance during a routine checkup at Siteman Cancer Center in St. Louis.

Let's take a little detour to April 2012...

When the technicians won't let you leave the post-mammogram room and immediately require you to get an ultrasound, you know yours is not a great mammogram result. The ultrasound was inconclusive, so they were going to reach out to my oncologist for next steps. Jason immediately flew in from Tampa (after I accidentally booked him a flight departing the wrong day...details, details), and I had a biopsy scheduled the following day.

"Hi...umm...it's not letting me check into my flight to St. Louis," Jason said politely to the Southwest agent at the TPA counter. "Let me see your driver's license," she replied. "Oh, you're not flying today," she replied with a smirk, handing him back his ID, "But you *are* booked on the same flight next month." Well shit. In my haste to get him to town as quickly as possible, I had chosen the correct date but the wrong month. "Right church, wrong pew," as dad would say! Sadly, this wasn't my first time doing this. Let's just say, I'm no longer in charge of travel arrangements for our family.

Ultimately, the biopsy confirmed the lump was benign, but they wanted to remove it anyway, given my radiation history and its likelihood to turn into something gnarly in the future. We didn't tell Dad and made up some excuse as to why Jason was coming to town. After what happened with Mom, I simply couldn't put Dad through the worry. Dad was still working part-time and was gone most of the morning hours, so it was easy to hide.

Since the biopsy came back negative for cancer, I urged Jason to fly home and get back to work. There was nothing to fuss about here. Marilyn could take me to my outpatient surgery, which was quickly lined up for the following Wednesday. The whole procedure was a debacle. They stuck what seemed like a straightened coat hanger into my breast while my boob was smashed inside a mammogram machine. Apparently, this was their way of marking the location of the tumor. Maybe they were being careful not to ruin my beautiful new breast implants. Who knows? Walking into the room in complete horror, seeing my bloody boob looking like a science project, Marilyn recalls them marking the wrong place.

After what seemed like hours, we finally got to the operating room, and the mass was removed. I forced the surgeon to text me a photo of the growth as soon as I came out of the anesthesia. It looked a little like the smelt roe on top of a piece of sushi. The next day, I flew home. I had a friend take me to the airport, so I didn't have to lift my luggage and checked my bag at the curb, happily tipping the Southwest porter. The recovery was no big deal, but the scar was a fairly large and thick gash. I made an appointment to have my stitches removed by the same plastic surgeon who had done my implants, and he seemed rather offended that his work had been compromised. "Next time," he said, "call me...I could have just gone around your nipple to take that out." I rolled my eyes, thinking *I hope there is no next time!*

Flash forward to 2014. I'm in the office with my Hodgkins oncologist, who is recommending a preventative double mastectomy.

I balked. "Chop off my girls?" I asked, "Now?" "Absolutely," the oncologist replied casually. "Another patient of mine did it recently, and she couldn't be happier!" I thought that was a pretty strange thing to be happy about, but whatever floats your boat. Suddenly, I was considering swapping my fertility treatment for yet another cancer-related procedure.

Fortunately, Marilyn came to the rescue, as she often does. Her sister-in-law, Susie, was a women's health nurse practitioner working for the premier fertility doctor in the St. Louis area. I called up Susie to get her take on my cause. "A double mastectomy feels pretty extreme. You're still in your thirties," she mused. "Let's just focus on getting you pregnant." When I brought up my doctor's concerns about fertility treatment and the onslaught of hormones I would face, there was a pause on the other end of the phone. "Let me ask you this," she finally said. "Is your oncologist overall agreeable with you becoming pregnant?" I was surprised at the question, because I'd never considered that she wouldn't be. But Susie went on to explain that the hormones administered during fertility treatment, though strong, were nothing compared to the amounts of those same hormones that would course through the body naturally during pregnancy. "If fertility treatment is a genuine risk factor for you," Susie explained, "then so is being pregnant." I called up the oncologist and asked if it was safe for me to become pregnant, which she immediately confirmed it was. I hung up without further question and called Susie back. We were off to the races.

Susie explained to Jason and me that the first step would be IUI, which stands for Intra-Utero Insemination. Basically, it's the turkey-baster method. They start out with some drugs that stimulate your follicle growth, which forces egg maturation. Once you've taken enough pills to get your eggs nice and juicy, you receive a shot to trigger ovulation. Then, within thirty-six hours, you get *inseminated*. (Such a sexy word, right?) Moo!

We did three rounds of IUI. For each one, I took the pills and trigger shot in Florida, then flew to St. Louis for the "big show," also known as being turkey basted. Incredibly, there weren't very many reputable fertility treatment centers in Tampa. We'd started fertility conversations at a Tampa clinic, but we didn't love the experience. Specifically, Jason hated the specimen collection process, which he described as "skeevier than a Times Square peepshow." The room was filled with old porno magazines with crumbled sticky pages, a VHS tape he refused to load, and a weird antiseptic smell from the frequent mopping between each so-called patient. Thank goodness for smartphones! The worst part, though, was the cheeky smiles he received from the nursing staff when he made the long walk from the collection room, back through the lobby, to the front door. At least at Susie's office, there was a door directly from the collection room to the parking lot. No walk of shame or cheeky smiles.

After three back-to-back unsuccessful IUIs, I was feeling despondent. IVF would be both a lot more expensive and a lot harder to orchestrate from 1,000 miles away.

Then, Dad had his first heart attack, and my entire focus shifted. There was a lot of starting and stopping during this period. If Dad was doing well, Jason and I would start fertility treatment. Inevitably, some of our tests would need to be redone because they were out of date. Sometimes, the fertility center needed approval from my oncologist before proceeding, which would cause more delays. By the time the oncologist responded, Dad would have an incident, and we'd have to put everything on hold again. Rinse. Repeat.

Even during the worst days of my cancer treatment, I'd never felt defeated. I'd always been a fighter, a survivor. Now, I didn't know what to do or where to turn. When Jason's brother called to let us know that his wife was pregnant accidentally for the second time, I burst into tears. I cried the entire car ride home, then felt deeply guilty afterward. I held myself back from confiding even in good friends like Lisa, for fear that she'd think I wasn't happy about her kids. I think she sensed the distance but didn't know what to say. Infertility can be so lonely.

Throughout all of this, I continued to focus on Dad's health. I never let on what I was going through or went to him for advice. As close as we were, that wasn't the kind of relationship we had. What Dad needed was stability in his life, and I wanted to be the person he could rely on. After all, he'd done that for me all those years. It was the least I could do in return. It was another time in my life I wished Mom was around to get me through.

Christmas 2017 changed things for Jason and me. It was another typical Christmas at Sharon's house, complete with more decorations and presents than could reasonably fit in the living room. There's nothing quite like seeing Christmas through the eyes of a child. As I watched my sister-in-law smile down at that new baby whose arrival had so wounded me, I felt myself soften a bit. It turns out, I could still be happy for other people. The jealousy in my heart began to be replaced with something I was a heck of a lot more familiar with: stone-cold determination. After all, when you can't have something, it only makes you want it more. After that, Jason and I agreed to start trying again in earnest. This time, we weren't going to take breaks to accommodate Dad's schedule or get on the test-break-test merry-go-round. We were going to take things seriously. Thankfully, my acupuncturist recommended an IVF doctor who was local to Tampa.

Jason and I instantly connected with this new doctor, who sat with us for well over an hour, answering questions and talking us through the procedures and options. We were sure we'd found the perfect person for us, but she left the practice as soon as our initial testing was completed. In past years, this setback would have been enough for me to put everything on pause again, but not this time. We moved on to the next doctor in the practice, despite the fact that he reminded me of an awkward dinosaur with very short arms and fat hands. If he could get me pregnant, his arm length didn't matter.

Anyone who's ever completed IVF will confirm that it's a huge pain in the ass, figuratively and literally. First off, you have to get your blood drawn multiple times a week. For me, that meant making a 35-minute drive (more if there was traffic) to Tampa General almost every other day. Once I got there, drawing my blood was always an ordeal. Because of not having a port throughout chemo, my veins were very small, tough, and difficult to draw blood from. They'd been through enough crap and were simply over giving, I guess. Every time I came in, I could sense the lab techs getting tense. In an effort to be helpful, I started bringing hand warmers to heat up my veins and try to reduce the number of unpleasant sticks I had to endure. I still often required at least three tries. On one occasion, when my veins were particularly fed up, the fertility doctor himself had to draw the blood. It was a Saturday, so none of the nurses or blood draw techs were in the office, but the tests were mandatory, so he had no choice but to work some magic. I could tell he was somewhat nervous, which probably didn't help. Finally, he found a tiny vein sticking out between my knuckles, and that's where he ended up stabbing me. It was not pleasant for either of us.

The point of all those blood draws is to make sure your follicles don't get overstimulated. This can lead to complications or even multiples. (Twins are one thing, but some women can mature up to 20 eggs on IVF or more. That's enough for your own TLC reality show!) Fortunately for me, I guess, the chemo had so wrecked my ovarian reserve that during that first round of IVF, there were only five follicles that had the potential to contain a mature egg. Once the doctors retrieved those follicles, they found three eggs in total. After insemination, there were just two that made it through.

The doctor called me that day to let me know that they had two fresh embryos, and they wanted to implant them right away. I took that call from the new hospice room that had just been set up in Dad's living room. *Well, this is convenient,* I thought.

A Slice of Ham: *Dad always dreamed of having vanity plates. That dream finally came true when he bought his bright red Impala LT and immediately started searching for any possible variation of his name that was available. This turned out to be surprisingly difficult. Guys named Ed love vanity plates, apparently. Finally, he managed to snag EZY-ED. The name stuck. From then on, Dad was Easy Ed to his friends. Perhaps that's how he got caught up in the love triangle.*

CHAPTER 15

EASY ED

Things with Dad finally took their ultimate turn for the worse one night while Jason and I were playing board games at a friend's house. We received a call from Donna informing us that Dad had broken his femur. Well, first he sliced his hand open pretty badly with a kitchen knife. Not wanting to worry anyone or make a fuss, he delayed getting stitches for several days. (Sound familiar?) By the time he did go into the emergency room, the cut had already started to heal, so all they could do was clean it and advise him to see a hand surgeon. It was on the way out of the emergency room that he tripped on a rug in the lobby and broke his leg.

This break was the true turning point in the downward spiral that would lead from palliative care to hospice. He needed emergency surgery to repair the break, but he was taking blood thinners. Surgery and blood thinners don't exactly go hand-in-hand, so, for a nearly a week, the hospital staff just tried to make him comfortable. Every time his surgery was scheduled, another emergency surgery would show up in the hospital, and he'd get bumped back. It took about five days before he could finally get the operation he needed. From a repair perspective, this went surprisingly well. His surgery took every bit of three hours, and he had some serious hardware installed alongside the two artificial hips he earned while working on the General Motors assembly line. The recovery, however, was not so great.

Insulin levels often have a hard time remaining in check after a big surgery. Dad's kidneys would be suffering, so the nursing staff would ease off his diuretic, which would cause too much fluid to be retained, and he'd end up in congestive heart failure. For months, we were constantly bouncing between the hospital and rehab center. Sometimes he'd be making great progress at the rehab center, and then, suddenly, his medications would get mixed up and he'd end up back in the hospital. Every time he'd enter a new facility, I'd come to his room that initial day and ask the first healthcare professional I met, "How's his blood sugar?" They would inevitably reply, "Why, is he diabetic?" SERIOUSLY! I wanted to tattoo all his chronic comorbidities on his forehead. During one of his return trips to the hospital, this time to insert a pleural catheter so they could more easily and routinely drain fluid from his lungs, his cancer had returned full blast on a chest X-ray.

During this time, Dad's moods would swing intensely. Some days, he would tell me with all sincerity that he was ready to give up. "This is too hard," he'd say. "I just want to see Mom again." The next day, he'd declare that he wanted to fight with everything he had. "I can still beat this," he'd announce. "Miracles happen every day." I wasn't sure which attitude was worse. I wanted him to be upbeat, but I didn't want to give him false hope.

There were a lot of conflicting conversations with doctors. Some would try to talk to Dad about options such as stopping his inpatient radiation. I had to constantly reeducate myself around Medicare rules, such as how long he could be in the hospital before he was kicked out. I was working with social workers, doctors, nurses, and anyone who might encounter us. Despite taking my laptop with me to Dad's condo, the hospital, or wherever he might be on a particular day, I didn't travel for work or visit a single customer for the better part of three months. There are a lot of false alarms during this time. Every time Dad would have a complication of any sort, we'd wind up back in the hospital. Enough days in the hospital would earn us a trip to the skilled nursing facility. The doctors would warn us that this was the end and that we should say our goodbyes. But Dad kept popping back up. I even started joking with my WWT manager that my dad had nine lives.

Most of this period was a blur, but one day stands out in photo-sharp memory. I was home for once, trying to get some work done on the couch, when I received a notification from 23andMe. I'd barely thought about that test since receiving the surprising result of being Jewish. Jason and Dad had both taken tests themselves, but their results were underwhelming. ("I could have told you I was Irish as fuck," Jason said.) Dad learned that he was very Italian, which is exactly what he'd always thought.

One interesting thing about 23andMe is that the results fluctuate. The more data they receive from more users, the more accurate their information becomes, so they occasionally send updates. In fact, I had grown considerably *more Jewish* since my original results. (L'chaim!) With the benign results from Jason's test, I'd mostly forgotten about 23andMe. I didn't need to check my profile every time my Jewishness increased a half percentile. But for whatever reason, on that momentous day, a random push notification prompted me to check out my 23andMe profile on my mobile device. What I saw would forever change my history and my understanding of myself.

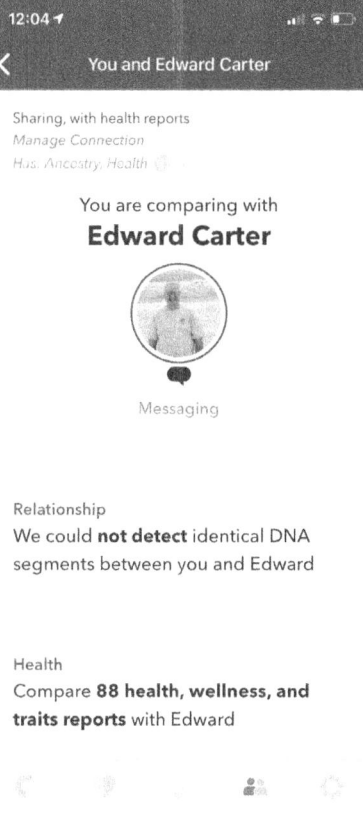

For a moment, I just stared at the screen, trying to make sense of what I was looking at. Then, I passed the phone to Jason, who gave what is probably the most profound understatement in the history of mankind: "That's weird."

It was indeed weird. My first thought was that there must have been some mistake. How could I not be related to my dad? Then, I was hit with one very grim possibility: maybe my mom cheated. Gasp!

I didn't even want to go there. My dad was probably nearing his deathbed, after all, still in and out of the hospital. He wasn't a particularly religious man, but the prospect of possibly seeing my mom again in the afterlife gave him a lot of hope. He was talking about it more and more as time went on. How could I possibly break this news to him now? And unfortunately, my mom wasn't around to ask. So, unable to broach these questions, I chose to bury them. It didn't really matter, after all. Not now. He was my dad, no matter what, and he was dying. Any questions I had may have to die along with him. Plus, we were still desperately trying to get pregnant before Dad passed away. I knew, logically, at this point, it was unlikely he would live long enough to meet his future grandchild. But I thought there was a real chance we'd be able to tell him there was a baby on the way. So, we kept pushing forward. On October 24, the fertility clinic performed the egg retrieval. The following day, while laid up on the couch with a heating pad, I received a call that Dad was going into hospice. It was finally happening. He'd had one setback too many. I went to his place to spend the night and started doing what I do best: compartmentalizing. In my mind, there is always a task that needs to be done, always something I can do to help. I started with the simplest task, which wasn't very simple at all. I called all our relatives, all Dad's friends, and Heather. She had moved back to the States (New York State), and our relationship had once again become a bit strange. Part of me definitely resented her for the lack of support caring for Dad in the later years. Then again, I never really expressed that to her or asked her for help. She called Dad regularly to check in, but the conversations were light and surface-level. She got the good news, chats about the weather, and conversations about Dad's next scheduled haircut.

Then, there was the fact of the 23andMe test. Heather hadn't taken one. I don't think she was particularly interested. I suddenly wondered, was Dad Heather's biological father? Or was her father someone else too? If we had different dads, that might explain so much, not just the fact that she had red hair and I had brown hair, but the fact that some days it felt like we came from different planets. I don't think she ever felt completely at home in our family after she went away to college. Maybe she was right. But I didn't have time to think about that now, and it certainly wasn't the time to break that news to her. I braced myself for her phone call, not sure how she'd react. It took several calls to get through to her. Finally, she picked up. "Dad's been put on hospice," I said, "It's only a matter of time." I don't remember much about Heather's reaction, other than she was conflicted about coming to visit because it wouldn't change anything. If I was being honest, it hurt that I was doing all of this alone. Thank goodness for Donna and Jason's support.

With that call out of the way, there was nothing left for me to do but return to the hospital bed in the living room and sit next to Dad. This was the hardest thing of all, because there is no good way to help someone die. You hold their hand, talk to them about mundane things, try to ease their fears, but it's not as if you know any better than they do what comes next. I did my best not to think about the million questions burning in my heart or the possible new life being created in a lab across the city. Instead, Dad and I reminisced. Or, should I say, I reminisced, and he nodded along, because he was tired and a bit fuzzy from the morphine. I talked about our menagerie of animals, about those Newfoundlands always getting stuck in the bathroom, about the Dogmobile. I confessed, for the first time ever, to taking that joy ride with Adam.

I talked about my cancer and thanked him for taking care of me and being my rock, about all those Relay For Life races over the many years, and all those hats. I realized that his love of hats may have come from that moment. I skipped the details about the various boyfriends. He didn't need to know. I told him about my travels abroad and all the places I'd been able to see. He smiled when I described the rolling hills of England, and I kicked myself for never taking him there.

I talked about Mom a lot too. Her free spirit, her love of animals and dog shows, and her later passion for fishing. I laughed, thinking of her up on a boat in Heaven, casting her fishing rod over and over to catch flying cloud-fish. I promised Dad from the bottom of my heart that he would see her again. I had to believe it. We both did.

When it came to the past two years, the memories became more complicated. I'd been there to meet doctors at the hospital or go to his appointments. Every time Dad had any medical issue, I focused on getting informed from a medical standpoint. I was so knowledgeable that I was often asked if I was a physician or a nurse. It was hard for people to wrap their heads around the fact that I was just his daughter. I did his meal prep, monitored his sugars, tried to manage every aspect of his health. All this because I loved him, of course. But he was never really on board with it. Instead, I spent time fighting a Sisyphean battle against nature and his will. He became unhappy. The funny, dad-joking, loving man who was fascinated by every mundane thing turned into a big, grumpy pessimist. "The world is shitting on me," he'd say. "My wife died. I have cancer. I can't eat shrimp, as it gives me gout. I can't eat salads, too much vitamin K." The excuse of a joke he'd bark was that his "optic nerve was hooked up to his asshole and that's why he had a shitty outlook on life." Charming, right?

It wasn't until I was sitting by his deathbed that I realized I could have handled things differently. I could have told him to go ahead and eat all the shrimp he wanted. "Sure, you're going to get gout, and it's going to hurt," I could have said, "But you only live once, and you love shrimp. It's your decision." I could have left his exercise routines up to him. If he wanted to walk, great. If not, oh well. I wish I'd listened more closely to what he wanted. In other words, I wish I'd spent less time barking orders and telling him what to do and more time loving him and accepting his choices.

Two days after Dad went on hospice care, I received the call that the IVF clinic had successfully created two embryos. Suddenly, I had another medical decision on my hands. They could either freeze the embryos to implant later or they could implant them both now as a fresh transfer. If I wanted to get pregnant this month, it had to be right away. I didn't hesitate. I felt a deep, mystical connection in all of this, something I couldn't put my finger on. My dad was dying, and I was getting pregnant. My dad had been a twin, and now we had two embryos. That had to mean something, right?

The main thing I remember about the IVF procedure is that it was extremely cold. I hate being cold. There were also blinding overhead lights, which made the whole thing feel more like an alien abduction than the miracle of life. The doctor was very kind, though, and talked us through the whole thing. We were able to watch on the sonogram screen as he inserted what looked like a large but thin turkey baster into my hoo-ha and shot the fertilized eggs up there. It was pretty cool, despite the weirdness of it all. Maybe it was even a little miraculous. After each one was released, you'd see a spark-like flash on the screen.

After the embryo transfer, I basically felt like I was having the worst period of my life. Aches, cramps, the whole bit. The doctors gave me valium and heat pads and told me to go home and rest. Like a Victorian invalid, I was told to avoid any strenuous activity and any stressful emotions. All I was supposed to do was lie on the couch for two weeks until they could confirm my pregnancy.

As soon as I got home and put my feet up, I received a call from Donna. Dad was not doing well, and I needed to get over there right away. The hospice nurse didn't think he'd make it through the night. It was finally happening. For real. I immediately forgot about my cramps and switched into crisis mode.

I spent that evening with Dad calling as many of his friends and loved ones as possible. We spoke to Heather and her family in Germany, Ingrid, Dad's Homie Russ, the whole crew. Dad was clearly very tired and mumbled a lot through the conversations. But he said what he needed to say to every person.

That evening, I posted this to Facebook:

Dad is presently trying on some wings to see which ones fit best. The hospice team has told us they expect he's going to be making that purchase in a few days.

He is home and surrounded by those who love him, and he's resting comfortably. Thank you, everyone, for your kind words and prayers. He knows how much he is loved.

He finally found the perfect pair of wings around 4:30 am that next morning. Just like that, the man who had raised me, who had been such an enormous presence in my life, was gone. Then, exactly fifteen days later, I saw that glorious little red plus sign on a cheap Walgreens pee stick. (Hooray for the Amish.)

If there was a baby boy, there was no question what I would name him. One question remained. Were there one or two hams in the oven?

A Slice of Ham: *Aunt Ingrid: "Well, the secrets out." Her Husband Ron: "What secret? The 'Who's the father secret?'"*

CHAPTER 16

WELL, THE SECRET'S OUT

I brought my 23andMe test results to my dad's funeral. Well, they were on my phone at least. I figured there had to be someone there who knew the truth. I imagined meeting a stranger who looked suspiciously like me, weeping over the mostaccioli. Or maybe I'd find a secret note tucked into the pocket of the casket, or someone would burst into the room with a secret message from my dad, unlocking the family's dark secrets. ("It was the Cable Guy, in the dining room, with the..." Never mind. Let's not go there.)

But there was no dramatic revelation – not yet. Dad's funeral went almost exactly the way he would have wanted it to go. We held the funeral in St. Louis so he could be buried next to Mom at Jefferson Barracks National Cemetery. He received full military honors, with an escort to the cemetery by the Patriot Guard Riders and a big American flag was draped across his casket. He would have gotten such a kick out of hearing all those motorcycles. He would have been so touched by how long that procession was. Friends and family from all across the country flew in to see him off that day, people who'd known him since elementary school, people he'd only just met, and even people he'd never met that I worked with and felt like they knew him. I was struck by how many people loved him and how they all talked about the same things: how genuine he was, how loyal, how delighted he was with the simplest things. Most of all, they talked about how much he loved his family: Mom, Heather, and me. We were his world. This is why it was especially hard for me to think that maybe Mom had deceived him all those years. It was equally hard for me to come to terms with the fact that Heather hadn't shown up for the funeral. She explained that Dad was already gone, and going to the funeral didn't do anything for him. I guess it never occurred to her that she could support her sister. I suppose we all grieve in our own ways, but this was tough for me to wrap my head around. It's not like she was still living in Germany, and she didn't have a bad relationship with Dad. She and Micah Facetimed me just before the wake, and I showed them the video presentation I had made, but she may as well have been on another planet. It all felt very cold and quite honestly, it hurt.

I couldn't allow my disappointment with Heather to cloud my entire experience, though. I spent the wake swapping stories about Dad and flipping through copies of the photo albums we'd scattered across the room. There were so many photo albums, so many memories, and so many questions. Every time I spoke with someone that week, a big one nagged at the back of my mind. "Do you know the truth?" When no revelations turned up naturally, I decided that if anyone in this family knew, it had to be Aunt Ingrid. It was just a matter of how to ask her.

The night before the wake, Jason and I had dinner with Aunt Ingrid and Marilyn at *Lewis and Clark* restaurant, a classic St. Louis institution serving things like burgers, taco salads, and the regional favorite toasted ravioli. I kept quiet about my big burning question all through the appetizers and the main course. By the time dessert came, Jason was making urgent eye contact with me, nudging me to get on with it. We had already asked for our check and had our credit cards on the table by the time I got up the nerve to do it. It was now or never. I took a deep breath and turned to Aunt Ingrid.

"By the way," I said with forced casualness, "do you have any idea what this is?" Then I showed her the offending screenshot on my iPhone, as if it were no more important than a photo of a plastic palm tree in a McDonald's parking lot. She took one look at the image and immediately burst into tears.

Of all the possible reactions, this is not one I could have imagined. This was Aunt Ingrid, after all, the toughest and sturdiest person I knew. The badass military woman, the purveyor of tough love. The poor waiter arrived at our table just in time to see this shocking display of waterworks and immediately turned around, not even bothering to pick up our credit cards. Even Marilyn, the queen of etiquette and poise, was at a loss for words.

When Ingrid was finally able to collect herself, she told me that my parents had struggled for years to conceive, with no success. The doctors determined that my dad was the infertile one and that the best option, aside from adoption, would be to use a sperm donor. Ingrid actually recalls there was a failed adoption that nearly broke my parents' hearts. In those days, it would be quite a wound to a man's ego to not be able to have children, so my parents never spoke about it. In fact, doctors often sugarcoated the process of sperm donation, mixing in donor sperm with the father's sperm and claiming that the donor sperm would "help theirs along." This way, men could tell themselves that there was at least a chance that the children were biologically theirs.

This news came as a huge relief to me. There was no affair, no terrible secret between my parents. It did hurt a bit that they never chose to tell me, but, given the social stigma of the time, it was understandable. There was also a smaller, but not insignificant possibility that Dad simply forgot. He was a very simple guy, after all. Things like genetics probably weren't all that important to him.

For Aunt Ingrid, on the other hand, this had all been downright torture. She was, and still remains, one of the most honest and straightforward people I've ever met, so keeping a secret of this magnitude wasn't in her nature. But she'd promised my mom she wouldn't tell, and she always kept her promises. She'd carried this burden for my entire life, and now, with both of my parents gone, she fully expected to carry it to her own grave. Those tears were as much relief as they were guilt. I made sure she knew she had nothing to feel guilty about. I didn't blame her one bit. Inside, however, I was still processing the shock.

Jason stayed quiet throughout the entire revelation, which extended our dinner another forty minutes until the waiter very gingerly suggested we continue our conversation elsewhere. It wasn't until we were walking out of the restaurant that Jason finally spoke. He looked at me with that charming grin and said, "Hey, at least you're no longer at risk for glaucoma." We both laughed until we cried.

The next morning at brunch I broke the news to Molly and Lisa, who reacted with the appropriate amount of shock. They also brought up some astute observations.

"So, when you had cancer and you had to give a family medical history, he never thought to mention that none of his history was relevant?" asked Molly. I hadn't thought of that.

"Guess not," I said.

"I didn't even know that technology existed back then," observed Lisa. I admitted that I hadn't either. It must have been very new. It also meant that my mom had been through IUI just like I had. If only I could have asked her about it.

"You could have a bunch more siblings," Molly chimed in.

Oh shit. She was right.

Edward Carter Obituary

Carter, Edward J. 71, passed away peacefully on October 25, 2018, at his home in Florida after a lengthy battle including multiple health complications. Beloved husband of Debra Doskal and the late Sonja Carter of 31 years. Loving father of Heather (Tom) O'Malley, Amanda (Jason) Dugger; dearest grandfather of Micah (17), Isaac (8) and Elijah O'Malley (7); cherished brother of Beverly Carter, dear uncle of Tre'von Giraud and beloved brother-in-law, nephew, cousin, and friend to many. Ed, a 1965 graduate of Riverview Gardens Senior High, joined UAW Local 2250 but was quickly drafted into the United States Army where he served as a Pershing Missile Electrical Master Specialist Instructor at the US Army Training Center, Field Artillery in Fort Sill, OK. He was honorably discharged in 1967 as an E5. He then returned to General Motors, where he primarily worked on the assembly line for 30 years before beginning retirement. Ed never met a stranger and frequently recycled his best jokes on all unsuspecting new friends. Explaining he graduated from the ever-so-famous university in Italy, "What's a Matta U," he told all that they could tell if he was lying (joking) if they could see his lips moving. An avid Cardinal fan, Ed was able to attend the 2011 World Series Game 7 and many Spring Training Games with his daughter in Florida. Throughout the years, he enjoyed his Honda Gold Wing, boating, water sports and was a member of the Alton Ski Club in the 70s, and the local St. Louis Glutton Club thereafter. In his later years, Ed conquered Facebook; never missing the opportunity to wish someone a Happy Birthday or Anniversary with one of his special digital cake photos. Last but not least, he was a hard-working family man and a true gentleman. He will be missed dearly by his family and friends. Services: The family will receive friends from 3:00 p.m. - 7:00 p.m. on Sunday, November 4, 2018, at Hutchens-Stygar Funeral and Cremation Center, 5987 Mid Rivers Mall Dr., St. Charles (63304). Graveside services will be held at 11:00 a.m. on Monday, November 5, 2018, at Jefferson Barracks National Cemetery. Procession departing at 10:00 am from Hutchens-Stygar Funeral Home.

PROTECT OUR FOOD AND NATURAL RESOURCES

When you travel...

Declare agricultural items

Don't pack a pest

Under no circumstance should you bring back ham to the US from the Bahamas!

U.S. Department of Agriculture
U.S. Customs and Border Protection

DONT PACK A PEST.com

A Slice of Ham: After Dad died, I felt like I saw messages from him everywhere. One message came in the form of a poster on the wall of customs enforcement on the way back from our vacation in the Bahamas. The poster warned that we could NOT bring any ham back into the United States. Too bad, I already had a little ham in the oven!

CHAPTER 17

AN HOUR FROM TAMPA GENERAL

I t's natural to search for patterns in life's ups and downs. It's comforting to think there is meaning hidden in the dark moments, a
mystical connection with Something Else, reaching out to us. My
parents had struggled with the same infertility I was struggling with.
We had that in common, even if I didn't share Dad's DNA. As I
waited to go in for my bloodwork, hoping beyond hope that my little
embryos took, I thought I understood exactly how my parents must
have felt. They wanted me more than anything, just like I wanted
these little ones more than anything. To my great joy, I found out I
was pregnant in mid-November 2018. To finally be pregnant after
all these years felt like a miracle. Amid grief, I was somehow lighter.
Could it be that Dad was sending me a message?

I did my best to try not to tell everyone, but after five years of trying,
I had to tell my best friends and a few coworkers what we were going
through. After all, it's so hard to take all the necessary time off work to
receive fertility treatments without raising some eyebrows.

After the funeral, Jason and I took a much-needed trip to the Bahamas. We needed to get away. After months of caring for a sick man, I was
more emotionally spent than I even realized. Jason has a way of knowing
when I'm worn out, even if I can't always tell myself. With very few of
us knowing that I was pregnant, the trip was also a bit of celebration.
Joy and grief mingled together on that trip, as they so often do in life.

During that week, I kept reflecting on a photo I had seen of my dad
as an infant, one of those professional photos taken while still in the hospital. Dad is lying in a hospital cradle next to his identical twin brother,

Elmer. Yes, Dad was a twin. Back in 1947, my grandmother had no idea she was pregnant with two until the day they arrived, both undersized. Elmer was only four pounds, and Edward, my dad, was an almost inconceivably tiny two pounds. They named Elmer after my grandfather because they assumed he was more likely to survive. The two boys lay side by side in their incubator for months, and the only way to tell them apart was my dad's habit of pulling on his left ear.

Eventually, the two boys were deemed healthy enough to take home. My grandmother must have thought it a miracle as well. But three months later, Elmer passed away suddenly in the night, a victim of a heart condition they either didn't recognize or didn't know how to treat. Dad often reminded us that he had a twin in Heaven, looking over us. I felt I was destined to have twins. Even though there was no way of knowing yet, if zero, one or two embryos had taken, I felt it had to be two boys. A symbolic nod to commemorate everything we had endured over the past few years.

I was wrong. After the trip, I went in for my ultrasound, bracing myself for another adventure with the Giant White Dildo Rod (GWDR for short). They informed me that I was pregnant with only one baby. My heart sank a little. I'd really been hoping for the two-for-one special. Still, we were elated that we were finally pregnant. Whatever message Dad was sending me, I was ready to hear it, or so I thought. The doctors told me to come back the following week. We would keep measuring to make sure everything was on track.

Another ultrasound, another GWDR, another day in the life of a geriatric, high-risk pregnancy, or as they liked to remind me, the combination of "advanced maternal age" and IVF. After assuming the position, I tried to relax as the doctor went in. I tried to read his facial expressions, but they were frustratingly blank. Finally, after removing the dildo, the doctor said the phrase everyone hates to hear. "There's no immediate cause for concern," he said. "Ah," I thought, "so I'll just schedule my concern in for later then." The doctor explained that, based on my baby's measurements, I was five weeks and six days pregnant. I was supposed to be seven weeks and five days pregnant. The doctor asked me to return in five days for another date with the big dildo. I tried my best not to think about what all this means. I'd had enough experience with doctors by this point to know they didn't always get the timing right.

Unfortunately, I never made it through those five days. I was at a friend's house decorating their Christmas tree when I noticed a light smattering of blood during a trip to the bathroom. I told myself it was just a little spotting and continued decorating. I didn't mention it to my friend or to Jason that night.

The next morning, I woke up to get ready for work as usual. When I went to the bathroom, I was relieved to see that all was normal. No blood. I mentioned nothing to Jason and sent him on his way to work. About an hour later, it all started. The moment I saw the blood, the sheer amount of it, the pain instantly hit me. I was surprised by the amount of blood I saw, which was far heavier than the heaviest period I'd ever had. More than that, I was surprised by the amount of pain I was in. I thought going through chemotherapy had prepared me for anything, but I was wrong. Nothing in my past had remotely prepared me for this level of physical anguish. I felt that my insides were falling out of my body. Which makes sense, because they were. I called Jason and told him what I already knew to be true; I was having a miscarriage.

I then called the doctor's office and was immediately able to talk to one of the nurses. She asked me to describe how much I was bleeding and if there was any pain. She was extremely empathetic and confirmed that I was indeed miscarrying. I would need to be seen immediately at the hospital, and she told me they would alert my doctor.

Jason was still at work, and it would have taken him forty-five minutes to get to me. Meanwhile, I was nearly an hour of rush hour traffic away from Tampa General Hospital, where I'd been receiving my IVF treatments. I knew I couldn't wait for him to get to me first, and I knew I couldn't drive myself. So, I went with Plan C: calling an Uber.

Uber drivers certainly see a lot on a daily basis, but a woman in the midst of an active miscarriage was probably a new one. I don't know how I made it through that long drive to the hospital without having some sort of breakdown or even moaning in pain. I'd packed my underwear with two super-absorbent Maxi-pads, but I could feel myself bleeding through them within a matter of minutes. I struggled to keep my face neutral, not wanting the driver to see the pain I was in, physically and emotionally. I tried not to think about Dad, and I tried not to do anything that would negatively impact my stellar Uber rating.

Gone. Gone. Gone. Our baby was slipping away moment by moment. The dream of a child who could have carried my dad's name, if not his genes. Everything that was tethering me to my old self, to my family, to my vision of the future. More than anything, this tiny little, microscopic being that I already loved so, so much was almost gone. I hoped against hope that I was wrong. But I knew I was right.

Somehow during this ride, I happened to catch sight of the date on my phone. December 4, the anniversary of my mom's death. I must have gasped when the realization hit, because the driver turned around.

"Everything okay back there?" the driver asked, with an uncomfortable concern in his voice.

"Oh yeah," I somehow chirped brightly, "Everything is good!" I'm confident he didn't believe me, as our obvious destination was set to Tampa General. Still, he nodded and kept driving. Later, I would give him five stars for not making eye contact.

I arrived at the hospital well before Jason did, so I limped down a long hallway, past the busy cafeteria, into the elevator on my own, clenching my knees together to keep the blood from spilling down my legs. I somehow managed to get myself checked in. The waiting room was so full of people, I ended up sitting on a piano bench (the seat closest to the elevator) while I waited for Jason to arrive or my name to be called. The pressure in my lower abdomen was intense. Every time I went to the bathroom, I saw more and more blood. There was nothing I could do to stop it.

Finally, Jason arrived, and I was taken back to the emergency bay area. It was the same room where I had been prepped for the egg retrieval and transfer. The same nurses, who had just seen me so hopeful a mere seven weeks ago, were back with me now, while everything was falling apart. Unfortunately, they saw this all the time.

The nurses approached me with a great deal of compassion but not pity. Thank God. I don't think I could have handled pity. They called the doctor as soon as I was in my gown for him to come in and confirm what we all knew was true. He proceeded to shove the giant white dildo wand up there. The screen was basically blank. No baby, no embryo, just blank. The doctor then proceeded to provide us with our options.

I could have a D&C. The D&C, or Dilation and Curettage, is when the cervix is expanded so the doctor can go in with a big spoon and scrape out the lining of the endometrium. Fun, fun, fun. Alternatively, I could use these large pills that you shove up your hoo-ha to accelerate the inevitable. Finally, I could just go home and let it happen naturally. I opted for the hoo-ha pills.

Since my ultrasound was already showing that there was nothing in my uterus. I'd expelled everything during the hour-long Uber ride and twenty-minute wait. Blood was still flowing, however. The doctor told me I could expect that to continue for several days. Basically, it was the menstrual period from Hell.

Jason and I left the hospital that day in total disbelief. I proceeded to lie on the couch and feel sorry for myself. I again began to meditate about the date. December 4. Did this mean anything? Maybe I was grasping at straws, but it felt significant. At that point, I was too tired to think about it. Instead, I placed an order on Shipt for elephant-sized maxi-pads, extra-strength ibuprofen, and lots of tissues for crying. When my package arrived, I discovered that the shopper had also included a king-size bag of chocolate M&Ms and a note saying "periods suck!" Even though it made my abdomen hurt, it felt good to laugh.

The following Monday, I was due to report to the World Wide Technology headquarters for the company's annual Leadership Conference. I had already called my boss earlier to alert him what was happening. I'm so thankful for the outpouring of support from the small group of co-workers who knew what happened. I did my best to allow myself to rest. I told myself I needed to stop looking for answers and hidden meanings and just sit with the emotions. Sitting with the grief, resting. This was the most challenging task of all.

One of the many emotionally painful things that they don't warn you about with miscarriage is managing your hormone levels. When you pee on a regular pregnancy stick, you're testing to see if your HSG is above five. That's what it means to have a positive pregnancy test. By the time you're at seven weeks (although in my case, I was only measuring at five), the levels of HSG hormone in your bloodstream are in the thousands. After my miscarriage, I had to go to LabCorp on a weekly basis to have my HSG levels measured. I couldn't be seen again for IVF until those numbers made it all the way back down to zero. The workers at the lab didn't know me or my situation. They always assumed I was coming in for a happy pregnancy test. I was, as the saying goes, only *a little bit pregnant.* I watched as the numbers fell: 2000, 1000, 500, 100, 50, 10, 5, 2.5, 0.5. My body, like my heart, couldn't quite seem to let go.

The mystical connection that I was holding on to, that tethered me to my dad's death, was unraveling. In its place was only empty space and a 23andMe profile that listed me as a child with no biological father.

At some point during that period, I found enough Dove chocolate quotes to cover my bathroom mirror. Here are a few of my favorites.

"Difficult roads often lead to beautiful destinations." – Letta L., Massachusetts

"After every storm there's a rainbow, no matter how long it takes to show up." – Grace V., Ohio

"You are never too old, and it is never too late." – Lauren P., Wyoming

"Everything will be okay in the end. If it's not okay, it's not the end." – Kayla Z., North Dakota

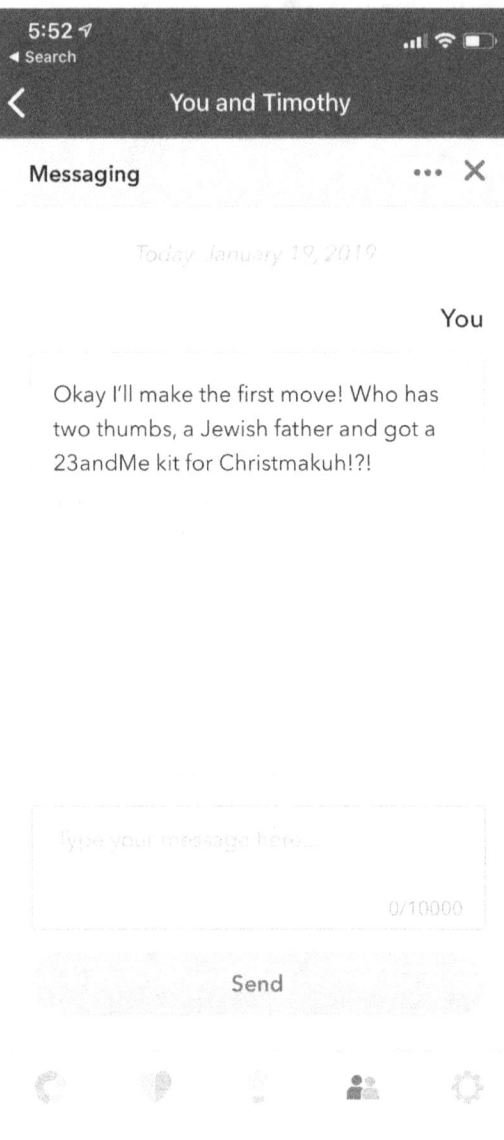

Messaging ··· ✕

Today, January 19, 2019

You

Okay I'll make the first move! Who has two thumbs, a Jewish father and got a 23andMe kit for Christmakuh!?!

Type your message here...

0/10000

Send

A Slice of Ham: In the early days of sperm donors, doctors would mix the hopeful father's sperm in with that of the donor. Men were told that the donor sperm was "helping theirs along." Anything to protect a man's ego!

CHAPTER 18

GIVE US
YOUR GRANDPA!

After the miscarriage, I did what any grieving woman would do: dive into a potentially life-altering quest to find her biological family. Or maybe that's just me. Either way, I started thinking hard about those 23andMe results. If Ed Carter didn't supply my second set of chromosomes, who did?

I broke the news to Heather not long after the funeral. Unsurprisingly, she took the news quite differently than I did. She wasn't devastated, but she was somewhat hurt by the lies. "It's not that I don't love them or I'm not grateful to them," she explained years later. "I just don't see why they couldn't trust us with the truth." I'd never considered it a lack of trust on their part. If anything, it was the lack of importance that Dad placed on our genetics. At least, that's my interpretation.

Somewhat ironically, Heather shared Dad's lack of interest in genetics, as evidenced by the 23andMe kit still collecting dust in her closet two years after I'd given it to her for Christmas. Part of me wondered if she had been offended by the gift. I never meant to imply that she wasn't my real sister! However, she was indeed the redhead in the family. Well, jokes on me. When Heather finally did send in her DNA, she learned that she too was the child of a sperm donor, and we were indeed half-sisters. But her interest in the mystery of her origins stopped there. She had little urge to join me on my quest. After all, we were only half-sisters and that meant we had different "donor dads." Fortunately, it wouldn't be long before I found someone who shared my curiosity.

A few weeks after Christmas, I received a notification on 23andMe that a new relative had been found. His name was Tim, and he wasn't some random third cousin that I shared 1.3% of my DNA with. He was my half-brother. In other words, he's just as related to me as Heather is. I barreled into Tim's DMs like a drunken Hurricane Irene.

Me: Okay, I'll make the first move! Who has two thumbs, a Jewish father, and got a 23andMe kit for *Christmakuh*!?!

Tim: I just received my DNA results this morning... and had a lot of questions for my parents. This is so insane, and I have no idea what to think.

Whoops. Maybe I came on a little strong there, I thought. I quickly typed in a more measured response.

Me: Sorry, I have a very sarcastic sense of humor.

Tim: Sarcasm. Is that genetic? ;-)

Oh yeah, this was certainly my brother. From then on, the conversation flowed naturally.

Newlywed Tim had received a 23andMe kit from his brand-new mother-in-law for Christmas. His wife's family was part German and part Syrian, so they were curious about their ancestry. Tim was included in the gift out of courtesy, but no one, least of all he, expected anything interesting to come of it. They all considered Tim's side of the family to be rather boring.

Tim describes his parents as "the loveliest but the most banal people you've ever met." They're grade school sweethearts who married right out of high school. They have no extended family, and Tim is their only child. They like peace and quiet and mostly keep to themselves. So, you can imagine Tim's shock when he found out he had a half-sister. "My first reaction was just... WTF."

His natural assumption was that his father had an affair. Were his parents secretly swingers? Were they part of a cult? Desperate for answers, he called his parents up to confront them. "I'm more than a quarter Jewish, and I have a half-sister named Amanda! Know anything about that?!?" When they finally explained the truth to him, that he was the product of a sperm donor, it was the first time they'd ever revealed the secret to anyone. (On the other hand, I'd since discovered that everyone and their mom apparently knew about Heather and me. Dad's cousins, friends of my mom, even neighbors all knew the truth and never told us.)

My first impression of Tim was that he was thoughtful and smart. He was an architect and loved geometry and science, just like me. Our friendship progressed quickly from that first message to emailing constantly to texting within a matter of twenty-four hours. He told me he lived in Los Angeles and, in one of those strange twists of fate, I happened to be visiting LA the following month for the WWT annual sales meeting. Before either of us had fully come to grips with what was happening, we were making plans to meet in person. I had a brother. A *brother*. And I liked him.

Even better, Tim shared my desire to find our biological father. We knew that if we put our joint mindpower to it, we could make it happen. Tim's approach was measured and careful; mine was energetic and a bit frenzied. But I loved having a puzzle to solve. I felt like a detective, or forensic scientist, tracking down clues and following them wherever they might lead. The best part was, despite everything that was happening to me, I wasn't feeling sad anymore. My dad had died, and I'd suffered a miscarriage, but out of nowhere, I had a whole new family. Maybe Dad was looking out for me after all. Maybe this was exactly the moment I was meant to find Tim.

The first big break in the case came when Tim texted me one morning about a possible relative.

"Did you see our cousin Rachel?"

Sure enough, I checked my 23andMe profile and saw that I had a cousin named Rachel Beard-Perry. We'd soon learn that 23andMe often can't tell the difference between a cousin and a niece because the relations share the same percentage of DNA.

"Yep," I told him, "Rachel comes up for me."

"GIVE US YOUR GRANDPA!" Tim declared.

The only problem was that, judging by her photo, Rachel was a teenager. Neither of us felt comfortable messaging her directly. Fortunately, that evening, a stranger with the last name "Beard" started following both Tim and me on Instagram. We figured this woman had to be Rachel's mother. However, when I snooped on her 23andMe profile, I saw there was no relation between her and us. This didn't make any sense. But when this woman, Chloe Beard-Perry friended us on Facebook as well, we knew she must know something. Finally, Tim got up the nerve to DM her.

"Who the heck are you?" he demanded.

He probably should have left the opening salvo to me. Fortunately, Rachel's mother was understanding.

"You're related to my biological daughter," she explained, "but my daughter was adopted."

You've got to be kidding me! My heart dropped, thinking this might be another dead end.

"I'm her mother," she typed. Wait a second, I'm so confused! She then explained that she and her husband got pregnant when they were 19 and 20, and decided to conduct an open adoption. Rachel had always known Chloe was her biological mother, and for her birthday, she asked for a DNA kit to learn more about her ancestry.

I explained our situation, that Tim and I were half-siblings through a sperm donor and that we were trying to find our biological father. After that, the chat went quiet. Tim and I wondered if perhaps we'd just hurled another family's life into chaos. Maybe our father was dead. Maybe he didn't want anything to do with us. Maybe this woman would vanish forever and take our chance at finding answers along with her.

Then, we saw those three little dots appear. Someone was typing... and typing...and typing. I could feel my heart pounding like a drum in my chest. *Boom. Boom. Boom.* Then, finally...

Chloe: "Gavin says he donated sperm back in the late seventies."

Tim: "WHO THE HECK IS GAVIN?!?"

My question exactly, Tim.

Chloe: "Rachel's grandfather. Your father."

A Slice of Ham*: I'll never know for sure why Dad kept the secret about my conception, or why he agreed to take the DNA test. Maybe he believed what the doctors said in those days, that I might be his biological child. Maybe he just didn't have the words to tell me. But, my friend Lisa has the best theory: Dad loved me so much, he simply forgot.*

CHAPTER 19

THE PERRYS

I n 1978, my biological father, John Gavin Perry, was a 24-year-old PhD student studying neuroscience at Washington University. His partner, Leah, was pregnant, and a friend mentioned he could earn fifty dollars by donating sperm—about five hundred in today's money. Gavin thought it was a good deal. "It's not like I wasn't doing it anyway!" he joked years later.

What began as a one-off donation quickly turned into a full-blown side hustle. He discovered he was in high demand. Many couples loved the idea of a tall, brown-haired, blue-eyed student at the medical school as their baby daddy. As they flipped through the "Daddy Catalogue", a booklet containing profiles of potential candidates, they often stopped on his page in the hopes that their child would also grow up to be a towering six-foot-five medical student. Gavin's ego swelled when he learned he had an unusually high sperm count. The handsome nerd from Boston had never been so popular. He donated repeatedly, even befriending the woman who ran the fertility program—who he suspected may have helped him secure more "picks." After a year and a half, he was told to stop; with so many biological children running around St. Louis, the risk of siblings meeting—and God forbid falling in love—was too high. In fact, several pairs of half-siblings grew up knowing one another and attending the same high schools. Gavin couldn't help but smile at the thought of his mini-me's populating the city. Maybe, he imagined, with their combined smarts and good looks, they could save the world.

Gavin's parents were Lucy Horwitz and John Perry, and meeting Lucy years later was a rare gift I will never forget. She was a force of nature. Born in Vienna in 1932, Lucy's family fled Austria to escape the

Nazis, eventually making their way to California. English being her third language, Lucy always felt most comfortable with numbers, becoming a Math and Philosophy major at UC Berkeley and later teaching Mathematics. Her life was extraordinary: activism, travel, scholarship, and adventure were constants. She bicycled through the Middle East and North Africa, attended MLK's "I Have a Dream" speech, and protested for justice until the end of her life. Lucy was brilliant, principled, and unrelentingly curious. Her own writings cover a wide range, from the textbook *Statistics for Social Change*, to several murder mysteries, to her memoir *Random Thoughts from an Aging Brain*. Lucy never lost her belief that the future could be better than the past, and she always strove to make it so.

Raised by this fiercely independent woman, Gavin describes himself as having been brought up by "a women's lib mom." Lucy was not naturally maternal; babies often baffled her, especially infants who couldn't hold an intellectual conversation. Yet her ideals shaped the world Gavin grew up in, inspiring a lifelong sense of purpose.

Gavin arrived in St. Louis for graduate school at Washington University in the summer of 1975. He and his partner, Leah, eventually met Kay Drey at the Missouri Coalition for the Environment (MCE), a non-profit, non-partisan organization based in St. Louis, dedicated to advocating for clean water, clean air, clean energy, and a healthy environment. Founded in 1969, the MCE serves as Missouri's first independent citizen-based action group, engaging in various environmental advocacy efforts, including monitoring government actions and participating in policy development.

Drey was among the first to raise the alarm about the dangers of nuclear dumping in several key areas around St. Louis, including right on the Washington University Campus. Back in the 1950s, naïve physicists had dumped nuclear waste from the labs that were processing uranium for the atomic bomb into large holes in an area called South 40. By the time Gavin arrived on campus, the university was building student housing in that section. Kay Drey was one of the few people questioning this decision.

Together, Gavin and Drey testified at many government hearings about the nuclear power plant being built in Fulton, MO, and to the Clean Water Commission about environmental pollution from uranium fuel processing in Herculaneum, MO. One of Drey's great concerns was Coldwater Creek. Gavin often heard her rail in frustration over the difficulty of convincing city and state officials of the dangers of tens of thousands of citizens living above groundwater contaminated with uranium and plutonium. "Everyone north of St. Louis is living in a deathtrap," she told Gavin, "and they have no idea." The injustice filled Gavin with a familiar anger, and he wondered why there weren't crowds protesting every day in North St. Louis. If his family had been living out there, you had better believe Lucy would be shouting down the walls of City Hall. But the people of North St. Louis weren't like Lucy, he realized. They were uneducated and blue-collar. Even if they heard the truth, they might not believe it. It was up to people like him and Kay Drey to fix this grave injustice.

After finishing his PhD at Kay Drey's insistence Gavin realized, to his great disappointment, that a large part of his life as a neuroscientist would be writing grants. This was not his idea of a good time. Plus, he was experimenting on monkeys, which felt like the height of hypocrisy for a committed vegetarian. After his third monkey died, Gavin took a hard fork into the budding field of computer technology. This was before the dawn of the PC, but Wash U's labs boasted 6-foot-tall computers with removable hard drives and a whopping 10 megabytes of storage. Gavin developed a system that could train monkeys (without pain) and pass data back to the computer. It was a huge success, and the Neuroscience labs continued using this system for fifteen years. Ultimately the systems Gavin built were utilized by many neuroscience labs across the university.

Gavin stayed on at Wash U as a roving technician for the university's labs. It was rare to find someone who understood both hardware and software, and his underlying knowledge of research made him the ideal man for the job. When different departments started arguing over who got to work with him, it felt almost as good as being at the top of the sperm donor list. Once again, Gavin was in high demand. He eventually created a university-wide electronics shop, which he ran for six years.

By the time I learned about Gavin's existence, I was no longer living in

St. Louis, so I met the other members of Gavin's bloodline before I met him. Only a few weeks after finding Tim on 23andMe, we were sitting across the table from one other at a Los Angeles taco joint. Coincidentally, WWT was hosting their big sales kick off in the same city where I had a half-brother, and I wasn't going to pass up this opportunity. Tim struck me as handsome, with a nerdy-cool style and a thoughtful manner of speaking. His wife, Julianne, was stunning. A filmmaker, she had a sort of effortless mystique about herself without being aloof. The whole meal felt like an out-of-body experience. Over tacos al pastor, Tim and I recounted our similar middle-class upbringings. It made my stomach churn a bit to realize just how close we'd been to one another. I was relieved that we'd never met, because with my promiscuous history, there was a chance we might have made out one night at the Morgan Street Brewery.

Tim's parents were still in denial about the whole thing. His dad claimed that his and the donor's sperm were mixed and "held hands" as they met the egg. He'd clung to this white lie from the doctors for decades, and no pesky DNA test was going to convince him otherwise. Tim admitted that he'd always felt a little out of place. His parents had little interest in education, content to live their lives in their little corner of the world, while Tim was constantly restless. Aside from the fact that neither parent was over five foot four and Tim was a towering six foot two, he felt there was something missing from his life that he couldn't put his finger on. So, one day, he packed up his Toyota and drove west to Los Angeles, never looking back. He never knew that he'd settled mere miles away from Lucy Horwitz, his biological grandmother.

A few days after eating tacos with Tim and Julianne, Celia, Gavin's sister (and now our aunt), took us to meet Lucy in person. She was in her early-eighties by then, and dementia was beginning to pull at the edges of her mind. Still, the force of her personality was evident. She was sharp-eyed and sarcastic, her quick wit cutting through her tenuous grasp on details. Although she repeatedly asked me how it came to be, she understood that I was her granddaughter. She asked me about the things that were most important to her: my education and my travels. She smiled approvingly when I gave her the summary of my life, and I must admit I felt relieved. Before I left, she gave me a copy of her book, *Random Thoughts from an Aging Brain*. She signed it "To my granddaughter, Amanda." She did the same for Tim. "What a badass," Tim whispered as we left.

The same experience can impact different people in different ways. For Tim, meeting the family meant discovering a missing piece of himself that he'd always longed for. Tim was no longer an anomaly. Gavin Perry was his father, and suddenly, everything made sense. Tim sees DNA testing as more than just an opportunity to learn about yourself, but also to learn about our connection to mankind as a whole. He says, "I'm not just a quarter this or an eighth that. I'm one ten-thousandth of the entire genome. We're all related. The more people who get that mind-expanding perspective, the better." I love the way Tim sees the world. As a self-described secular humanist, Lucy would be proud to hear that.

That visit stirred something in me. After our miscarriage, connecting with my DNA family gave me a sense of continuity and belonging I hadn't known I needed. I could see traits inherited from Gavin and Lucy, yet I knew a deep truth: Ed Carter was still my dad. No amount of new connections could change that.

That week, getting a tattoo to honor my parents felt right. I'd been contemplating the idea for a while. Marilyn had the perfect suggestion: the word "believe." Believe had always been our personal motto and the sign-off on most of our emails. Even to this day, she will sometimes just text me the word as a reminder to keep on going no matter what. I decided to get this word tattooed on my arm in a combination of my parents' cursive handwriting.

I found a letter that my mom had written to my grandpa Louie, and sent a photo of it to my cousin, who is a graphic designer, along with one of the many writing samples I have of my dad's. (Probably something about a colonoscopy.) My cousin created a design with combinations of letters in their handwriting. I absolutely loved it. So, only a couple of hours after meeting Lucy, I walked into an LA tattoo shop and showed them my design. I would leave that trip feeling physically closer to my parents – Ed and Sonja, that is – than I had since they passed away.

...

A few weeks later, I had an opportunity to meet Gavin on a freezing cold February day in St. Louis. Did I mention yet that Gavin worked a mere 300 feet from me for years? After an executive briefing at WWT, I literally drove across the street. I parked my car in front of the Meridian Electric building and sat there for a few minutes, psyching myself up. Once I'd finally worked up the courage, I got out of the car and walked into the lobby. As soon as I asked the secretary at the front desk if Gavin Perry was there, I heard his voice.

"Over here!" He popped his curly-haired head out of a door, looking like a mad scientist. "Come on in!" he said with a gesture.

We borrowed one of his coworkers offices for our conversation. It was stuffed from top to bottom with paperwork. A table full of busted LED lights that Meridian customers mailed back were staged for Gavin to analyze for quality assurance. At that moment, he was fixated on an ancient-looking crockpot someone at the company decided he should repair. He seemed desperate to keep it from going to a landfill. He then took me into his "lab," more like a large closet with benches full of wires, connectors, and equipment for analyzing LED performance. Despite the chaos, I was certain he knew exactly where everything was. After the quick tour, we returned to the office to chat.

For most of our hour-long conversation, Gavin gave me an electronic tour of his research articles and told me about his family. When we talked about me, it was to point out places where our physical traits or personalities intersected. He was also delighted to learn about my career in technology. Last, but certainly not least, he seemed to have a morbid fascination with my cancer story. He kept leaning forward and asking me to repeat where exactly I'd grown up. When he finally informed me about Kay Drey's research, I understood. My cancer was another connection between us, albeit this one seemed more tied to fate than DNA. "You got your cancer from Coldwater Creek," he told me with confident finality. I agreed that it was possible, but reminded him that you can never really know for sure. "I know," he interrupted. "That's what happened." Overall, we had a good first visit, but the whole experience was a bit overwhelming. I eventually snagged a selfie on the way out and headed back across the street to WWT headquarters.

Genetically speaking, I lucked out not being blood-related to Ed Carter. I hit the jackpot with Gavin and Lucy –smart, healthy, sharp-minded people. From Ed, I could've inherited high blood pressure, glaucoma, or diabetes. I do feel like I got the best of both worlds in the nature versus nurture department. I'm thankful Gavin donated sperm and helped my parents' dreams come true. It was also Ed's steady hands, his quiet strength, and his blue-collar, Midwest work ethic that shaped who I am. He was nurturing, present and deeply kind.

Meeting my DNA family was more than discovery—it was a bridge, connecting the past, present, and future in a way I had never imagined. It reaffirmed my roots, broadened my understanding of identity, and deepened my gratitude for the people who shaped me—by blood, by choice, and by love.

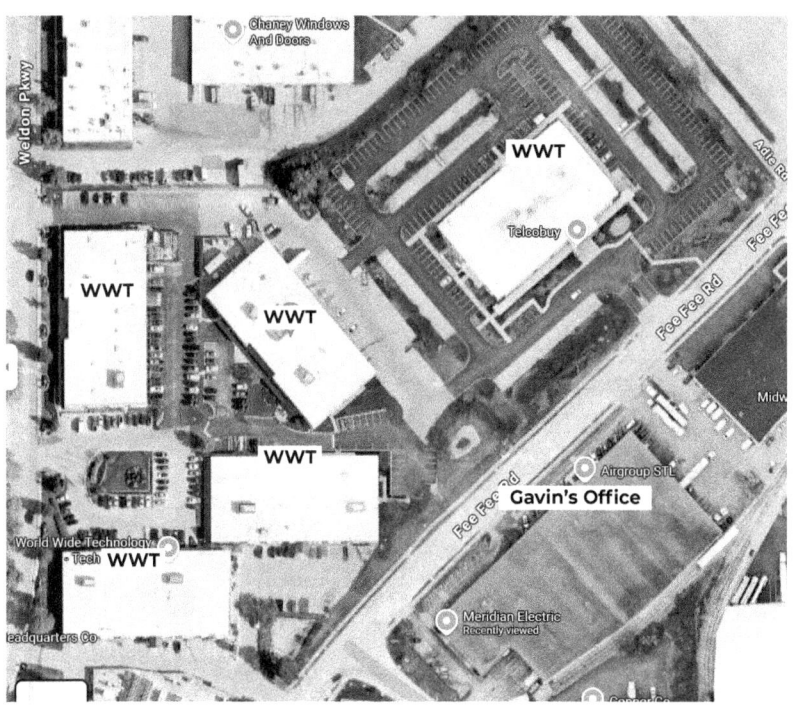

A Slice of Ham*: The hospital Dad took me to multiple times to undergo radiation treatment was the same hospital he went to when I was being created. What must have been going through his mind when we sat in all those waiting rooms together? Unfortunately, it was also the same hospital where we said good-bye to mom. Some real circle of life memories.*

CHAPTER 20

PELVIC REST

The good thing about having lived through cancer is you learn to be very proactive about your medical treatments. (The bad thing is everything else.) My oncologist continued to warn me about the risks of pursuing IVF, citing the increased risk of breast cancer. Still, there was zero doubt in Jason's and my minds that we would try again as soon as humanly possible. To be honest, I feared the possibility of another miscarriage much more than I feared cancer. We agreed that we would try IVF up to two more times. After that, we might have to stop, not because of cancer risk but because the emotional toll would be too intense. The good news was I had solid reasons to believe that the second time around would be more successful than the first.

To begin with, frozen embryo transfers have a higher success rate than fresh transfers. In a fresh transfer, the doctors implant the fertilized embryo(s) right away. This means there's no opportunity to check for genetic defects that could result in a miscarriage. In a frozen transfer, the embryos are allowed to develop in a petri dish for three days. Only healthy embryos are then frozen and later implanted. This significantly reduces the risk of miscarriage due to a genetic defect. Then, there was the simple fact of experience. Having been through the process before, I knew what to expect and what to focus on. Because I understood my medical treatments inside and out, I requested that they reconsider the every-other-day blood testing I'd endured during my first round of IVF. There was no risk of my follicles getting overstimulated due to my severely depleted ovarian reserve, therefore, very little chance of triplets in this creaky uterus. Thankfully, they obliged, and I was able to avoid the constant painful needle sticks.

By April, I was going in for my egg retrieval. I had two eggs. (Call me Fertile Myrtle!) Both were successfully fertilized and, a few days later, a biopsy confirmed that one precious embryo was healthy. A cheerful embryologist, Dr. Choi, who introduced herself as "The Babysitter," filled us in on the next steps. The healthy embryo (known as Baby D) would be frozen while I prepared my body for the procedure. Once the hormone cycle was completed, the fertilized embryo would be implanted. It was showtime, baby.

Until it wasn't. Only a few days after my egg retrieval, the fertility clinic was shut down for six weeks to undergo an audit. Chalk it up to my famous good luck. My precious Baby D was frozen solid, like a microscopic Hans Solo, while some unknown government entity combed through the records (and who knows what else) of the fertility clinic. This was terrifying. Naturally, I wanted to know why exactly this lab was being audited. Was this routine, or had something raised a red flag? How good of a babysitter was "The Babysitter"? I worried constantly about the embryo getting defrosted, lost, or switched with someone else. What was going on behind the scenes at this place? I never would find out. However, only six months later, the two primary doctors at the clinic would move their practices elsewhere, and the entire place would shut down for good. But not before my frozen embryo transfer procedure.

During the window between the audit completing and the fertility practice being shut down for good, I was able to prepare myself for the transfer. I similarly had to prep my body with daily shots to fake it into thinking it was pregnant. Looking back, the whole audit debacle didn't exactly instill confidence, but by that point, I wasn't asking questions. Jason and I had foregone a Caribbean vacation to Antigua, several work obligations, and family functions for months, so we could be ready at a moment's notice. When we finally got the call that the clinic was open for business, we made sure we were at the top of the list.

Once my oven was successfully preheated, the day finally came to go in for egg transfer. On July 30, my check-in time was 9:30 a.m. at Tampa General. The prep for the procedure was pretty easy. I was to empty my bladder at 9:45 a.m., take a valium at 10:00 a.m. and drink 32 oz of water by 10:15 a.m. I changed into the lavender Bear Hugger Warming Gown, where two hoses hooked in and provided a temperature-controlled forced air system (basically hot air blowing up your skirt). Not only did it keep me warm and cozy, it reduced infection and gave me the feeling of being super naked and slightly horny. Let's get pregnant!

After you have a frozen transfer, you must continue to trick your body into thinking it's knocked up by injecting yourself with hormones to support maturation of the embryo. Twice a day, I stabbed myself in the ass with an enormous, angry needle containing progesterone in oil. The oil is very thick, so it needs to be injected straight into the muscle with a thick gauge needle; hence, the butt being the best place to stab yourself. At the beginning, Jason gave me the shots. He didn't enjoy this and had a hard time stabbing me. By this time, I was basically immune to needles, but that didn't stop me from getting giant knots all over my rear end. I'd be careful to massage the injection site each time, but it didn't make much of a difference. I had the lumpiest, bruised ass Jason had ever seen.

And just like that, I was pregnant the second time. Jason and I were obviously very happy, but I hesitated to say I was over the moon. My experience the first time around had taught me that nothing was certain. I wasn't going to start reading any hidden meanings into this pregnancy, much less daydreaming about baby names or picking out nursery colors. I tried not to think about anything at all until after the first trimester.

About a month later, I noticed red spotting in my underwear. "Oh God," I thought, "Not again." At least this time, Jason was with me. We rushed to the hospital, sure that all our worst fears were being confirmed.

"Baby is just fine," the nurse told us, moving the giant dildo around casually, "See!" Indeed, my teeny-tiny little baby was just fine. It had been a false alarm. Only now did I finally allow the full joy of being pregnant to wash over me. This time was different. This time, I really was going to be a mom. Still, because of the "near miss," the doctors decided to take one extra precaution. I was put on pelvic rest for the rest of my pregnancy. That meant no sex until at least we graduated from the fertility clinic and were released to our chosen obstetrician at thirteen weeks. What a drag!

Aside from the ban on sex, the remainder of my pregnancy was a breeze. I've always been an anxious person, but after crossing that first trimester barrier, all the anxiety melted away. My biggest challenges were heartburn, intense cravings for Tijuana Flats Mexican takeout, and cervical checks. Can we talk about cervical checks for a second? Holy Smokes! Anyone who's been pregnant knows about this rite of passage, so it would have been nice if someone had warned me. If you've never been pregnant, let this serve as your warning. Starting at about 35 weeks, they're going to start digging for gold in your hoo-ha. I'm talking spelunking *all the way back* to see how dilated you are. Not fun.

The first cervical check left me with terrible cramps, but when I got home, I got to put my feet up in Baby Nacho's nursery. (We'd nicknamed the baby Nacho in honor of the aforementioned desire for Tijuana Flats tacos.) After crossing into the second trimester, I'd allowed myself to go into full nesting mode, and this nursery was the apex of all my efforts. With our dog Barley curled up on the area rug, I sat back in my rocking chair, admiring all the perfect gender-neutral gray tones. Hanging over a white dresser, was the framed 4,997-piece *Under the Sea* puzzle that took Jason nine months to complete, a green and blue rocking horse in the corner, cactus crib sheets adorning a dark gray and white crib, curtains with colorful puppies on them, a beautiful handmade patch quilt, and bookshelves stacked with book staples such as *Cuddle Bug*, *I've Loved You Since Forever* and *Snuggle Puppy*. When we were finally pregnant, I promised myself that I wouldn't get too carried away with any one theme. Our baby's nursery screamed, "We have no idea what we're having," which is exactly what I wanted. I was exactly where I was supposed to be, doing exactly what I was supposed to be doing. For the first time in a very long time, I thought nothing could possibly go wrong. Did I mention this was late 2019?

In February 2020, Jason and I went on a babymoon over my 40th birthday. Jason was horrifically ill for several days the week prior and couldn't shake the nasty cough well into the birthday weekend. In retrospect, I don't think it was a typical cold. Contagious diseases aside, the Ritz in Naples was lovely, and while driving home that Sunday, we passed the town of Ellenton, Florida. I kept saying Ellenton in my head as we continued to drive, and then it hit me. "Wouldn't that be a perfect baby girl name? Ellenton, Ellington...Duke Ellington...Jason loves jazz music." So, onto the famous iPhone Note of baby names it went.

A few weeks later, I attended a World Wide Technology event at Top Golf. I have a video of myself extremely pregnant, attempting to swing a golf club. Mostly though, I was interested in the disco fries. (Hey, I was very pregnant!) While munching on a french fry, I received a text message from Jason with a link to an article about a strange virus that was showing up somewhere in China. "It's not if it's coming here," Jason wrote, "It's when." I rolled my eyes a little. Jason was always ahead of the news!

He asked me to pick up some masks and hand sanitizer at Walgreens on the way home. "This is going to be a big money-maker for the Amish," I thought. I hoped my dad was laughing somewhere. To my great surprise, there wasn't a mask or a rubber glove to be found at any of the three pharmacies I visited on the way home. I settled on some "Maui Breeze" hand sanitizer masquerading as perfume for a preteen. I was eight months pregnant and COVID-19 was about to rear its ugly head.

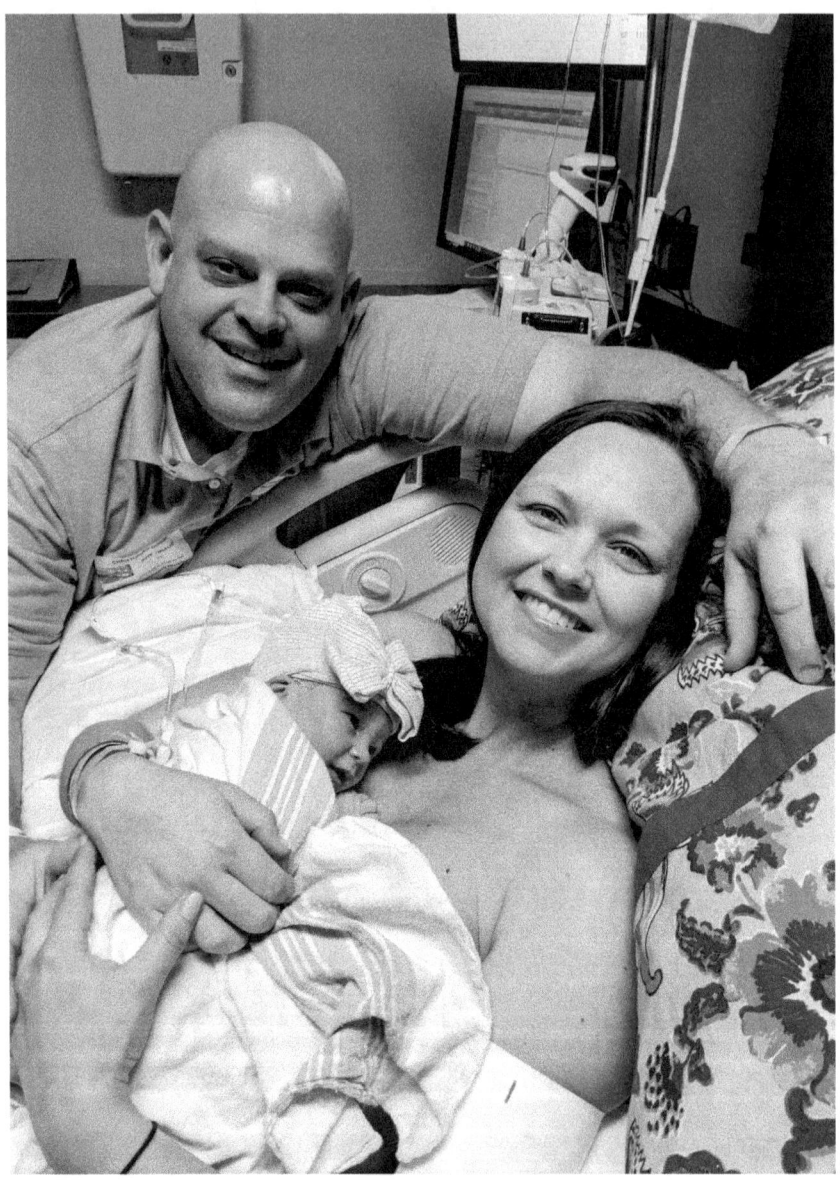

A Slice of Ham*: Jason and I had originally planned for him to stay in the "northern hemisphere" during baby's birth. After so much pelvic rest, why interfere with the sex life? But due to COVID restrictions, that wasn't an option. He not only had to help me breathe, but he also had to hold my left leg and get up close and personal with the miracle of life.*

ELLINGTON

It was March 12, 2020, and the sign I held up read "Little Nacho. 35 weeks pregnant. Due Date: April 17th. Craving: Ice cream sandwiches." Baby Nacho was almost five pounds, and I had enough heartburn to melt a glacier. The sign also read: "This week: The sky is falling... Corona Virus." By now, it was official. We were in a global pandemic, and no one had any idea what was going on. No one should wear a mask. Everyone should wear masks. Masks should be saved for only those who really need them. Stay inside. Go take walks. Who knows?! Clearly, this was the ideal moment to bring a baby into the world.

By the following week, mandatory social distancing had been enacted, and Jason could no longer come with me to the weekly doctor appointments. I nervously asked my doctor if Jason would be able to come to the hospital when the baby arrived. The doctor gave me that super reassuring deer in the headlights look and calmly replied, "I honestly don't know." Ah, don't you just love hearing that from your physician? By 37 weeks, "shelter in place" orders had finally been enacted across the state of Florida. I could no longer just walk right into the office for my checkups. I had to call when I arrived, get my temperature taken at the door, and wait for any previous patients to leave. They were only allowing one patient in the office at a time. At 38 weeks, my triple X cankles and I had our last day of work at WWT - the day just prior to Florida's governor extending the "shelter in place" order. The entire world seemed off-kilter, like we were all living through the plot of an action movie and any moment now Nick Cage was going to burst through the window of the CDC holding an ancient antidote and save the day. Unfortunately, that wasn't going to happen any time soon.

Safe within the walls of our home, however, life was strangely idyllic. I was too pregnant to want to go anywhere anyway, and my weird sense of calm carried on despite the madness outside. We'd narrowed down our baby name list to two boy names and three girl names. Finnegan Michael and Finley Rose were out. We were down to Miles Vinson and Bennett Lewis for boys, and Kennedy Rose, Raegan Elizabeth and Ellington Carter for girls. Most were family names. I was convinced we were having a boy, and Miles Vinson was the leading contender.

Because Nacho was an IVF baby combined with my "advanced maternal age" of forty, I was to be induced at 39 weeks. Compression socks and all, we checked into the hospital at 8 p.m. on a Thursday evening. The waiting room was eerily quiet, with only a handful of couples chatting quietly. No relatives or friends waited eagerly with balloons. The gift shop was closed. There was no valet. The security guard looked bored.

Once I was quickly admitted, the nurse, Janet, gave me my first dose of Cytotec. (By the way, that's another pill they shove up your hoo-ha.) We had a long way to go, as only the day before I'd been dilated at a full zero during my office cervical check. The nurse told me I may need three to four doses of the Cytotec before we start Pitocin in the morning. WRONG! I started progressing and got to two centimeters rather quickly. I also had to get up and pee every 30 minutes, although my friends would later say that's quite normal for me. Eventually I started having light contractions.

At 1:45 a.m., on one trip back from the bathroom, my water broke. You'll definitely know when this happens, ladies! It felt like I'd peed all over myself. Almost right away, the contractions sped up and became painful. The nurse immediately kicked up the saline drip, as they apparently can't give you your epidural unless you have a full liter bag through your IV. It took a full 45 minutes to accelerate the bag of saline with a blood pressure cuff looped around it to continually squeeze it in my thirsty veins. By the time the anesthesiologist came to give me the epidural I was in full on Tourette's cursing mode. (Not that that's too far from the ordinary.) Thankfully, once the epidural hit, I didn't feel a thing.

Once I was numb, the doctor told us to get some rest, as it would still take several hours before I was dilated enough to begin pushing. But, getting rest isn't exactly easy when you have a blood pressure cuff going off every 15 minutes and the baby's heart rate monitor sounding like a horse galloping next to us. Listening to the sound of a heartbeat magnified ten times isn't exactly calming, and I started to get anxious, which of course only made it worse. Finally, I asked the nurse to turn down the sound and turn the monitor away from us. They complied and adjusted the blood pressure cuff so it would only go off every 30 minutes. Sweet relief! We napped a bit, but I can't say it was the best sleep I've ever had.

They came in to check me at 3 a.m., and I was three centimeters. At 6:30 a.m. I was at seven. By 7:30 a.m., they were calling my doctor. She didn't arrive until 9:30 a.m., which I still don't understand. After that, I pushed for two hours. One thing they don't tell you about getting an epidural: pushing is hard. Sure, it didn't hurt, which is great, but the downside of not feeling anything is you have no idea how hard you're pushing. You only know if you're succeeding by how much the labor and delivery nurse is yelling at you. They want you to push like you're taking the biggest poop of your life. And, you may. I did. Don't sweat it. I literally pooped three times. Shit happens.

This made the experience even more... let's say romantic... for Jason, who was an active participant for the full two hours of my active labor. We hadn't really intended for Jason to play the part of male nurse, considering he had exactly zero medical experience and I wanted to maintain a little mystery, thank you very much. But due to all the scaled down pandemic staff, the poor guy didn't really have a choice. He got right down in there like a champ, though. Thankfully, he doesn't regret it one bit. The doctor didn't arrive until the last fifteen minutes of labor, just in time to catch the baby, along with Jason, and stitch me up. (Thankfully, not along with Jason.)

Our most perfect baby was born at 11:38 a.m. Just like we had planned; the doctor let Jason announce the gender. He shouted, "It's a girl"! I was both surprised and elated. They placed her on my chest while they did all the initial screenings. It's the most indescribable feeling, holding your child for the first time.

There was a small scare when she wasn't crying enough at first, so they took her over to the warming area in our room. The pediatrician came, and she got all checked out. She was fine. She was perfect. And they eventually brought her back over to me. She lay again on my chest, and thankfully everyone left us alone for a full hour. I'd never been so content. Once everything was quiet, Jason and I stared at one another in amazement that we finally had this perfect baby girl. I've never felt so much love. Ellington Carter Dugger was born on Good Friday, 7 pounds, 4 ounces and 20 ½ inches long.

We ended up staying an extra night in the hospital because of slight jaundice. Breast feeding wasn't coming easy for me (does it for anyone, really?), and, after several visits from the lactation consultant, we started supplementing with formula. Eventually, the jaundice improved, and we were able to return home on Easter Sunday. When we turned onto our street, we saw our lawn was filled with signs, and "Welcome Home, Ellie!" was written in colorful chalk across our entire driveway. All our friends and neighbors had come by to decorate and leave us some much-needed meals on the porch.

I texted our next-door neighbor, Erin, to come over into the yard and snap a photo of our new family of three in front of the front door. Sleep deprived, super bloated, and wearing my hospital bracelets there we stood, Jason holding Ellington like she was a football. Everything was perfect! Who cared that there was a global pandemic. We had our healthy baby girl, and I was delighted to shelter in place with this happy new normal.

A Slice of Ham: *The first time I visited Dad's grave, I brought a ham sandwich from Subway. I sat beside his headstone, eating it, and cried a little. But not so much that I couldn't finish the sandwich.*

CHAPTER 22

THE GREAT WINNEBAGO TOUR

When my milk finally came in, my boobs got huge, lumpy, and hard as basketballs. They were also so lopsided I looked like I might tilt over. The right boob, Ol' Reliable, consistently produced four healthy ounces of milk anytime I pumped. The left side would produce only one measly ounce, if that. It was Milk Dud. I was somewhat concerned about this lumpy boob situation, but everyone I spoke to assured me that it was normal. Everyone has a "Super-boob," I was told. Still, it seemed like milk was coming into my left breast but not going out. I tried to massage the breast in the shower, standing under streams of hot water in the hopes of working out a few of the lumps, but to no avail. My lymph nodes were like giant golf balls bursting out under my left armpit. For someone who had lymphoma, seeing this was quite alarming.

But my doctor assured me that everything was normal. "This happens," she said. "Just wait and see if it goes back down." Fortunately, the lymph nodes eventually receded back into my armpits, and I figured that everything was fine. Breastfeeding just sucked.

When Ellie was three weeks old, and after being hunkered down from COVID for over a month, Jason and I took her to the Lazy Days Big RV Store. Aside from the park, it was our first real outing as a family. COVID safety measures prevented us from taking her even to the grocery store. But we were on a mission to get to Memphis. I wasn't going to let Coronavirus stand in the way of Jason's mom getting to meet Ellie. We shopped for about five hours, and, by the end of the day, settled on a 29-foot Winnebago, our new home away from home. The following weekend, we did a "test run," spending the night in the parking lot of Lazy Days. The week after that, we loaded up the dog and all the baby shit and drove to Tennessee.

Ellie was a dream traveler, snoozing through most of the ride and only waking up to eat. I was still fumbling my way through breastfeeding –each attempt brought a sharp, burning pain in my left breast. We'd started supplementing with formula early on, and somewhere along the "Tour du Winnebago," I began to wean off the pump. After everything I'd already faced in life, I wasn't about to let breast milk become my breaking point. Some things just aren't worth the mental load.

When we first arrived in Memphis, we found an RV park only a couple of miles from where Jason's mom lived. We called her up to let her know that we had arrived, but we weren't going to make it to her place until the following day. In true grandmother form, she was at that RV park within fifteen minutes, driving around looking for us. She found Jason and me pushing Ellie in the stroller, stopped and rolled down the window. I immediately scooped Ellie up and passed her through the window of the car. Seeing the two of them together made all the years of struggle worthwhile. I didn't think my heart could possibly get any lighter.

By the time my return date to World Wide Technology rolled around, I was seriously reconsidering my life. With a new baby, collecting frequent flier miles was significantly less appealing. I wanted to be home with Ellie, and I was ready for a new challenge. (As if being a mom isn't challenging enough!) All summer, I had been finding ways to contribute more to DGR Systems, which, at this point, Jason had been running for 11 years. I took on a big marketing project to revamp the DGR website and social media. As part of the rebrand, we considered what it would mean for DGR Systems to be a Certified Woman-Owned Business. For that to happen, I would need to work there full-time, and we would have to pass an extensive audit. I'd already resigned from World Wide once, and it hadn't turned out great. But this time it felt different. So, after several long conversations, Jason and I decided it was time for me to become CEO of DGR Systems. I let my boss know that I would not be returning to WWT. This time, it was for real.

Life had truly never been so good. Jason and I were blissed out on cloud nine with Ellie, and the excitement of going all-in on our own business was an absolute thrill. Even though Ellie was barely four months old, and my periods hadn't even started up again, we already knew we wanted to have another baby. We found a new fertility clinic (the old one had already shut down due to whatever dealings were going on there) and scheduled a virtual consultation. "You two are definitely nuts," the doctor assured us, "but, sure, I can help." "Time isn't really on our side," I explained, "I just want to know what our options are."

The doctor was great. He spent forty minutes with us on that Zoom call trying to get caught up on all my medical history. He assured me that we could perform an egg retrieval as soon as I went through some of the testing again, which must happen between days one and three of my period cycle. Post testing, they could perform an egg retrieval as soon as I was six months post-partum. I could bank those eggs so that by one year post-partum, I'd have eggs to implant. We had a plan, and it felt good to know what the future could hold.

Unfortunately, the Winnebago tour had other plans. I started my first post-partum period while on our second two-week road trip to Memphis. I was heartbroken. This meant I would have to wait another month to get my tests done, delaying the entire process. IVF never happens the way you want it to.

While Jason worked from Memphis, I took Ellie on her first trip to St. Louis. On the way up, we stopped at one of Dad's favorite restaurants. Lambert's, in Sikeston, MO, "The Home of the Throwed Rolls." The schtick of this place is that you order a main course, and then people walk around with carts to offer you all-you-can-eat sides. When the buttered rolls cart comes by, you raise your hands, and they throw them across the room at you to catch. You can see why Dad loved his place. We would always stop there on the way back from dog shows. All these years later, it was completely unchanged. (The pandemic didn't seem to have had much impact on it either. Maybe throwing the rolls from six feet away counted as social distancing?)

In St. Louis, Ellie and I posted up at a hotel, so friends and loved ones could visit us. Lisa brought the kids to swim in the hotel pool while we chatted and caught up. Marilyn came over as well, and I got to see her hold Ellie for the first time. I was sure to dress Ellie in the onesie Marilyn had sent her and get a photo of the two of them together. I always had a knack for remembering the gifts that are given to us, and there were several special gifts from this trip.

After visiting with friends, I took Ellie to meet Gavin and his wife, Lynn. We sat out on the porch, a respectable distance away. Gavin gave me some produce from his garden, a few tomatoes and a squash. I wasn't sure what I was supposed to do with those, considering I was hundreds of miles from home, living in a hotel room, but I thanked him all the same. I was sure to thank Lynn for the hand-knit sweater she made for Ellie and the books they sent her. It was a really nice visit.

The final thing Ellie and I did together on that trip was visit my parents' grave. It was only the second time I'd been there since Dad passed, and the weight of that felt heavier than I expected. Maybe it was postpartum hormones. Maybe it was the fact that I was standing there with my daughter—their granddaughter—in my arms, and they weren't there to see her. Either way, up until that moment, I don't think I had ever missed them more.

I stayed composed or at least tried to. Even though Ellie was just a few months old and didn't understand a thing, I didn't want her first impression of that sacred place to be her mom sobbing into a burp cloth. So instead, I smiled and talked to her about them. I told her how much they would've loved her—how my mom would've rocked her for hours and called her "sweet pea," and how my dad would've taken one look at her cheeks and declared, "She's gonna cost you a fortune in snacks."

I snapped a photo of her propped up in front of the headstones—awkwardly, lovingly—while blinking back tears. It wasn't the moment I'd dreamed of, but it was the one I had. And in that quiet, bittersweet visit, I felt something shift. I wasn't just mourning them—I was introducing them to her. And somehow, that made it a little easier to walk away.

The day after we returned from Memphis, September 1, 2020, I had my first well-woman visit post-partum. Dr. Sheran, the same doctor who delivered Ellie, was doing a normal breast exam when her expression suddenly changed. "Oh wow," she said, "you have a lump here." It was on the left side, the same one that had given me so much trouble while I was trying to breastfeed. The same one that had the benign lump removed eight years prior. This was the first time I'd had a lump in my breast that I could feel. I'd had issues (repeat mammograms, ultrasounds, etc.) with the left breast in the past, but never something I could discern by touch. Fortunately, my routine mammogram was scheduled for the very next day. "That's great," Dr. Sheran said when I told her, "But we need to make sure that it's a diagnostic mammogram, not just a routine mammogram." She changed the order for the imaging and gave me a new paper order.

What I didn't do was check ahead of time to make sure the clinic I was scheduled with offered diagnostic mammograms. Honestly, I had no idea there was a difference. So, when I went in the very next day, they informed me that they couldn't fill the order for my test. I felt my stomach drop. I had a gut feeling that something wasn't right with this lump, and I needed to press forward. I asked them where I could go, and, of course, they named a place very close to my house. That clinic, however, couldn't get me in until two days later. I made an appointment. Then, I called Jason on the verge of tears.

"Something isn't right," I told him. "I know it." I couldn't wait two days. "You know what? I'm just going to go and see if they've had any cancellations." I drove straight to the clinic, even though I didn't have an appointment. I marched right up to the front desk and told the nurse my situation. "I have a lump in my breast. I have a five-month-old baby at home. I have a sitter today. I was supposed to get a mammogram today at your other location, but they can't do it because this is diagnostic. Do you have any cancellations?" I think she saw the desperation in my eyes as I regurgitated these facts at record speed, and she got me in.

You can tell when a nurse is looking at an image that concerns them. I'm not sure what they do; maybe they press a button that alerts the radiologist behind the wall. What I do know is they don't let you leave. The mammogram was concerning enough that they immediately ushered me to another room to perform an ultrasound. The ultrasound was performed by the radiologist himself. He spoke quite plainly to me. "First of all, know that what's on the screen right now is magnified by like thirty times, so don't panic. But this is concerning enough that you need a biopsy, especially with your history of radiation to your chest." He told me he would send in the order for the biopsy. I asked him where the biopsy was going to be done and for the phone number for that office. That way, I can call them. I never wait for anyone to *effing* call me to schedule anything. Pro Tip: As long as you have an order in the system, call the scheduling line and book yourself! Read that sentence again, people. Don't wait for people to schedule you.

Two days later, a Thursday, I was going in for my biopsy. They did it all under local anesthesia, so I drove myself as I didn't want Jason to have to take time off. I was doing my best to keep Jason focused on running the company, and Ellie was with a babysitter. During a needle biopsy, they insert a tube, almost like the part of a pen that holds the ink, into your tumor and suck out fluids like a cord from the hole. It wasn't painful, but I had a lot of anxiety around how quickly I could get the results back. I wanted to go balls to the wall and figure everything out immediately. I called the following day to ask if my results were ready yet, but the nurse told me no. They had to send some patients' slides back for additional "staining." Not to worry, she told me, they had to do that a lot. I would receive my results after Labor Day weekend. SIGH!

I had no choice but to wait. Fortunately, Aunt Ingrid was visiting that weekend, so I had her to distract me. On Monday, we went to Lazy Day's RV Store to investigate upgrading our RV. Why not!? The roads were still empty, and gas was less than $2 a gallon. Assuming I didn't have cancer, we had a few more road trips in mind. I also went for a massage and got my nails done. Priorities.

When I called back on Tuesday, the nurse told me she still didn't have my results. The truth was, she did have them. She just hadn't had an opportunity to tell my doctor yet. What I didn't know at the time was that the additional staining wasn't exactly routine. My slides had been sent back so the doctors could see all the various characteristics of my cancerous tumor. It was already confirmed. I had breast cancer.

A Slice of Ham*: During Dad's radiation treatments, he wore a special shield over his head that made him look like a medieval knight headed into battle. Like everything, the headshield became a source of humor. On the day of his last treatment, they offered it to him as a parting gift. Never being someone to pass up a freebie, Dad jumped at the opportunity to capture a souvenir. Dad buckled him in, adorned him with sunglasses and texted me this photo once he got home. Pretty progressive for someone who couldn't figure out how to text a space some years ago.*

CHAPTER 23

LOP 'EM OFF

There are three main indicators for breast cancer: stage, grade, and hormone receptors. Stage refers to how advanced a tumor is and if it has spread to other parts of your body, grade refers to how abnormal the cells look under a microscope, and hormone receptors are proteins found on breast cells that tell the cells to grow. When I was first diagnosed, I knew little about these categories, so I dove into scientific researcher mode to find out everything I possibly could.

The simplest thing to understand, because it had the most direct correlation to Hodgkin Lymphoma, was that my cancer was Stage 1, although only technically. Stage 2 starts at two centimeters, and my tumor was 1.9 cm. Still, this was good news. It meant we had caught my cancer early, and there was a good chance it hadn't spread. The grade was less good news. On a scale of one to nine, I was a nine. My tumor was the most abnormal possible and growing aggressively at the fastest possible rate. If we didn't control the cancer immediately, it could turn deadly. If this news wasn't scary enough, there was the issue of hormone receptors. I was hormone receptor negative (both "ER"-estrogen and "PR"-progesterone), which meant there were no hormone-related treatments that could be offered to combat my cancer. This also confirmed my fertility treatments and being pregnant didn't cause my breast cancer which was a big relief.

Aside from the hormone receptors, there are two basic categories of breast cancer: HER-2 Positive and HER-2 Negative. Thanks to Molly being named as one of my medical providers and passing me all my test results as they came in via eFax, I knew that I was HER-2 Positive. What I didn't know was what that meant, so I turned to my trusty sidekick,

Dr. Google.

Pro Tip: Don't turn to Dr. Google.

As soon as I typed "HER-2 Positive Breast Cancer" into the search bar, my stomach dropped. Phrases like "Low Survival Rate," "Negative Outcomes," and "Aggressive Recurrence" swam across the screen. According to the Google machine, there was about a 90% chance that I would be dead within the next three years. The ground spun beneath me. Was I about to leave Ellington without a mom? What would happen to Jason? What about the Winnebago!?

For those lucky enough to have no idea what HER-2 is, it's a hormone receptor that basically operates like a light switch. When it's turned on, it overexpresses itself and results in fuel for cancerous cells. Even if doctors can beat down breast cancer, it will keep coming back as long as this switch is turned on. Every time cancer returns, the treatment is harder, and the outcomes are more dire.

Back in the '90s, when I was first diagnosed with Hodgkin Lymphoma, there was a lot of talk about finding a so-called "cure for cancer." But cancer is not one disease. Every type of cancer is different, and every individual person's cancer is different. The end of cancer is not going to be one singular discovery, but a steady stream of innovation that will beat back cancer one invention at a time. Immunotherapy is one such innovation. Before immunotherapy, HER-2 Positive breast cancer was a losing battle. Because doctors had no way of switching off the over-expressed gene, the cancer would return in as little as a year after treatment ended, like a game of grotesque whack-a-mole. HER-2 Positive breast cancer was essentially a death sentence.

Immunotherapy, nonexistent decades earlier, would make all the difference in my battle with breast cancer. Thanks to this treatment, doctors can "turn off the switch" on the HER-2 receptor, improving the survival rate from 10% to 80-90%. (Side note: There's a pretty good movie about the creation of the immunotherapy agent, Herceptin, the first drug to target the HER-2 gene. It's called *Living Proof,* and it stars Harry Connick Jr. Give it a watch. Stiffler's mom is also one of the patients.)

While I was relieved to learn that I wasn't on death's door, I was still pissed about having cancer again. Who wouldn't be? I had a business to run and a daughter to raise. I'd already more than fulfilled my lifetime quota for hospital stays. Plus, my insurance situation was a mess. All this was added stress during a "global pandemic."

After I resigned from WWT, I had the option to stay on their health insurance through COBRA. According to federal law, if an employee from a company the size of WWT departs, they must be given the option to stay on their healthcare plan for eighteen months, provided they pay the premiums themselves. This is nice in theory, but I had no intention of paying $2,400 per month for health insurance. So, I tossed those COBRA papers right into the garbage the moment I received them. I don't think I even opened the packet.

Being a much smaller company back in 2020, DGR Systems had a level funded plan, which means a portion of what isn't used comes back as credit in the following year to offset costs. This is great for, say, young single males who never visit the doctor. It's less great for cancer patients. Oh, and the plan our family was on didn't cover any healthcare outside the state of Florida. Sound the alarms!

The lead physician at BayCare, where I was first diagnosed and referred, was a general oncologist and not exactly up to date on the latest breast cancer-specific protocols. His recommended course of treatment included heavy doses of the Red Devil, which I'd already maxed out years ago. While the surgeon at BayCare was lovely, she was only one year out of her fellowship. She did spend a lot of time with us and even gave me a little booklet of different types of mastectomy scars with handy, horrific photos to reference. There were nipple-sparing mastectomies, non-radical mastectomies, mastectomies that hid the scars, etc. Still, something wasn't sitting right with me. I needed to expand my care options.

First and foremost, I wanted to pay a visit to my first OG (original) oncologist in St. Louis, who was the only doctor offering me an elusive PET Scan. These tests, though highly useful, are rarely covered by any insurance, so many doctors need to be begged to order them. I called the DGR Systems insurance broker and explained the situation. "I've just been diagnosed with cancer, and I need to leave the state for testing. Is there anything we can do?" The agent told me she would make some calls on my behalf, and, not even a few hours later, she called back. There was no way to switch from an in-state to an out-of-state plan without "a major life event." Being diagnosed with cancer apparently did not qualify as a major life event. Jason would have to fire me or divorce me. We considered it briefly, but decided getting divorced sounded unpleasant, to say the least. Plus, I didn't really feel like planning a second wedding. By this time, I was starting to seriously regret throwing out those CO-BRA papers.

After calling WWT and speaking with their amazing human resources team, I learned that I only had three weeks left to apply for COBRA. Fighting a creeping sense of panic, I got the papers together, filled them out, faxed them in with a check, and moved the entire family over to the WWT insurance plan within a few days. In the meantime, I started planning for my "National Cancer Tour." It was like the Winnebago national tour in that it only went to three places, but it was unlike the Winnebago world tour in that it wasn't any fun. My first stop would be Siteman Cancer Center in St. Louis for the PET scan. After that, MD Anderson in Houston, Texas who was considered the premier cancer facility in its region, right up there with Moffitt Cancer Center in Tampa. I knew that some people were treated in tandem by both hospitals, so I wanted to explore that while I sat on the wait list at Moffitt, ironically, the closest hospital to me with the longest lead time for an appointment.

My COBRA insurance came in only a few days before I was set to fly to St. Louis. Meanwhile, both hospitals had been calling me repeatedly, asking for my insurance information, and threatening to cancel my appointment. (The out-of-pocket cost of a single visit to MD Anderson would have been a whopping $14,000.) Jason drove me to the airport, but he didn't get out of the car. I don't think either of us wanted to really admit what this trip was for. He was staying in Tampa with Ellie, and I was on my own, yet another aspect that this sucked compared to the Winnebago tour.

This was September 2020, still the height of COVID, and the airports were strictly enforcing masking and social distancing. The Tampa airport was eerily empty, with every food stand and store closed. There wasn't even a Starbucks. I had just taken my first real COVID test, and my nose felt weirdly sore. (You remember the early ones where the nurse tickled your brain.) The flight was even emptier than the airport, with just a few scattered passengers, masked up and avoiding eye contact with one another. I wondered what in their lives was so pressing that they too had to get on a plane.

I arrived in St. Louis for the PET scan, and my friend, Mary, carted me around to meet a breast oncologist that I ended up not clicking with. She did mention an up-to-date trial that was informative, but she certainly wasn't worth traveling to St. Louis for. On to the "Big Barnes" hospital, I arrived for my PET scan. During a PET scan, the provider shoots you up with "radioactive stuff" (that's a medical term) which attaches itself to high glucose cells, including cancer cells. Then, they have you lie down in a large, white, tube-like machine that looks like something out of Star Trek. On the scan, my left breast lit up like a light bulb along with my first lymph node on the left side, which meant that I likely had regional metastasis. The good news was that nothing else lit up. With this information duly noted, I flew on to Houston.

When I arrived at my appointment at MD Anderson, I was informed that the hospital had not received all my insurance information. I sat in the waiting room feeling incredibly alone. I'd spent the night before in a nearly empty hotel, paid for with a friend's unused Marriott points. There had been virtually nowhere to order food from, nowhere to pass the time. All I could really do was sit alone with my thoughts, wonder what would happen next, and try not to worry about my insurance.

After a few tense phone calls, the insurance information did come through, and I was allowed in for my appointment. The oncologist there was wonderful and spoke with great clarity and confidence. "You're very lucky," he assured me. I responded that I didn't feel particularly lucky given that this is the second time I'd been diagnosed with cancer. "You're right," he asserted, "cancer is awful. And your cancer is particularly aggressive." I appreciated the fact that he didn't mince words. "But you caught it early," he assured me, "which means you're going to be okay." I felt a massive weight lift from my shoulders. "Also, there's no need for you to be treated here," he concluded, to my great surprise. "I'd make the same recommendation as Moffitt would. You should go there." He proceeded to give me some really great recommendations on diet and exercise to keep me cancer-free post-treatment. I should probably dig those up. So back to Tampa it was.

"I don't care what you say," Jason told me sternly, "You should call him." I was back home in our living room, relaying the events of my cancer tour. The *him* Jason was referring to was the Chief Technology Officer at Moffitt Cancer Center, someone we knew personally through DGR Systems, working with their Information Technology teams. I'd been stubbornly refusing to lean on him, choosing instead to sit on the waiting list like everyone else. But my husband had had enough. Within an hour, I had a text from our friend. "I can't believe you haven't called," the text read. "I can help you." Insert God Wink! Within a few days, I had an appointment with the CTO's favorite surgeon, Dr. Cole Kirell, the man who would become my knight in shining armor. (Sorry, Jason!)

From the moment I met Dr. Kirell, I knew I was in good hands. I sat in the exam room with Jason on video via a Moffitt provided tablet, discussing my treatment options. (Jason had to call in from the parking lot because, well, COVID.) Dr. Kirell listened patiently to my history of cancer and the aggressive treatment I'd received as a young adult. He shook his head, grumbling, when he learned that a previous physician had recommended the Red Devil. "You already have neuropathy, cardio-toxicity, and a damaged immune system," he observed. "More intense chemotherapy will only make that worse. And radiation is out of the question." Dr. Kirell believed that, if we started with surgery, I'd have the best chance of preventing it from spreading further.

I left Dr. Kirell's exam room and proceeded to meet with the medical oncologist. "Chemotherapy has to be first," the oncologist said matter-of-factly. "Otherwise, there's no chance to see if the chemotherapy is working." Doctors often recommend doing chemotherapy first, so they can re-conduct imaging mid-way through treatment to confirm your tumor is shrinking. The oncologist explained that she would never recommend starting cancer treatment with surgery first.

"Don't you people talk to each other?" Jason piped in from his tiny screen. Within five minutes, we were marching back down the hall so the doctors could confer with one another. After some intense back-and-forth, they came to a decision: they were undecided. The doctors agreed that my case was unusual enough that they would have to take it to the hospital's Tumor Board for further review. But before I left, Dr. Kirell had a question for me. "What do *you* want?" he asked, his kind and curious eyes resting patiently on mine. "They're just boobs," I shrugged. "Lop 'em off." Dr. Kirell smiled and replied, "If I had my sword, I'd do it right now."

My case was unusual. In most cases of breast cancer, doctors opt for *neoadjuvant* chemotherapy. That is, chemo before surgery. The hope is that chemo will shrink the tumors down enough that a full mastectomy isn't necessary. The reason for this is simple: mastectomies suck. Both physically and psychologically, losing your boobs is not a walk in the park. Even in my case, where I was pretty sure I wanted *adjuvant* (after surgery) chemo, I was shocked when I learned what my scars were going to look like. The boob book was out the window. I was going to be left with a huge, angry purple V across my chest. I would have absolutely no nipples. It would take several more surgeries for my body to look anything close to normal again – but that is another story. In the short term, the important thing for me was to survive. To be given a chance to be a mom to Ellington for as long as possible.

By doing surgery first, the doctors could get a more accurate picture of how large my tumor really was and whether it had really spread to my lymph nodes. Based on that assessment, they could give me exactly the appropriate amount of chemo and immunotherapy, and no more. Science had come a long way since I was a teenager, when standard treatment was simply to blast the patient with as much radiation and chemotherapy as possible. Ultimately, the board voted with Dr. Kirell. He called me himself with the news while I was out pushing Ellie in her stroller around the neighborhood. I would lose the boobs immediately. There was only one problem: I was number 50 on the waiting list for a mastectomy.

When you have cancer, every day it's not being treated is a day you feel like it's multiplying and spreading all over your body. The idea of sitting still for a full month while the tumor in my body grew and possibly spread to other places was terrifying to me. Fortunately, Dr. Kirell had my back (or should I say, my boobs?). Although Fridays were his clinic days, he opted to switch around his schedule. He borrowed an operating room from a doctor who was on vacation. My surgery was scheduled for the following week. It was barely three weeks after I'd been diagnosed with breast cancer, and I was getting a double mastectomy. Winner, winner chicken dinner!

"Now, this is a teaching hospital with USF, but don't worry," Dr. Kirell assured me. "I will be the one performing your surgery. You will see the whites of my eyes when you wake up."

The night before my surgery, Jason and I went out to eat at the Island Way Grill near Clearwater Beach. I got dressed up in tight jeans and a deep V-neck blouse, showcasing plenty of cleavage. It was the girls' last outing, after all. It was a lovely sunset dinner. I had a single martini and king crab legs. The next day, I switched out the blouse for a black t-shirt that read "Wicked Witch of the Breast – *out!*"

An hour before the surgery, a tech came into my room to inject blue dye with a radioactive tracer into my nipples. Yep, you read that right. The blue dye is used to trace and identify your lymph nodes through your milk ducts. During the surgery, the doctor traces these nodes and removes them one by one, as if blocking the exits on the highway. Then, they look at the node under a microscope to determine if there is cancer. If yes, they go on to the next one and repeat until they are all clear.

In my case, they only found Isolated Tumor Cells (ITC) in one sentinel lymph node on the left side, but thankfully, none on the right side. Although my nodes did show isolated cancer cells, the cancer had not fully spread. This meant I was still a Stage 1 versus 2, and I'd receive less chemotherapy and immunotherapy drugs. Doing the surgery first was the right decision.

...

I woke up freezing, like I always do after surgery. Jason was at my side, looking pale.

"I'm so glad to see you," he said, eyes watering. "I thought you died."

"WHAT?!"

Apparently, during the three hours I had been unconscious, Jason had been sitting alone in a completely deserted waiting room. Suddenly, a Code Blue came over the speaker. Jason Googled this and, to his horror, discovered that Code Blue meant that someone was coding on the table.

As soon as he read that, his name was called.

He approached the nurse's stand, terrified and preparing himself for the worst news of his life. "She's out of surgery!" the nurse chirped. "You can see her now!" Jason barely had time to relay this story to me before the nurse came in and announced that visiting hours were over.

"He's staying the night," I said, confused. "Sorry," the nurse said, somewhat sheepishly, "Because of COVID protocols..."

Jason and I had both been under the impression that he was staying the night. We'd even lined up a rotation of six different babysitters to hand off Ellington to one by one. Jason mused that maybe he should just go home and take over Ellie's care from our former neighbor, who was watching her overnight.

"You're not allowed to go home," I said firmly. "Ellie doesn't need you right now. I need you right now." Home was nearly an hour away, and I wanted Jason there first thing in the morning. So, cashing in those trusty Marriott points, we got him a room at the nearby Fairfield Inn. This turned out to be a good thing because the moment he got to the hotel, he crashed. There's no way he would have gotten as good a night's sleep in my hospital room, which was so small that, if I got out of bed, I immediately tripped over the toilet. It was an odd setup for sure, and the toilet was totally out in the open like a prison cell.

Fortunately, thanks to my wonderful community of family and friends, there was plenty to keep me occupied during that first night in the hospital. While I ate my rubbery chicken dinner, my body warmed up by the purple hospital gown with the hot air hose, I read letters and opened gifts. Our sitter sent photo after photo of Ellie—who, in an unexpected miracle, slept through the night for the very first time. Ingrid sent me a lucky coin etched with a breast cancer warrior saying. Billy Pope, a friend and former customer—and an Air Force Colonel—mailed me a folded flag that had seen combat, along with a moving letter and one of the patches from his uniform. I also had a smooth, glassy guardian angel rock tucked into my purse—the same one my dad carried in his pocket for years after Mom passed away.

Lying there, sore and swollen but surrounded by all these tokens of love, I didn't feel alone. I felt held. I felt rooted. Not just in my body, which was now forever changed, but in the incredible web of people who showed up for me—some in person, some in spirit. In that tiny, awkward hospital room, I realized something simple and true: healing doesn't begin with medicine. It begins with people. *Genuine Humans*.

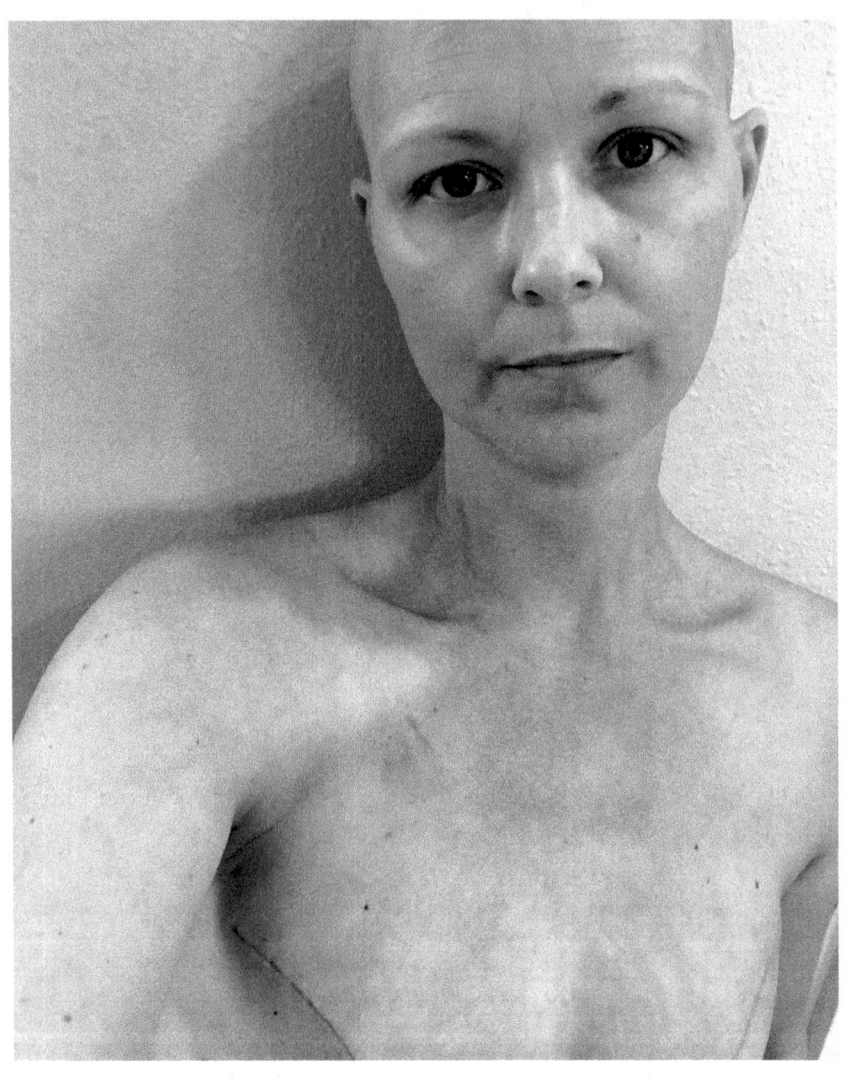

A Slice of Ham: *Dr. Kirell didn't sugarcoat it. There'd be no dainty, nipple-sparing techniques or precision sculpting in my case—just the complete and unapologetic removal of everything that made my chest mine, except the breast implants from a surgery long ago. "It's like carving out a watermelon," he said, "we have to remove every bit of pink without breaching the rind." It was a vivid and horrifying metaphor, and it stuck. That was the reality of a double mastectomy: not a delicate procedure, but a controlled demolition—necessary, brutal, and final.*

CHAPTER 24

IT TAKES A VILLAGE

Even with the warnings, I was shocked when I came out of surgery. I've never thought of myself as a vain person, but I've never been insecure about my appearance either. There's nothing wrong with being confident! There's also nothing wrong with having breast cancer and getting a double mastectomy. Okay, there's plenty wrong with it, but the physical aspect isn't typically listed in the top three things that suck about having breast cancer. But when I looked in the mirror the first time after that surgery, I felt my stomach drop. There was an angry, red and purple, V-shaped scar covering my entire chest. Nasty, brown liquid oozed from my wounds into tubes and bottles that were sewn and attached to my body. I didn't have any nipples. Yes, I expected this, but nothing prepares you for the shock of not having nipples. The nipple is a pretty essential visual.

Of a more practical concern than nipples was the fact that I couldn't lift my arms over my head, let alone lift a 5-month-old, 25-pound baby. The doctors told me it would be another six weeks until I was allowed to lift anything heavier than a gallon of milk. It would also be six weeks until I was allowed to bathe, which is exactly as gross as it sounds. (Side note, I found out quickly I could shower, but avoiding the giant incision was not particularly easy.) I was incredibly grateful to be alive, don't get me wrong, but this recovery was going to absolutely suck. I wanted my nipples back, and I wanted to be able to do shit. The thing about cancer, and life in general, is that some things are completely out of your control. Sometimes it takes 100% of your energy just to heal. When that happens, you need your people to step in. Fortunately for me, they did.

When I arrived home from the hospital, I expected to feel exhausted, broken, maybe even a little lost—but what I walked into was a scene of love in full bloom. A crowd of friends had gathered around my dining room table, their faces lit up like they had just been waiting to exhale until I walked through that door. I was immediately enveloped in a cascade of flowers, laughter, and a box overflowing with handmade cards and notes. One of my favorites was from my nephew Elijah, one of Heather's boys. In his endearingly practical tone, he'd written, "I hope you don't get COVID-19!" Same, buddy. I pinned it to the fridge like it was sacred.

By 8:45 p.m., we were all crowded around the table playing Exploding Kittens like it was any other Friday night, not the end of one of the hardest weeks of my life. My arms were awkwardly perched on these round, underarm pillows that volunteers sew for mastectomy patients, and I was dripping hot sauce from my Tijuana Flats tacos all over them. I couldn't have cared less. I was sore, bandaged, and a little loopy, but I was surrounded by the people who knew me best and still managed to treat me like myself—not like a patient or a project, but Amanda. It was messy and funny and oddly perfect. In that moment, I felt held—not just physically, but emotionally, spiritually. I wasn't alone. I was home.

Over the next six weeks, a rotating cast of friends flew in to help me care for Ellie while Jason was running the company. Molly came first, and her training as a nurse practitioner was essential to getting both my pain under control and a teething and often hysterical infant to sleep through the night (not!). That first night I was in the hospital, when Ellie slept through the night, turned out to be a complete fluke. Molly also helped, twice a day, with the unglamorous task of emptying and measuring the amount of fluid draining from my boob tubes. We had to keep meticulous records of the amount of gunk and report back to the hospital every other day.

Also, during this time, I had planned to throw a baby shower for my friend Kayla. Naturally, everyone agreed I was a bit unhinged, and Kayla begged me to cancel, but I refused. I needed a task, and barking orders while my girlfriends packed baby shower lunches and cut out decorations fit the bill perfectly. I attended Kayla's shower at a local Bed & Breakfast, boob tubes, oversized shirt to hide them and all. It was a beautiful event for her, but it was equally important for me. As much as possible, I was determined to minimize the number of things cancer was going to take from me. As time went on, my community of supporters found increasingly innovative ways to empower me and keep me doing the things I love.

After Molly, Lisa came for a week—and it's hard to put into words what it meant to have her there. Lisa and I have been best friends for over thirty years, which means she's been there for every version of me: the awkward, the confident, the heartbroken, the reckless, the stubborn, the successful, and now, the post-mastectomy, pain-medicated me living in a $1,500 recliner we were forced to overspend on due to COVID supply chain issues. It now holds our decorative pillows when we go to bed at night. Bargain!

Lisa didn't flinch. She folded right into the chaos of our household like it was the most natural thing in the world—helping with the baby, cooking our family meals, making sure my drain tubes weren't dragging on the floor like haunted house props. She even helped me shower and blow-dried my hair.

But it was more than the help. There's something sacred about having someone beside you who remembers who you were before everything cracked open—someone who doesn't need a map to find you. Lisa didn't treat me like I was fragile, but she knew exactly when to slow down, when to make me laugh, and when to just sit quietly while I tried to piece myself back together. Having her there reminded me that, even when your body is unfamiliar and your life feels hijacked, love like that doesn't waver. It holds. It shows up with snacks. It makes space for who you are and who you're trying to become.

Lisa stayed a full week, even coming with me to Ellie's six-month pediatrician appointment. On the way back, we received a call from Ingrid. When I picked up the phone, she was hysterically crying. Now, the last time I heard Aunt Ingrid cry was the day I learned that Ed Carter was not my biological father, so it's safe to say I was alarmed. I was not exactly in a state to receive any more traumatic family secrets. Still, I took a deep breath and counted to five. "All right. Just say it" I said, "rip off the band-aid."

"I… HAVE… COVID!" Ingrid wept. My first reaction was to laugh.

All that for COVID? But she was admitted to the hospital, gasping for air, and sounded practically on her deathbed. After being assured she would recover, I looked over at Lisa, and her face was pale, her eyes were as wide as saucers. That's when I realized a problem: Ingrid was the next person in line on my care team. She was supposed to take over for Lisa two days later. Who could I possibly get to come take care of Ellie and drain my tubes for an entire week during the pandemic while Jason was working day and night?

Marilyn, the dog trainer, that's who! It seemed that fate was on my side, because Marilyn just so happened to be in Florida at that very moment. She was in the process of closing on a home in The Villages. Now, if you've never heard of The Villages, it is a lovely golf and retirement community. If you have heard of it, it was probably because it made the news a few years ago for having the highest rate of sexually transmitted infections per capita in the United States. They live large in The Villages. (Marilyn claims the "loofah code" is a myth, but maybe she's just not hanging out at the right community center.)

Marilyn was extremely gracious and immediately agreed to switch around her entire agenda and come stay with us for ten days. The only problem was that Marilyn had absolutely no idea how to take care of a baby. Dogs were no problem, but infants were another story entirely. She had rarely changed a diaper or mixed a bottle of formula. Thankfully, one of Marilyn's closest friends had triplet granddaughters several years prior. When they were first born, Marilyn often went over to help, but she had never taken care of a baby for more than a few hours. We were so grateful for her help and were too desperate to decline her offer. Ultimately, Marilyn did great, and she and Ellie formed a lasting bond.

Once Marilyn left (and Ellie was properly clicker trained to crawl), we still had about three weeks left to fill where I couldn't lift Ellie out of the crib. Our former neighbor, Andrea, would stay one or two nights a week, but it wasn't practical for her to stay every night. This is when we developed a morning wake-up system. The other mornings, our friends Matt and Kayla (remember baby shower Kayla?) would pull into our driveway at 6:00 a.m. I'd unlock the door and settle into the recliner. They would quietly breeze in, pick Ellie up, change her diaper and place her in my lap. It was good practice for them as Kayla was now eight months pregnant. After making the bottle for me, I was able to feed Ellie myself. It's hard to put into words how much it meant to be able to feed my own child. The thoughtfulness of this gesture, the simple humanity of it, will stay with me for the rest of my life. Matt and Kayla made sure that I didn't miss out on a single moment with my daughter. Talk about taking a village.

The boob tubes finally came out on October 16, and Jason treated me to a big ass margarita and tacos. Around that time, my friends started selling pink T-shirts that said *Believe* on them in white script. This matched my most recent tattoo: the script of a combination of my parents handwriting designed by a cousin and tattooed on my left arm. I got it as a reminder post miscarriage, post dad's passing and while in Los Angeles meeting Tim and Lucy. It was a reminder to never give up, no matter what.

Between the shirts and a *Go Fund Me* my friends set up, they were able to raise about $6,000, which we used to offset the costs to hire a nanny for Ellie for the duration of my recovery. They also gave me a digital picture frame, so I could flip through the photos of everyone I knew wearing their *Believe* shirts. It was an important reminder, on the toughest of days, of how many people were there to support me, and just how big my village was. Thanks to all of them, I was able to breathe a little easier.

I had a short break between getting the tubes out and the next phase of treatment: chemotherapy and immunotherapy. The weekend before chemotherapy started, Jason, Ellie, and I took a mini vacation, just the three of us. We stayed two nights at the Sand Pearl Hotel, a beautiful spot on Clearwater Beach about forty minutes from home. The hotel had a glorious resort-style pool that looked up at the blue sky and was warm even in October. It felt like summer all weekend.

Due to the doctor's orders that I wasn't to submerge myself in water for another week, I sat on the side of the pool, dangling my feet in the water while Jason pushed Ellie around in her little blue float. The water looked so cool and clean and tempting. I ran my finger along the top of my scar, visible above my one-piece suit. It was smooth and there were no open sores. I figured that was good enough.

I was never good at following rules. As I slowly lowered myself into the water, I felt a shiver up my spine. I waded over to Ellie, and she splashed her feet with joy, hitting me in the face with little sprinkles. Jason raised an eyebrow at me, questioning, and I shrugged in return. I took the float from his hands and began pushing it myself, making little motor noises that made her giggle even more. I wasn't afraid of a little water. If there's one thing cancer makes crystal clear, it's that you only live once, and there's no way of saying for how long. Just get in the pool.

By Tuesday, I was back in the hospital ready for my first chemo treatment. The hospital chaplain paid me a visit, carrying a wooden business card holder with the word *Believe* emblazoned in cursive across the top. The script closely mimicked that of my tattoo. I scooted up in my chemo chair, eyes wide. Another God Wink! The chaplain gave me a wooden cross, which I held onto tightly throughout my treatment, regularly packing it in my "go-bag." Somehow, at that moment, I knew I was going to be okay. Months later, when Kayla was hospitalized with pre-eclampsia during pregnancy, I would pass that wooden cross on to her, a small symbol of how much she and Matt had supported me. When the roles were reversed, I would not let her down.

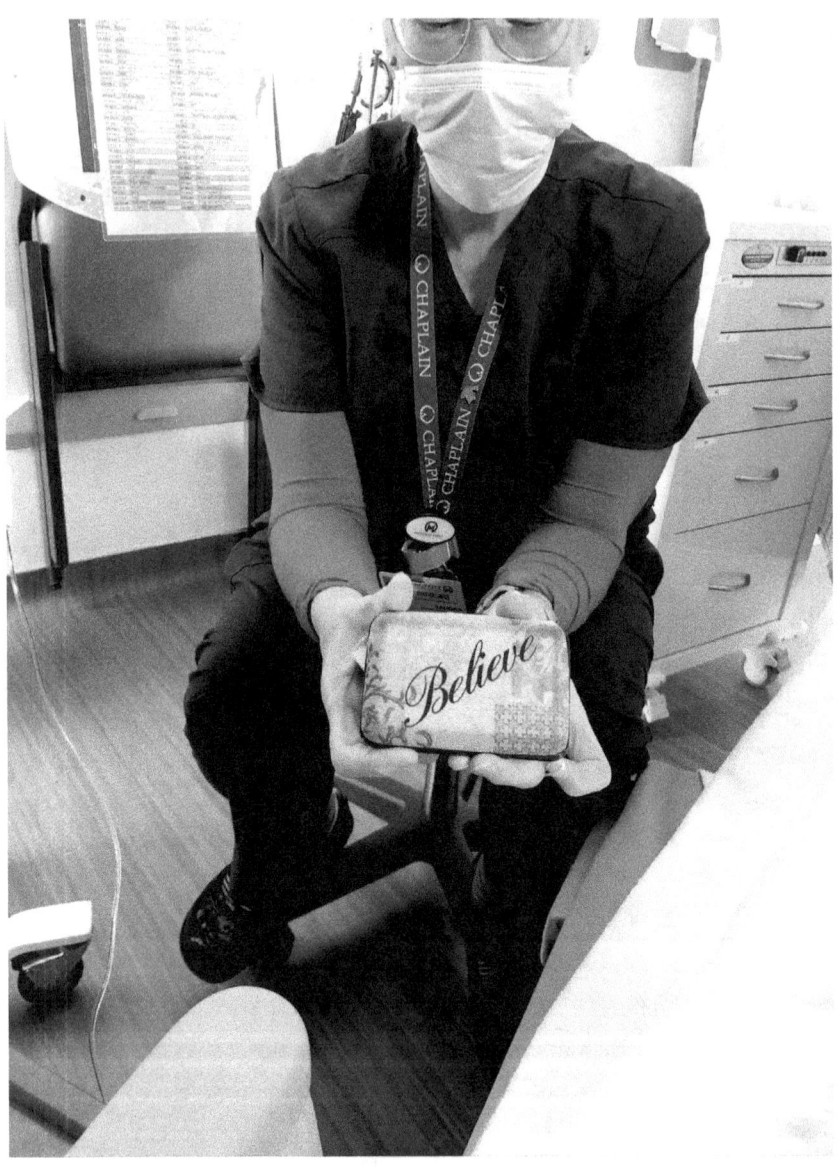

Throughout the next stage of treatment, I kept my mind on my dad and what I was sure was his message to me: *Believe, and keep on believing.* I believed I would be there for Ellie, for Jason, for my friends and family. I believed I would see the other side of this.

Because when life strips you down—physically, emotionally, spiritual-ly—it's not the scars or the surgeries that define you. It's the people who step in and say, "We've got you." My village didn't just show up—they carried me. With every text, every flower, every hot sauce-soaked taco, they reminded me I wasn't fighting this alone.

Cancer may have tried to break me, but love rebuilt me. I had miles to go, but I wasn't afraid. I was tired, yes. Bruised, absolutely. But I was also held, tethered by something stronger than fear: faith, friendship, and the fierce determination to keep showing up—for myself, and for everyone who had shown up for me.

This was the beginning of my second cancer journey—but this time, I already knew the most important truth: healing doesn't happen in isolation. It happens in community. And because of that, I didn't just believe I'd make it through.

I *knew* I would.

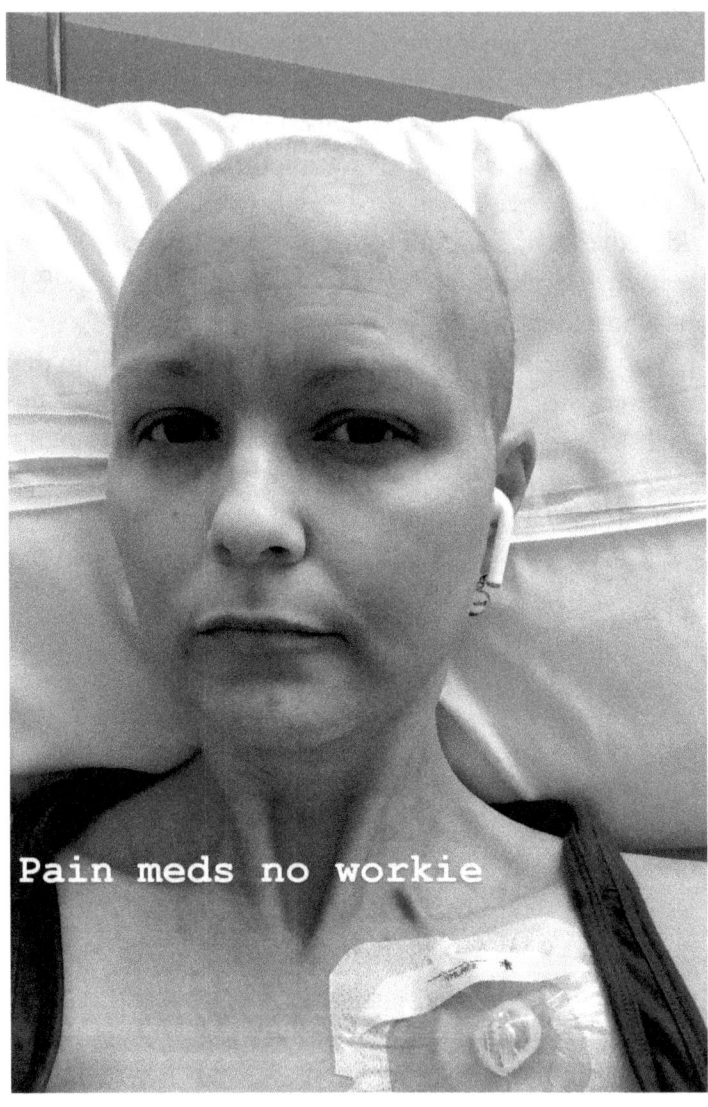

Pain meds no workie

A Slice of Ham: *One of my favorite quotes is "Just because someone carries it well, doesn't mean it isn't heavy." We all have our "stuff," and we often put on a smile to hide the underlying pain and emotions we are feeling. My guidance is for everyone to find their outlet. Whether that be an anonymous Facebook group, or a friend you can truly share all the feelings with. Don't purposely go through all the pain alone.*

CHAPTER 25

C·A·N·C·E·R.:
THE ONE WHERE
I BEAT IT TWICE!

Chemotherapy sucked. I'd say it was at least twice as difficult as my first time at bat. For one thing, I was 40 now, not 20. I was also a sleep-deprived new mom attempting to navigate the COVID pandemic. On top of all this, the pain was intense. I couldn't get through a full chemotherapy infusion without experiencing searing pain in my femurs. Every single Tuesday, it felt like a freight train hit me mid-way through treatment. I coped by taking the pain medication Tramadol before and after every treatment, then retreating home to my bed for what was often a four-hour nap.

I didn't want to burden Jason with the full responsibility of my care, so we relied heavily on our village for support. I created a virtual Care Calendar where friends could sign up to babysit Ellie while he was at work, drop off casseroles, or be my "chemo buddies" for the day and take me to treatment. Because of COVID, these friends weren't allowed to come into the infusion room with me, so they would often sit for hours in the waiting room, masks on, until I was finished.

Chemo days went like this:

First, my Chemo Buddy would pick me up from our house. I'd kiss Ellie goodbye and hand her off to her babysitter. We'd drive the 45 minutes from Safety Harbor to Moffitt McKinley Center and walk from the parking garage to the lobby. (We left the valet parking for the old people.) There was always someone stationed in the lobby to take everyone's temperature. (Remember COVID?) Once it was confirmed that everyone was healthy (aside from the pesky cancer), I'd be bombarded with questions at central check-in. Had I fallen in the past 30 days? (No.) Any issues completing your daily activities? (Um, obviously.) Has your insurance changed? (No.) Can I see your ID? (Why would anyone pretend to be me right now?) Do you have someone with you today? Do you have a port or a pic line? Can we text you on your mobile phone? (Check, check, check.)

After a fun game of 20 Questions, we'd head off to the blood draw center. Here, I'd be checked in again. Again, they'd ask about my port and if they were allowed to text me. Finally, after about a 15-minute wait, I'd actually receive said text. "Blood draw is ready for you in Bay 3." I'd leave my Chemo Buddy temporarily and walk around the corner to Bay 3 and sit in the blood draw chair. The nurse or medical assistant would put on some seriously thick rubber gloves, open a bunch of very sterile materials, and tap the port on my chest like it was a keg at the worst college party of all time. They'd use this sticky plastic cellophane stuff to tape down the access line to my chest and suction my blood into tubes.

Finally, we were off to the infusion floor, floor 5. We could wait there for an hour or more. There were always many different faces that passed in and out of the very long and narrow waiting room. Over time, some of them became familiar. Even all these years later, I was often the youngest one there.

When it was time for me to check in (yes, again), they would ask a series of very similar questions. Again, I would receive a text letting me know whether to come to door B or C to be processed by a medical assistant. They would take my weight, blood pressure, temperature, pulse, and oxygen stats. They would ask me more questions about my current medications. I would again verify that I had not fallen in the past 30 days. Then, I'd be dismissed back to the waiting room until a chemo bay became available.

Despite the long and bureaucratic process of getting into the chemo chair, I never felt like a number. The staff at Moffitt, from the parking lot, lobby, check-in, blood draw, medical assistants, and nurses, were always so caring and compassionate. We were all navigating a completely unknown situation, cancer treatment during the height of the pandemic, and I knew they were doing their absolute best to keep me safe. They always called me by name and asked how I was feeling. It didn't necessarily make the tedium any easier, but I was grateful to be under their care.

When my lucky number was finally called, I would receive another text message. "Meet at door A." I'd leave my Chemo Buddy in the waiting area and head to the tiny infusion room. They were about 5-feet by 5-feet, adorned with a cozy "medical recliner," a folding chair for the person who was not allowed to join me, and a TV on a swing pole that no one uses because everyone streams content from their personal devices.

I always brought my chemo bag, which carried a thick fuzzy blanket from Mary, my laptop, and a sweary "F-Cancer" coloring book. (I highly recommend this if you ever get cancer.) Once you were fully hooked up to the life-saving poison by one of the amazing nurses, they would offer you one of their mediocre lunch options. They were always good enough that I wasn't tempted to brown bag it, but not so good that I'd turn down an offer of a Chick-Fil-A run when my Chemo Buddy offered it.

I went through this process on a weekly basis for 12 continuous weeks, getting to know the nurses and other staff by name. I managed the excruciating pain by taking so much Tramadol and Benadryl that it was sometimes hard to wake up, and I was often super constipated as a result. So glamorous! After only two treatments, my hair started falling out. (What a weird way to feel young again, right?) I recalled how much it had helped to feel in control the first time around, so I made plans to shave my head on my own terms. I mentioned this to my friend Jeff, and he immediately contacted his hairstylist, who came over to my house and shaved both of our heads.

Jeff was one of those friends I could share anything with. We teamed up as the Client Exec and Consulting Systems Engineering team serving the Special Operations Command customers during my time at WWT on the DoD team. We traveled together, looked out for one another's careers, and provided completely unfiltered advice. His wife, Katie, was a nurse and was always super helpful in assisting me with managing my medications and subsequent constipation. During the head shaving, we took a ton of photos and videos to commemorate the special moment. No one rocks a shaved head like me!

Every third chemotherapy treatment also included immunotherapy, the new drug that was going to save my life. Immunotherapy is an incredible technology, but it is not a miracle drug. Few things in science really are miracles. Like chemotherapy, there are tons of adverse reactions. Unlike chemotherapy, these reactions aren't always clear or easy to predict. Once, a woman next to me suddenly found herself unable to breathe. I was keenly aware that Dad's immunotherapy filled his lungs with fluid and put him in the ICU, which wasn't the most comforting thought. Fortunately, the staff watch you like a bunch of hawks. The slightest sneeze, the smallest twitch, and they're at your side. This process is nerve-racking and yet another test for my general fear of being out of control. But it's so much better than the alternative. Without immuno-therapy, I probably wouldn't be here today.

In addition to the potential immediate side effects of immunotherapy was the cumulative cardiotoxicity. I had to receive quarterly echocardio-grams to keep an eye on the ejection fraction percentage of my heart. Your ejection fraction is the measurement of the percentage of blood leaving the heart each time it contracts. A normal percentage is 55-70%. Values below 40% may indicate reduced heart function and potential heart failure symptoms. Thankfully, my first echo was 55-60% and I never fell below 55%. Once treatment is completed, your heart does recover.

Christmas that year fell directly between my eighth and ninth chemo-therapy treatments, so we were unable to take our usual trip to Memphis for Ellie's first Christmas. Instead, we took her to the Zoo Lights, the same event that had been so special for my dad. Biology aside, there was no doubt that she was Ed Carter's granddaughter. She loved the lights as much as he did. She crawled around nonstop, pointing excitedly at every animal she saw, until she exhausted herself and fell asleep in Jason's arms, the twinkling lights dancing on her face.

Christmas Day was quiet, with only me, Jason, Ellie, and our dog, Barley. Ellie, of course, had far more toys to open than she needed and predictably overlooked them in favor of playing with all the paper, boxes, and bows. Despite it being a little sad to not be surrounded by the usual family ruckus on Christmas Day, there was something sweet about this peaceful Christmas. I'll treasure the memory of Ellie's first Christmas, despite the tumult that surrounded it.

Very soon – too soon – it was back to reality. My ninth chemo treat-ment was on December 26. By then, the pain was so intense they decided to lower my chemo dosage by 20%. It didn't help. Still, I had no choice but to push through. My new strategy was to request a room with a bed rather than a chemo chair, so I could bury myself in the covers and try to sleep through the pain. Once I got home, I'd sleep some more, sometimes not waking up until 6 p.m. when it was time for the babysitter to leave and me to take over the bedtime routine.

My final chemo appointment, big number 12, was on January 15. However, I wasn't fully out of the woods yet. I still had immunotherapy infusions every three weeks until October. Fortunately, immunotherapy wasn't nearly as hard on my body. I gradually started to feel better during the weeks between treatments, despite sometimes feeling out of breath. You know, minor details.

The longer breaks between treatments meant increased freedom for us. On a few occasions, we'd leave on an RV trip the day after treatment and not return until two weeks later. I loved these trips, which felt like mini-escapes from the realities of cancer. We took a two-week trip in the new super-sized Beyonce Bus (we also nicknamed Stevie Nicks...because the brand was called Fleetwood) to Lake Toxaway near Cashiers, North Carolina. Aside from having to work with two customers who had been hit with ransomware attacks the day after we arrived, it was a lovely trip. Jason would work several hours in the morning, we'd pack our lunches and go hiking at a national park, find a waterfall, and return by Ellie's naptime. Jason could then check on the DGR team and get a good amount of work in via our RV's satellite internet connection.

The steep trail climbs were pretty tough for me, but I pushed through while glancing back at Jason carrying Ellie in one of those backpacks. She'd get antsy (as any 14-month-old would), so we'd retrieve random rocks and leaves for her to play with along the way. On this trip, we discovered Ellie's love of apples, so we would take a few bites out of one at the start of our hike, and she'd gnaw on the rest of it the entire way, being completely entertained.

My hair also started coming back over the summer. Naturally, upper lip and chin whiskers returned first, followed by the sprouts on my head, which of course emerged a glistening gray. Beautiful! Still, things were looking up. I saw the light at the end of the tunnel as my very last day of treatment drew near.

In September of 2021, I had my first breast reconstruction revision. Our former neighbor, Andrea, took me as I mandated Jason not waste the Eric Clapton tickets I had gotten him for his birthday. It didn't turn out as well as I had planned. They switched my old 2008 model saline implants for newfangled silicone ones of the same size. I never wanted my girls to look "fake." Clearly, 250 cc on top of an original B cup of breast tissue looked great. 250 cc on top of a carved-up flat chest looked deformed and lumpy. My plastic surgeon at Moffitt and I agreed we'd need to go a little bigger and transplant as much fat as they could suck from my stomach and thighs to pad around the implants. The problem was, I didn't have all that much to give. I ended up having a second revision surgery the following January, but I can't say I'm completely thrilled by how unnatural they still look and feel. I also didn't come out of the anesthesia very well, so I vowed to stop trying to aim for perfection and just moved on to finding new nipples.

It had been a long, grueling haul—more difficult than I imagined, even with experience on my side. My body ached in ways I couldn't have predicted, my spirit bruised by the daily grind of pain, paperwork, and uncertainty. But still, I kept going. We kept going.

I found small joys where I could: in Ellington's giggles, in the quiet of our RV escapes, in the steady return of stubble and strength. My community never wavered. Their support—relentless, creative, and full of love—carried me through the worst of it. Even as the pain dragged on and the treatments stacked up, I could see something shimmering on the horizon.

I wasn't at the end yet. However, I was getting close.

....

It was October 21, the eve of my last cancer treatment. Jason had hinted at a few surprises, so I was already buzzing when Ingrid and Tre'von walked into our date night dinner at the Salt Shack in South Tampa. I was high on life, sipping a cocktail in my pink T-shirt with C.A.N.C.E.R. spelled out in the *Friends* TV show font and the words "The One Where I Beat It Twice" underneath.

Then my phone rang. It was Molly. She was talking a mile a minute—something about being in Tampa (wait, what?), doing a cadaver lab at the Air Force base (seriously?), and needing dinner recommendations for her team. I was only half-tracking her story when she and Ryan walked up behind me, grinning. *Total* Molly move. We cracked up for a solid ten minutes over how ridiculous the whole thing was. Then came news that Lisa was on her way—she was flying in, too. She wouldn't make dinner, but they'd be in town for the weekend. My heart was already full.

October 22, the morning of my final treatment, was a blur of emotion and preparation. Jason and I both wore our matching pink "Believe" shirts, and I adorned myself in *everything* I owned with the word Believe on it—bracelets, pins, tote bags. I had a box of custom "boobie" cookies made for the staff—each cookie shaped like a sideways capital "B" and decorated to reflect all kinds of post-surgical realities: some with nipples, some without, all with their own unique shapes, sizes, and scars. The cookies were a hit.

By 11 a.m., I was plugged into my final infusion. The same chair, the same beeping pumps, the same sterile smell—but this time, the weight felt different. Around noon, the CTO and Director of IT from Moffitt stopped by to wish me well, and for the first time ever—thanks to relaxed COVID restrictions—Jason was allowed back into the infusion room. He kept ducking out, and I figured it was for work calls. It was a Friday, after all. I didn't know he was orchestrating something far bigger.

Once I was unhooked, the nurse led me out to ring the survivor bell. Every staff member who had treated me followed. Someone announced to the entire waiting room that I had completed my last cancer treatment, and the place erupted in applause. I rang the hell out of that bell. Jason and I locked eyes—both of us misty—and silently agreed: *Let's GTFO.*

We hopped in the elevator and took the long hallway toward the parking garage. Outside, something was going on. I could see a sea of pink—streamers, shirts, balloons, a piñata shaped like the bell I had just rung. A table of beautiful cookies sat off to the side, and about twenty of my favorite people lined the walkway, cheering. It took my brain a moment to register that this was all for me. I was handed flowers, wrapped in hugs—and then I saw Ellington. That was it. The tears came fast and hard. So much joy. So much release. The air itself seemed lighter, charged with a kind of hope I hadn't felt in months. We were done. This speed bump—one that had jarred us to our core—was finally behind us.

Lisa and Me outside Moffitt

Our family walking out of my last infusion treatment

The rest of the day felt like a dream. We stopped for lunch with another group of friends who had shown up for me in every possible way—casserole deliverers, chemo buddies, babysitters, morale boosters. Of course, we ate tacos and toasted with margaritas. My body was bone-tired, but my spirit was floating. When Jason said, "You should probably rest... there's another event," I croaked back, "What kind of event? How long can I nap?"

Post what felt like the quickest one-hour power nap ever, we headed to World of Beer in Tampa for a full-on celebration. Lisa and Jason had planned the whole thing—an open bar, a balloon arch in the shape of a pink survivor ribbon, and friends from every stage of my life and career. People flew in from St. Louis and Atlanta and joined video calls from around the country. To see those faces—some I hadn't seen in years—show up just for me was overwhelming in the best way. For once, I wasn't the one holding everything together. I got to simply receive. I felt impossibly, beautifully loved.

By 7:30 p.m., I was completely spent—but the bar tab wasn't. We hadn't come close to hitting the food and beverage minimum. After a few rounds of expensive cocktails, we quickly realized this was an uphill battle. I ended up negotiating with the bar manager and taking home more than a case of Belle Glos Pinot Noir. I left that night with wine in my arms and gratitude in my heart, and collapsed into the couch—finally back to our new normal.

The following week, on October 28, I had my port removed. The scar left behind was small, but it felt monumental—like my body was reclaiming itself inch by inch. Two weeks later, I was in Birmingham visiting my friends and customers. On November 19, Jason and I headed to Key West to attend a wedding and a long-overdue vacation. Life moves on. You do your best to step back into it. But the truth is, you never step back as the same person. You carry the lessons, the scars, the unshakable awareness that nothing is promised.

I poured myself into work at DGR Systems, picked up momentum with fundraising for Genuine Human, and began leading the Membership Committee for Tampa Bay Tech. Each commitment, each meeting, each new project felt like a stitch pulling me back into the fabric of everyday life. The cadence of normalcy was comforting, but I also noticed how much sharper my instincts had become about what really mattered and what I was willing to let go of.

Some days, it's hard to believe it's over. Other days, it feels like just another crisis I had to navigate in the wild and wonderful chaos of my life. Nevertheless, here's what I know for sure: no achievement, no promotion, no resolution means more than the people who stand beside you in the fire. From lifelong soulmates to strangers-turned-heroes, community is everything. Cancer taught me that resilience isn't about being unbreakable—it's about finding the hands that help you rise when you fall.

So, love big. Laugh often. Make someone feel seen, valued, and cared for. And always—*always*—be your own fiercest advocate. No one is more qualified to carry your flag than you.

The end.

GENUINE HUMAN

After my first go-around with cancer, fundraising became a hobby, and one I was damn good at. I consistently offered my time and efforts toward American Cancer Society Relay For Life events, St. Baldrick's Day head-shaving endeavors, and the American Heart Association. But I knew I wanted to expand my efforts beyond the world of cancer and health research. There were people out there making an impact in ways I couldn't imagine. Soon, I began to toy with the idea of starting my own foundation. But where would I begin?

When Jason and I joined a local church in St. Petersburg, Florida called BridgePoint, we got involved in a ministry called Build-a-Bed. Every four to six months, a few dozen of us would gather at a local warehouse to assemble all the components of a twin-sized bed. There would be a station for the headboard, another for the footboard, and others for the side rails and wooden slats. Twice a month, the delivery teams (we participated in this as well) would load up and deliver the beds across Pinellas County, Florida. We would enter homes where children were previously sleeping on floors, couches, or squeezed in with their parents and put the beds together with a few bolts. Then, we'd dress the beds with sheets and comforters. The looks on these kids' faces, to have their very own bed (sometimes the first they ever owned), was one of the most rewarding experiences Jason and I had ever been part of. Through Build-a-Bed, Jason and I got our first taste of the fruits of volunteerism on a local level.

Then came Mike Rowe. In 2017, Mike Rowe had a show on Facebook Watch (Facebook's failed streaming platform) called Returning the Favor. He would crowdsource suggestions from people in the community, whom he called "Bloody Do-Gooders," people who were making a difference with innovative and impactful volunteer work. Then, he would pretend to do a documentary on that person's efforts and surprise them at the end of the episode with a hefty check to further their efforts. I watched these episodes over and over until I'd mastered the formula in my mind. I knew that's what I wanted to do. I would put my fundraising skills to work to build an organization that would support the most impactful change-makers in our communities. What began as a tiny seed of an idea began to take root and blossom into a mighty tree. However, before I could start fundraising in earnest, I needed to give my foundation a name.

I first coined the term "genuine human" to describe a friend and coworker of mine, Oladipupo (Ladi) Adefala. Ladi, ouNigerian-born former World Wide Technology colleague, was truly one of a kind. From the moment he joined our circle, he fit right in, even though on paper he was the least likely match for our ragtag crew. We spent countless nights hopping between bars and dance clubs, laughing until closing time. Ladi never once judged us for our antics—he didn't drink, didn't need the blur of alcohol to loosen his joy, and yet he was always the brightest light in the room.

What made him remarkable wasn't just his kindness, but the quiet, unwavering way he carried it. He never preached, never lectured, never put himself above anyone else. He simply lived his faith with a gentleness and consistency that left an impression on all of us. His presence made you want to be better, without him ever saying you should. He was the kind of man who knew God well and reflected that love through how he treated people.

I used to say over and over, "He's just a genuine human." The phrase became our shorthand for him, but it also became something bigger—a way of recognizing the rare and beautiful souls (many mentioned in this book) who move through the world with love, integrity, and grace. It was Ladi who inspired the name of my foundation, Genuine Human, which exists to give back to others in the same spirit he modeled every day.

To this day, whenever I think of kindness, humility, or grace in action, I think of Ladi's infectious smile and steady, welcoming presence. He was, and will always be, the embodiment of a genuine human.

A *Genuine Human* is the salt of the earth, honest to a fault, *human* in the deepest sense of the word. When I chose to name my foundation *Genuine Human*, it was to honor every genuine human, but especially to honor my dad. Whatever stuff he was made of, the more of that we have on this planet, the better.

From the beginning, my goal for *Genuine Human* was simple. Raise as much money as possible and give it to people making a difference. So far, our grants have been modest, but the results have been astounding. Take the case of Tim Emmerson, for example. When his granddaughter Synnove (Sin-oh-vee), that's Scandinavian for Sunshine, was born, the family wasn't sure how she would overcome her severe physical and developmental limitations. For the first few years of her life, their only focus was survival. However, as time moved on, they realized that Synnove yearned to move around and explore, just like other kids.

To qualify for an electric wheelchair, the family had to demonstrate that Synnove could operate it herself, which, unfortunately, was not possible with her rare condition. But Tim, a retired engineer for Procter & Gamble, was not about to give up so easily. He built a personalized remote-controlled scooter for Synnove that her parents could operate on her behalf.

When Synnove's scooter proved to be a huge success, Tim knew he wasn't done. He started building *Sunshine Scooters* out of his garage. He uses a Computer Numerical Control (CNC) machine, 3D Printers, and custom programmed circuit boards to build the state-of-the-art devices. The remote-control feature, now accessible through an app, allows kids to receive their scooter earlier, no matter what their condition. Over time, kids can learn to operate the scooter themselves.

"Mobility in children is not just about getting from place to place," Tim explains, "It is also about exploring the world in a way that allows for independence and healthy brain development."

When a neighbor offered Tim his garage to expand the workshop, *Genuine Human* stepped in. We contributed funds he needed to upgrade his CNC machine, so he could create scooters for older children, as well. Now, Tim is proud to make as many as 60 scooters a year, working 8 months out of the year for nearly 50 hours a week. While electric wheelchairs can cost as much as $10,000, a Sunshine Scooter only costs about $600 to make, which largely comes from donations. Some families don't have to pay a cent.

Sunshine Scooters is just one example of an organization that *Genuine Human* has helped support over the years. We've also provided feminine hygiene supplies for women left stranded by Hurricane Ian, run a toy drive for St. Louis Children's Hospital, and helped fund free flights for sick children who can't fly commercial airlines so they can go to treatment or summer camp. And, we're just getting started. All we need now is for more Genuine Humans to get on board. And there's no better time than right now.

Now is the part of the book where I make my pitch. If you've come this far, you probably have a pretty good idea what it's all going to be about. The short version: do what you can with the time you have left.

It might be a bit of a cliche to tell people to live in the moment, but this advice is especially urgent when coming from a two-time cancer survivor. Most days, I do my best not to dwell on how much or how little time I have left. I allow myself to get busy with work and being a mom. During these hectic times, I sometimes allow my fledgling foundation to fall by the wayside. Then, out of nowhere, someone in my Hodgkins survivor Facebook group will die. This happens around once a month.

Those of us who were treated for Hodgkin Lymphoma between the early '70s through the early 2000s have a special understanding of the fragility of life. We were blasted with so much radiation that our hearts are calcified, and there are spots on our livers. People post in our Facebook groups with long lists of inexplicable symptoms. Then, a few months later, they'll be gone. If I focus too much on this, I might end up in a tailspin. But keeping it right on the edge of my mind is a powerful motivator. I try to live in the moment, but I always have that extra bit of awareness of just how fragile life is. As much as I would like to control the future, to assume that I'll be around to see Jason walk Ellington down the aisle, I can't. All I have is right now. While this reality might be more tangible for me, it's no less real for you. None of us know how much time we have left. Some of us, like my mom, pass away suddenly, without any inkling that everything is about to change. In some ways, I'm fortunate. When you're constantly reminded of the fragility of life, it is harder to stay complacent.

The people that I support through *Genuine Human* are those who have refused to become complacent. They are using the time they have on this earth to change it for the better. By helping me to help them, in a small way, you can be a part of their stories. Right now, my goal is to touch as many lives as possible and to let the good I can do multiply. I hope you will help me do that. I hope you will become a *Genuine Human* as well.

When I look back on the genuine humans in my life, I am knocked right off my feet with blessings. From Lisa, my earliest childhood friend, to Molly, Marilyn and Mary (my holy trinity of M's), and Aunt Ingrid. I know I wouldn't be where I am today without you. To those who were there for me during my first round of cancer, and those who stuck with me through the bitter battle of infertility, and those who rose up to fight when breast cancer reared its ugly head – thank you. To my brother Tim, my first surprise sibling, and the eleven additional (donor side) half-siblings I've located so far, you may not have been what I expected, but you all came into my life at the times I needed you. My life wouldn't be complete without you.

Most of all, to Jason, the love of my life and the absolute best father to Ellington anyone could ask for, thank you for being there for me through thick and thin. Thank you for being there for me from the butterflies and date nights to the grief, the mess, and uncertainty. This has been one heck of a journey, and I wouldn't want to do it with anyone but you. You and Ellington are the reasons I keep believing. (Side note: Go ahead, date your boss! I recommend it!)

Finally... for those who have passed on. Mom, I miss you every day. I know you are looking down and smiling at Ellington. There are so many things I wish we could have talked about. And, to my dad, Ed Carter, the ultimate genuine human. You taught me how to love and how to keep laughing, even during the hardest times. I know that I will see you again one day and that you will smile at me and tell me how proud you are.

Then you'll remind me that there's ham in the fridge.

The end. Or is it?

If this story moved you, inspired you, or made you feel seen, I invite you to learn more and get involved at www.genuinehuman.org. Let's keep showing up for one another.

www.ingramcontent.com/pod-product-compliance
Lightning Source LLC
Chambersburg PA
CBHW071721120626
46550CB00001B/334

* 9 7 8 1 9 6 4 2 3 9 3 9 2 *